EAT WELL
Stay Healthy

Editor: Sally Taylor
Art Editor: Gordon Robertson
Consultant Nutritionist: Inger O'Meara

Published 1985 by Hamlyn Publishing, a Division of
The Hamlyn Publishing Group Limited
London   New York   Sydney   Toronto
Astronaut House, Feltham, Middlesex, England

Produced by Marshall Cavendish Books Limited
58 Old Compton Street
London WIV 5PA

ISBN 0 600 32465 6
D. L. TO: 1426 -1984

Typeset by ABM Typographics Limited, Hull, England

Printed and bound in Spain by Artes Graficas, Toledo, SA

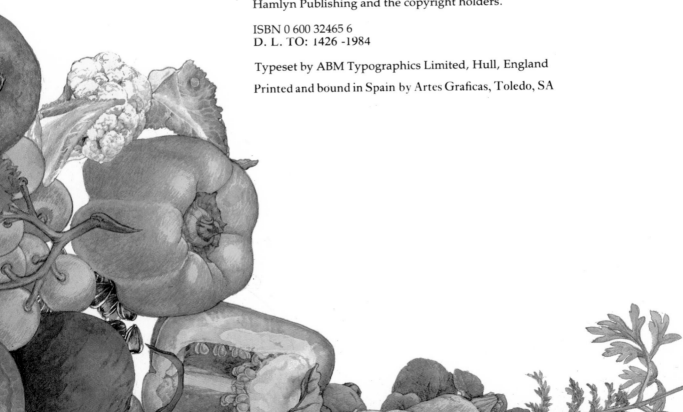

EAT WELL
Stay Healthy
Pamela Westland

HAMLYN
London · New York · Sydney · Toronto

Contents

Introduction

At last, after years of eating all the foods that money can buy, we are starting to question the effect that diet has on our general health and happiness. And not before time! Almost without our noticing it, the march of progress has taken us ever further from the natural foods of the soil and seasons, and ever closer to a diet of refined and artificially flavoured and coloured substances that leave us not properly nourished nor satisfied – and so clamouring for more.

It is almost certainly because so many of the foods we eat are processed, supposedly to make them easier to prepare, quicker to cook, faster to eat (not, usually, cheaper) that we have got into the habit of over-eating. The less we feel that we have 'had a good meal', the sooner we shall be ready for the next one. And the more we give way to this all-too-easy form of self-indulgence, the

more we resort to a crash diet (often an exaggerated form of foods that are healthy and good for us) to get back into shape.

Many processed foods have the dietary balance upside-down. They give us instant energy in the form of concentrated sugar – wasted calories, dieticians call them – and yet starve us of the natural nutrients and dietary fibre we need.

The recipes in this book show you how easy and how very good it is to turn back the clock and enjoy again the flavours and the real benefits of food as it used to be.

The first chapter, plunging in at the deep end, takes one of the most controversial of ingredients,

meat, and shows that there is a place in a healthy diet for this high-protein food – in reasonable quantity. When it is combined with vegetables, pulses, whole grains, dried or fresh fruits – or with wholewheat pasta – the meat content takes on a different perspective and you can actually serve less, yet still produce a thoroughly satisfying – and much healthier – meal. Many of the recipes show the 'dry-frying' method of cooking meat, where the hidden fat is fried out and discarded before other ingredients are added. Marinating meat before cooking in aromatic blends of vegetable oil, wine or vinegar and herbs and spices tenderizes it and adds flavour. Grilling, covered roasting on a rack, simmering, boiling, steaming, these are the healthy ways to cook meat that are explored fully on the coming pages.

As anyone who has followed a slimming diet knows, fish supplies a valuable amount of protein and other nutrients, but comparatively few calories. And so it is a perfect food for a healthy eating programme; and it has that extra, so-important ingredient, too – variety. Baked in fruit

juice, simmered in wine, steamed in a marinade, fried in polyunsaturated oil, served on a bed of high-fibre spinach or brown rice, it can be served in so many ways.

Next there is a bumper crop of vegetable recipes, but not just as accompaniments. Vegetables are too full of nutrients, fibre and flavour to be confined to such narrow limits. Make them into clear or creamy soups, hotpots, casseroles, thread them in all their colourful variety on to kebab skewers, stir-fry them in moments, toss them in spices, bake them in foil or stuff them with fragrant fillings.

Fruits are gifted with many of the same virtues, and so they feature prominently in the section devoted to delicious desserts. Fruit salads with not-too-wicked dressings, fruits combined

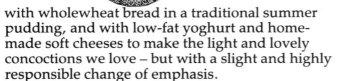

with wholewheat bread in a traditional summer pudding, and with low-fat yoghurt and home-made soft cheeses to make the light and lovely concoctions we love – but with a slight and highly responsible change of emphasis.

Yoghurt is one of the natural ingredients that has brushed aside earlier prejudices and become widely accepted as a healthy substitute in puddings, drinks, dressings and savoury dishes for high-fat ingredients such as thin and thick cream, butter and oils. Subtly and softly, yoghurt can do so much to make a healthy eating plan enjoyable that it makes sense to make your own. Prepare it from low-fat skimmed milk and stabilize or thicken it so that it can be readily added to hot foods or cooked in casseroles and sauces.

In a cookery book it seems like cheating perhaps to have a whole section devoted to raw foods. And yet here is a way to enjoy all the delights of the dairy, with low-fat cheeses, cheesecakes and puddings; to experiment with timeless Oriental

ways with uncooked fish, and to revive traditions of salting, marinating or brining. Salads with fruits as well as vegetables, suspended in herb-flavoured liquids or in yoghurt, no-cook fruit soup and long, iced drinks – the makings of lazy summer days and of radiant health.

Summer or winter, cold or hot, what we drink is just as important as what we eat. An injudicious splurge on sugar-ridden bottled drinks, and the calories pile up like a mocking meter. Fruits, vegetables, yoghurts liquidized and blended together make vitality drinks for breakfast, for no-cook starters or between-meal refreshers. Recipes like these are perfect ways to make a meal in a glass for family members who insist they haven't a moment to spare to eat anything. All the scents of the herb garden and many of the remedies of the past are revived in a pot-pourri of tisanes, hot or cold 'comforters' of herbs, spices and flowers. Some of them in days gone by were even supposed to offer a cure for over-indulgence in possets and mulls. Recipes here are quite innocuous, the alcohol but not the enjoyment surreptitiously diluted.

One of the largest sections looks into the whole question of bran and fibre, what it means in terms of health and how we can include it in the meals we plan. Recipes draw unashamedly on cultural favourites from all over the world, combinations of pulses, grains, wholewheat flour, wholewheat pasta, fruit and vegetables. With so many dishes to choose from, it is the easiest – and most sensible – thing in the world to include one high-fibre dish in at least one meal a day. Evidence mounts all the time that this change of emphasis in our diet could be the single most important step in the right direction.

With the importance of natural foods stressed from cover to cover, the chapter devoted to the natural way to eat concentrates on the flavourings that give such widely different personality to the 'staples' of our diet. Raw brown sugars, untampered with and full of all their original nutrients – and calories – honey, molasses and dried fruits, the delicious sugar-alternatives are discussed and explored in recipes from all over the world.

Nuts and seeds, vitally important ingredients in a vegetarian regime because they are so protein-packed, add crispness and crunch to salads and milk puddings, savouries and cakes.

Herbs and spices, the original flavourings that have given the different characteristics to cuisines throughout the world, are the 'goodies' of any healthy eating plan. In a lifetime you couldn't exhaust the permutations of flavours they offer.

Throughout the book stress has been laid on the importance of a healthy eating pattern or plan – not on a 'diet', which has all too many connotations of a crash course thankfully discarded after the first boring couple of days. But one chapter is devoted entirely to a diet, both for people who have been medically advised to follow a low-fat regime and to those who would like to do so as a prevention rather than a remedy. A little of the background, the why's and wherefore's show the importance of restricting the intake of saturated fats, and the following recipes prove, we hope that it is a diet of exciting opportunities rather than wistful deprivation!

The more we get into the regular daily habit of eating wholefoods, healthy foods, the more likely we are to restrict our intake of calories without even trying. For wholefoods, healthy foods, are more filling and satisfying, and long before we have eaten to the point of over-indulgence, we suddenly feel full. However, counting calories is a measure of energy consumption we all understand. And so each recipe has the approximate number of calories and the amount of protein that each portion contains. This cannot, clearly, be absolutely accurate and will naturally vary a little depending on such widely different factors as the actual size of a piece of fruit you use, the amount of fat you fry away and discard and even, to an extent, on the climate. Sun-soaked fruit will be sweeter and have more calories than fruit harvested in a year of permanent cloud!

Generally speaking, women leading a moderately active life require about 1800-2200 calories per day to keep their weight steady, although this will vary with the individual. Men require about 500 calories more. The recommended daily intake of protein for women is about 55 grams (men, 70 grams) with a minimum requirement of 38 grams. Aim to achieve a balance between healthy eating and full enjoyment of your food that is just right for you. So that you can EAT WELL, STAY HEALTHY!

Healthy Meat Cooking

According to nursery rhyme tradition, Jack Sprat must have been one of the healthiest characters around. For Jack, you remember, 'would eat no fat' and therefore, through the lines of the children's song, had a lesson for all of us. History doesn't relate what awful fate befell his wife who, on the other hand, would eat no lean. But present-day medical thinking would lead us to believe that with such a high intake of animal fats she may well have fallen victim to heart disease.

A high consumption of animal fats is now held to present a risk to health. Because of this, all of us who wish to eat well and stay healthy would do well to adopt a gradual change of emphasis in the foods we eat.

This does not mean giving up eating meat altogether and becoming vegetarian. But it does make sense to select the meats that have the lowest fat content; to cut off and discard all the visible fat, and whenever possible draw off (by dry-frying or grilling) and discard the invisible fat – the hidden gremlin present in seemingly lean cuts of red and smoked meats.

The meats highest in fat, and therefore the ones to choose only occasionally, are pork in all its guises – bacon, ham, sausages, smoked sausages and pâté – beef, lamb, goose and duck. Those with the lowest fat, which we can enjoy more often, are chicken, turkey, rabbit and veal.

Of course, the way we cook meat plays a large part in its nutritional value, or de-value. As our aim should be to subtract rather than add fat it is best to grill meat or dry fry it in a good-quality non-stick pan; pour off melted fat from fry-start casseroles, and meticulously skim the top of soups, sauces and casseroles. Many dishes are even more delicious cooked a day in advance and then re-heated. The flavours blend and mellow, and the fat sets like ice on a pond.

Marinating

Marinating meat before cooking opens the door to an infinite variety of new flavours. Each different blend of oil, fruit juice, herbs and spices tenderizes the meat, moisturizes dry cuts like chicken and turkey, and enhances the flavour. Experiment with a mixture of a vegetable oil such as sunflower or corn oil; wine, wine vinegar, lemon or orange juice or cider; flavouring vegetables like chopped onion, leek and garlic cloves; fresh or dry herbs; whole or ground spices, and special flavourings such as soy sauce or anchovy paste.

Grilling

Grilling is a healthy way to cook both red and dry meats. Red meats cooked under high heat drive off the fat, which can then be discarded. Dry meats are cooked at a lower temperature and, unless they were marinated, need brushing with oil to keep them from drying out.

Kebabs are a perfect way of presenting a modest portion of meat with flavour and style. Alternated on the skewers with bright green and red peppers, button mushrooms, mini onions, tomatoes or courgette slices, the meat – whether it is chicken, turkey, lamb, beef, bacon or offal – becomes part of a calculated combination of textures and colours – and it need not be a very large part. Serve the kebabs on a bed of brown rice or wholewheat pasta and the meal is satisfying in every way.

Pan-grilling meat in a ridged iron or cast aluminium frying-pan over high heat, gives steak and chops the appetizing criss-cross 'charcoal look' and can be as healthy as grilling, as the fat drains away into the channels at the base of the pan.

Chicken bricks

Chicken bricks, thick clay pots with lids, are designed to cook a chicken or a small joint of meat to crisp-on-the-outside, tender-on-the-inside perfection without added fat and without basting. Line the base of the brick with aluminium foil or greaseproof paper. Season the meat well with salt, pepper and, if you wish, other spices or garlic and brush it lightly with oil. Close the foil over the top, put on the lid and put the brick in a *cold* oven. Set the temperature to 260C/500F/gas 10 and cook a 1.4 kg/3 lb chicken or piece of meat for 1½ hours without peeping. You can add your own choice of extra flavourings in the form of vegetables, herbs and spices.

Steaming

The Chinese have been steaming meat for centuries, but it is a method only now becoming widely popular in the West. If you do not have a special steamer pan, or an electric steamer, you can fit a bamboo steaming basket, colander or metal folding steaming 'fan' into a saucepan with a well-fitting lid.

Meat to be dry-steamed is placed directly on the grid and cooks very quickly in the fierce heat of the jets of steam. Stock instead of water in the base pan produces steam with built-in flavouring potential and juices dripping into the stock will flavour it still more.

In many Oriental dishes the meat is marinated first, and then cooked in the sauce. To do this, put the meat and marinade into a heatproof dish and stand it on the steaming trivet.

Cooking times vary considerably with the size of

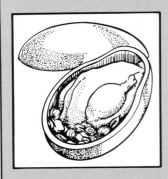

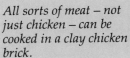
All sorts of meat – not just chicken – can be cooked in a clay chicken brick.

Special steaming equipment is available, but without it, improvize (see below).

the meat portion. Thinly sliced beef cooked in a marinade is steamed in about 8 minutes. To cook a whole 1.4-kg/3-lb chicken, simmer it in stock first for 30-40 minutes, then steam it over the stock for a further 30 minutes; the texture of the meat will be perfect, not too moist and not too dry.

Cooking 'en papillote'

Another way to cook meat over steam, and to include minced meat in the repertoire, is to wrap it in little parcels. In Chinese dishes the meat would be wrapped in lotus leaves; we could use vine leaves, lettuce or spinach leaves, or go completely with the times and use foil. Season the meat well, sprinkle it with onion, garlic, mushrooms, tomatoes or celery, moisten it with stock or a sauce and seal all this flavour into the little parcels.

Covered roasting

Some covered roasting methods are like grown-up cousins of the little foil parcels. This method has definite advantages over open roasting for the not-quite-top quality cuts of meat. Best end of neck or breast of lamb, or topside or silverside of beef, become really tender with the minimum of shrinkage when cooked in this way.

Foil parcels of meat and flavourings can be steamed, boiled, baked or grilled.

As a substitute for a covered roasting dish, use foil or special roaster bags.

Fry-start casseroles can make delicious use of second-grade cuts of meat.

A flameproof casserole with a well-fitting lid is essential for braising.

Fry-start casseroling

This is a perfect way to adapt an established cooking method to healthy meat cooking. Instead of tossing the cubes of meat in flour and frying them in butter or other fat, heat a non-stick pan and dry-fry the meat. Pour most of the fat away, leaving a little to fry the onions and other vegetables. Then you can stir in wholewheat flour or semolina until it forms a roux, cook until it browns for the traditionally rich-coloured beef dishes, and just until it is blended for pork, veal, chicken and rabbit. Stir in the stock until the sauce is smooth and slightly thickened, then bring it only just to boiling point. Cover the casserole and cook it over a very low glimmer on top of the stove or in the oven at about 150C/300F/gas 2 – or 180F/350F/gas 4 for chicken. The sauce should never be at more than a gentle simmer.

Another high-fibre way to thicken the sauce is to purée the stock with all or some of the cooked vegetables. With all the original vegetables masked in this way, you can serve others, crisp and colourful, as accompaniments.

Cold-start casseroling

This is the way to bring the very cheapest cuts of meat, the real 'toughies', to tender submission! Frying these cuts – leg and shin of beef, scrag end of lamb and so on – has irretrievably disappointing results. The sinews contract and harden and positively gang up on you, so that no amount of gentle treatment thereafter makes them tender.

Electric slow cookers are perfect for cold-start casseroles, in which all the ingredients are put in the pot together. Cut the meat into very small cubes or the thinnest of strips to expose the largest possible area to the liquid, which will eventually penetrate the meat fibres and reduce the sinews to a jelly. As the meat juices are drawn off the liquid takes on more and more flavour and is not usually thickened, except by potatoes collapsing after long, slow cooking. Again, the liquid should never be at more than simmering point. An oven temperature of 150-160C/300-325F/gas 2-3 is usually right, with 180C/350F/gas 4 for poultry.

Braising

Whole joints or portion-sized pieces of meat, often marinated first, are laid on a bed of chopped root vegetables, a mirepoix, with very little liquid added. The meat cooks in the rising steam and the liquid is reduced to little more than a coating sauce.

Tandoori Chicken

1.5-kg/3½-lb chicken, skinned,
  washed and dried
5 ml/1 tsp chilli powder
5 ml/1 tsp salt
2.5 ml/½ tsp ground black pepper
30 ml/2 tbls lemon juice
25 g/1 oz polyunsaturated
  margarine, melted
paprika

For the marinade
275 ml/10 fl oz natural yoghurt
5 ml/1 tsp salt
5 ml/1 tsp garam-masala
5 ml/1 tsp turmeric
5 ml/1 tsp chilli powder
2.5 ml/½ tsp ground ginger
2.5 ml/½ tsp cumin seed
1 garlic clove, crushed
2 bay leaves, crushed
15 ml/1 tbls tomato purée
15 ml/1 tbls lemon juice
sliced onions, tomatoes and green
  chillies, quartered lemons
chapattis or naan, to serve

With a sharp knife, make gashes in the thighs and on each side of the breast of the chicken. In a saucer, mix together the chilli powder, salt, pepper and lemon juice. Rub this paste well into the chicken on all sides and into the gashes. Set aside for 20 minutes.

Meanwhile, mix together all the marinade ingredients. Transfer the chicken to a large bowl, pour over the marinade and rub it into the chicken to coat it thoroughly. Cover the bowl and refrigerate for 24 hours, basting the chicken with the yoghurt mixture occasionally.

Soak a chicken brick in cold water for 15 minutes and line the base with a large piece of foil. Place the chicken in the brick, pour on the remaining marinade and the melted margarine and close the foil over the chicken. Close the brick and put it into a cold oven. Set the temperature at 250C/500F/gas 9½ and cook the chicken for 1 hour 20 minutes.

Reduce the oven heat to 190C/375F/gas

5. Remove the chicken from the brick, allowing the excess marinade to drip back into the brick. Place the chicken on an ovenproof dish and rub it all over with paprika pepper. Return the chicken to the oven to dry for 10 minutes.

Meanwhile, strain the marinade and juices from the brick and reheat them gently in a small pan.

Spoon a little of the marinade sauce over the chicken to glaze, and garnish the dish with sliced onions, tomatoes and green chillies and wedges of lemon. Serve the remaining sauce separately.

Serve with chapattis or naan.

Serves 4
Calories 1140 (4755 kJ)
Protein 150 grams

Sesame Soy Chicken

1.5-kg/3½-lb chicken
cornflour for coating
25 g/1 oz halved blanched almonds
75 ml/5 tbls sesame oil
4 spring onions
60 ml/4 tbls soy sauce
75 ml/5 tbls chicken stock
2 garlic cloves, chopped
sesame seeds (see recipe)
spring onions cut into 'frills'

Cut the chicken into small serving pieces, toss them in cornflour and shake off any excess. Heat the sesame oil in a heavy frying-pan, over medium-high heat and fry the chicken pieces with the almonds for 5-6 minutes, or until they are crisp on all sides. Pour off the remaining fat.

Trim the spring onions, cut them in halves and split them in half lengthways. Add the soy sauce, stock or water, garlic and spring onions to the pan, cover and simmer over low heat for 20 minutes, or until the chicken is tender. Check occasionally and add more stock or water if the sauce is drying out

Transfer to a warmed serving dish, sprinkle with sesame seeds and garnish with the frilled spring onions.

To cut the spring onions into 'frill' shapes for the garnish, trim them and cut them in halves. With a sharp knife, cut criss-cross slits down from each end, almost to the centre, and soak them in iced water for 30-45 minutes. Drain.

This dish, which comes from Korea, is usually served with Kimchi, pickled cucumber with red chilli, and rice.

Serves 4-6
Calories 1570 (6555 kJ)
Protein 142 grams

Chicken Ginger

1.5-kg/3½-lb chicken
salt and ground black pepper
15 ml/1 tbls lemon juice
25 g/1 oz polyunsaturated
    margarine
15 ml/1 tbls vegetable oil
1 medium-sized onion, chopped
2 green peppers, thickly sliced
5 ml/1 tsp ground ginger
2.5 ml/½ tsp grated nutmeg
a pinch of ground mace
275 ml/10 fl oz chicken stock
50 g/2 oz stem ginger, sliced
100 g/4 oz button mushrooms
15 ml/1 tbls cornflour
275 ml/10 fl oz natural yoghurt,
    stabilized
30 ml/2 tbls blanched almonds,
    halved and toasted
15 ml/1 tbls chopped parsley

Skin, wash and dry the chicken and cut it into 8 serving pieces. Season them well with salt and pepper and sprinkle with the lemon juice. Heat the margarine and oil in a pan and fry the chicken pieces over moderate heat for about 5 minutes on each side, until they are evenly golden brown. Remove the chicken and keep warm.

Fry the onion in the fat remaining in the pan for 3 minutes, stirring occasionally. Do not allow it to brown. Add the green pepper and fry for 1 minute. Stir in the ground ginger, nutmeg and mace and gradually pour on the stock, stirring. Bring to the boil, replace the chicken joints and cover the pan. Simmer for 30 minutes, add the stem ginger and mushrooms and continue simmering for

15 minutes, or until the chicken is cooked.

Transfer the chicken and mushrooms to a heated serving dish and keep warm. Blend the cornflour with a little water, stir into the stock and bring to the boil, stirring. Boil for 1 minute. Remove the pan from the heat, stir in the yoghurt and reheat gently without boiling. Taste and adjust seasoning if necessary.

Pour the sauce over the chicken and garnish with the almonds and parsley.

Serves 4
Calories 1455 (6080 kJ)
Protein 157 grams

Greek Lemon Chicken

1.5-kg/3½-lb chicken
30 ml/2 tbls vegetable oil
1 large onion, sliced
2 garlic cloves, finely chopped
15 ml/1 tbls flour
125 ml/4 fl oz lemon juice
275 ml/10 fl oz chicken stock
salt and ground black pepper
450 g/1 lb small potatoes
225 g/8 oz baby carrots
15 ml/1 tbls chopped mint, or
    parsley
1 lemon, quartered

Wash and dry the chicken and cut it into 8 serving pieces. Heat the oil in a large pan and fry the chicken for about 10 minutes, turning it often until it is evenly browned on all sides. Remove the chicken from the pan and keep warm.

Add the onion and garlic and fry for about 3 minutes without browning. Stir in the flour and cook for 1 minute. Gradually pour on the lemon juice and chicken stock, stirring, and bring to the boil. Season with salt and pepper.

Return the chicken to the pan, cover and simmer for 20 minutes. Add the potatoes, halved if they are not really small, and the carrots. Stir well, cover and continue cooking for 20 minutes, or

until the chicken and vegetables are tender. Adjust seasoning if necessary.

Transfer to a warmed serving dish and garnish with the chopped herb and lemon wedges.
*You can reduce the calorie count considerably by skinning the chicken before frying.

Serves 4
Calories 2990 (12470 kJ)
Protein 186 grams

Steamed Chicken

Place the sliced chicken breasts in a shallow dish and pour over the sherry or sake. Cover and leave for at least 1 hour at room temperature. Remove the chicken, reserving the marinade.

Arrange the chicken in a single layer in the upper part of a steamer, or a colander that fits inside a large pan. Pour hot water into the base pan and fit on the upper part and lid. Steam over boiling water for 10 minutes.

Heat the grill to high.

To make the sauce, pour the reserved marinade into a small pan. Add the sugar, soy sauce and monosodium glutamate if used. Bring to the boil, stirring, then remove the pan from the heat.

Transfer the chicken to the grill rack and brush with the sauce. Grill for 3 minutes on each side, basting occasionally with a little of the sauce. Transfer the chicken to a warmed serving dish, pour over the remaining sauce and serve.

To serve as a main course, double the recipe quantities and serve with rice.

2 whole chicken breasts, skinned, boned and cut into 2.5cm/1-in slices
175 ml/6 fl oz dry sherry or sake
15 ml/1 tbls sugar
5 ml/1 tsp soy sauce
1.5 ml/¼ tsp monosodium glutamate (optional)

Serves 4 as a first course
Calories 320 (1350 kJ)
Protein 49 grams

Cock-a-leekie

Wash the chicken, put it into a large pan and cover it with about 1.7 L/3 pt of water. Bring to the boil and skim off any scum that rises to the surface.

Cut off the roots from the leeks, discard the discoloured outer layers and wash thoroughly under cold running water.

Add the leeks, celery, carrots, pearl barley and the bouquet garni to the pan and season with salt and pepper.

Cover the pan, bring to the boil and simmer for 1½ hours, or until the chicken is very tender and the meat is falling off the bones. Remove the pan from the heat. Discard the bouquet garni and transfer the chicken to a plate. When it is cool enough to handle, cut all the meat from the bones and cut it into small pieces. Skim off the fat from the top of the stock.

Return the meat to the pan and reheat the broth gently. Taste and adjust the seasoning if necessary.

Pour the broth, meat and vegetables into a warmed serving dish and sprinkle with the parsley to garnish.

Any broth remaining can be used as the basis for a delicious soup, with the addition of more root vegetables.

1.5-kg/3½-lb chicken
8 medium-sized leeks
4 stalks celery, sliced
2 carrots, thickly sliced
40 g/1½ oz pearl barley
1 bouquet garni
salt and ground black pepper
30 ml/2 tbls chopped parsley

Serves 4
Calories 1450 (6075 kJ)
Protein 189 grams

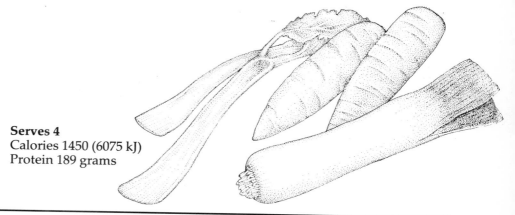

Chicken Kebabs

1.5-kg/3½-lb chicken
4 large courgettes, sliced
4 small tomatoes

For the marinade
2 medium-sized onions, sliced
150 ml/5 fl oz olive oil
60 ml/4 tbls red or white wine
5 ml/1 tsp dried oregano
2 bay leaves, crumbled
salt and ground black pepper
2.5 ml/½ tsp paprika

Mix together the ingredients for the marinade and set them aside.

Wash the chicken and cut the flesh away from the bones. Use the bones to make chicken stock for another dish. Cut the meat into about 32 neat pieces and add any small trimmings to the stockpot.

Add the chicken to the marinade, cover and leave for at least 2 hours – or overnight, if that is more convenient. Drain the chicken, reserving the marinade.

Thread one tomato half on to each skewer and then alternate with the chicken pieces and courgette slices, finishing with a halved tomato. Brush the kebabs with the marinade.

Heat the grill to high.

Grill the kebabs, turning and basting them frequently with the marinade, for 15 minutes, or until the chicken is cooked.

Serve the kebabs on a bed of boiled rice, with green salad or sweetcorn cobs.

Serves 4
Calories 2035 (8450 kJ)
Protein 130 grams

Veal Chops with Orange

Mix together the ingredients for the marinade. Lay the chops in a shallow dish, pour over the marinade and cover. Leave to marinate at room temperature for about 6 hours, or overnight if more convenient. Turn the chops at least once.

Heat the oven to 200C/400F/gas 6.

Peel the oranges, cut away any white pith from the flesh and cut out the segments (see page 140).

Sprinkle the chopped onion and tomatoes over the base of a roasting pan. Drain the chops, reserving the marinade. Arrange the chops on a rack set over the onions and tomatoes and cook in the oven for 40 minutes. Arrange orange slices on top of each chop, sprinkle with cayenne pepper and return to the oven for 5 minutes.

Transfer the orange-covered chops and vegetables (using a slotted spoon) to a warmed serving dish. Pour off any fat and strain the marinade into the pan. Add the stock and thyme, stir well and bring to the boil. Simmer for 3 minutes, then pour over chops.

Serves 4
Calories 970 (3977kJ)
Protein 143 grams

4 large veal chops
2 oranges
1 medium onion, chopped
4 tomatoes, skinned and chopped
1,5 ml/¼ tsp cayenne pepper
150 ml/5 fl oz chicken or veal stock
15 ml/1 tbls chopped thyme

For the marinade
grated zest and juice of 1 orange
150 ml/5 fl oz dry white wine
15 ml/1 tbls medium sherry
1 small onion, finely chopped
30 ml/2 tbls chopped thyme
1.5 ml/¼ tsp cayenne pepper

Veal and Mushroom Rolls

8 veal escalopes, weighing about
   450 g/1 lb
40 g/1½ oz polyunsaturated
   margarine
1 medium-sized onion, finely
   chopped
1 garlic clove, crushed
100 g/4 oz mushrooms, finely
   chopped
5 ml/1 tsp chopped sage
25 g/1 oz pine nuts
salt and ground black pepper
125 ml/4 fl oz chicken stock
4 fresh sage leaves
15 ml/1 tbls thick cream
sprigs of fresh sage

Beat the veal escalopes out flat with a rolling pin and set aside.

Melt the margarine in a pan and fry the onion and garlic over moderate heat for 3 minutes, stirring occasionally. Add the mushrooms and fry for a further 2 minutes. Take the pan from the heat and remove the vegetables with a slotted spoon. Stir the chopped sage and pine nuts into the mushroom mixture and allow to cool.

Divide the mushroom filling between the 8 escalopes and roll them up tightly. Secure each roll with a cocktail stick or toothpick, 'stitching' the meat so that the stick lies along the side of the roll.

Gently fry the veal rolls in the fat re-maining in the pan until they are evenly brown. Add the stock and sage leaves, increase the heat and bring to the boil, stirring and scraping up all the pan juices. Season the sauce with salt and pepper, stir in the cream, reduce the heat and simmer for 15 minutes, or until the meat is tender.

Transfer to a warmed serving dish and pour the sauce over. Discard the sage leaves and garnish with sprigs of fresh sage.

Serves 4
Calories 1035 (4320 kJ)
Protein 108 grams

Rabbit and Lentils

900 g/2 lb rabbit pieces
100 g/4 oz continental whole
   lentils, soaked overnight
1 stalk celery, sliced
1 medium-sized carrot, chopped
1 bouquet garni
salt and ground black pepper
450 g/1 lb small potatoes, washed

For the marinade
150 ml/5 fl oz red wine
30 ml/2 tbls olive oil
1 medium-sized onion, chopped
1 garlic clove, crushed
5 ml/1 tsp dried oregano
4 parsley stalks, chopped
a few black peppercorns, crushed

Mix the marinade ingredients in a bowl, add the rabbit, cover and set aside at room temperature for at least 8 hours, or overnight, turning at least once during this time if possible.

Lift the rabbit pieces from the marinade and put them in a large pan. Strain the marinade, add this to the pan with the lentils, celery, carrot and bouquet garni. Add just enough water to cover and season with salt and pepper. Cover the pan, bring to the boil and simmer for about 2½ hours, or until the rabbit is very tender.

Lift the rabbit from the pan and keep warm.

Strain the lentils and other vegetables, reserving the stock. Discard the bouquet garni. Rub the vegetables through a sieve and mix them to a thick, coating sauce with about 200 ml/7 fl oz of the reserved stock. Or put the vegetables and measured amount of stock into an elec-tric blender and reduce to a purée.

Rinse the pan and return the rabbit and vegetable purée. Taste and adjust the seasoning if necessary. Reheat very gently over a low heat, taking care not to allow the thick sauce to 'catch'.

Meanwhile boil the potatoes in their skins. Arrange the rabbit on a warmed serving dish and surround it with the potatoes. Garnish with chopped parsley if you like.

Steamed chopped cabbage is a good accompaniment.

Serves 4
Calories 1790 (7555 kJ)
Protein 172 grams

Veal with Watercress

Season the flour with salt and pepper. Toss the veal in the seasoned flour to coat thoroughly and shake off any excess.

Melt the margarine in a large frying-pan and fry the spring onions for 3-4 minutes, stirring occasionally, until they are soft and translucent but not beginning to brown. Remove the spring onions and keep warm.

Fry the veal, turning it frequently, for 8-10 minutes or until it is evenly brown. Stir in the stock, wine and mustard and bring to the boil, stirring. Simmer for 40-45 minutes, or until the veal is tender. Test it by piercing with a fine skewer or sharply-pointed knife.

Wash the watercress, discard the stalks and reserve some of the best sprigs to garnish. Chop the remaining sprigs and stir into the pan.

Turn the veal into a warmed serving dish and garnish with the reserved spring onions and watercress.

Serves 4
Calories 1495 (6265 kJ)
Protein 198 grams

30 ml/2 tbls flour
salt and ground black pepper
900 g/2 lb breast of veal, trimmed
    of excess fat and cut into
    2.5 cm/1-in pieces
50 g/2 oz polyunsaturated
    margarine
12 spring onions, chopped
125 ml/4 fl oz beef stock
125 ml/4 fl oz white wine
5 ml/1 tsp mustard
2 bunches watercress

Rabbit with Prunes

Mix the marinade ingredients together in a bowl, add the rabbit pieces and stir to toss them in the liquid. Cover and leave to marinate at room temperature overnight. Stir once or twice before cooking if possible.

Soak the prunes in the tea for 8 hours or overnight.

Skin the onions and blanch them in boiling water for 3 minutes, then drain.

Heat the oven to 180C/350F/gas 4.

Using a slotted spoon, lift the rabbit pieces from the bowl, reserving the marinade. Pat them dry with kitchen paper.

Melt the margarine in a flameproof casserole and fry the rabbit pieces over low heat for about 12 minutes, turning them often, until they are evenly brown on all sides. Remove the rabbit and keep warm.

Sprinkle the flour into the casserole and stir until it just browns. Gradually pour on the stock and stir until it thickens. Strain the rabbit marinade and the prune liquid into the casserole and bring to the boil, stirring. Add the rabbit, prunes and blanched onions and season with salt and pepper.

Cover the casserole and cook in the oven for 2 hours, or until the rabbit is very tender. Taste the sauce and adjust the seasoning if necessary. Remove the rabbit and prunes and keep them warm.

Cut the butter paste into small pieces, add this beurre manié to the casserole and stir over moderately-high heat to reduce and thicken the sauce. Return the rabbit and prunes to the casserole and gently heat through.

Serves 4
Calories 2115 (8445 kJ)
Protein 149 grams

900 g/2 lb rabbit pieces
225 g/8 oz prunes
575 ml/1 pt strained tea
12 small onions
50 g/2 oz polyunsaturated
    margarine
15 ml/1 tbls flour
275 ml/10 fl oz chicken stock
salt and ground black pepper
25 g/1 oz butter mixed to a paste
    with 15 ml/1 tbls flour

For the marinade
150 ml/5 fl oz medium sherry
30 ml/2 tbls olive oil
1 medium-sized onion, chopped
5 ml/1 tsp dried thyme
4 parsley stalks, chopped
4 allspice berries, bruised

Lamb and Lemon Kebabs

900g/2lb lean loin of lamb, boned
1 large green pepper
8 small tomatoes, quartered
1 lemon, quartered

For the marinade
75 ml/5 tbls olive oil
juice of 1 large lemon
2 medium-sized onions, sliced
2.5 ml/½ tsp salt
2.5 ml/½ tsp ground black pepper

Mix together the ingredients for the marinade.

Cut any excess fat from the lamb and cut the meat into 2.5 cm/1-in cubes. Put the meat into a shallow dish, cover with the marinade and stir to coat it thoroughly. Cover the dish and leave to marinate at room temperature for 8 hours, turning the meat at least once.

Heat the grill to high.

Trim the green pepper, discard the seeds and white pith and cut the flesh into 25-mm/1-in pieces.

Using a slotted spoon, remove the lamb and reserve the marinade. Beginning and ending with a piece of tomato, thread the pieces of meat, to-mato and green pepper on to 4 kebab skewers. Strain the marinade and brush it over the kebabs.

Grill the kebabs for 4 minutes, turning them once. Reduce the heat to moderate and grill for a further 6-8 minutes, or until the meat is just cooked, turning the skewers occasionally and basting them with the remaining marinade.

Arrange the kebabs on a bed of rice in a warmed serving dish and garnish with the lemon wedges.

Serves 4
Calories 1970 (8220 kJ)
Protein 164 grams

Lamb Cutlets in Mint Aspic

To make the aspic jelly, put the sherry, wine, lemon juice and vinegar in a large pan with the onion, carrot, celery stalk and seasoning. Simmer for 30 minutes.

Separate the egg, add the white and crushed shell to the stock and bring to the boil, whisking. Boil without stirring until a thick scum forms on top. Strain twice through a sieve lined with muslin. Allow to cool slightly, dissolve the gelatine in the stock and stir in the chopped mint. Leave to cool but not set.

Have the meat in two pieces of 4 cutlets each and ask the butcher to chine the meat but not chop the bones across.

Heat the oven to 160C/325F/gas 3.

Trim the flap from the meat, peel away the skin and clear 2.5 cm/1-in at the end of each bone. Place the meat, fat side down, in a roasting pan, season and cook for 20 minutes on each side. Cool.

Divide into cutlets, put them on a wire tray and spoon over just enough aspic to run down the sides. Leave to set for about 1 hour. Served garnished with paper frills if available.

*Calorie count assumes that you eat only the lean meat!

Serves 4
Calories 985 (4140 kJ)
Protein 127 grams

75 ml/5 tbls dry sherry
75 ml/5 tbls dry white wine
zest and juice of 1/2 lemon
25 ml/5 tsp red wine vinegar
1 onion, quartered
1 carrot, halved
1 stalk celery, sliced
2.5 ml/1/2 tsp salt
4 black peppercorns
1 small egg
25 g/1 oz gelatine
small bunch of mint, chopped
8 best end of neck lamb cutlets
   (see recipe)

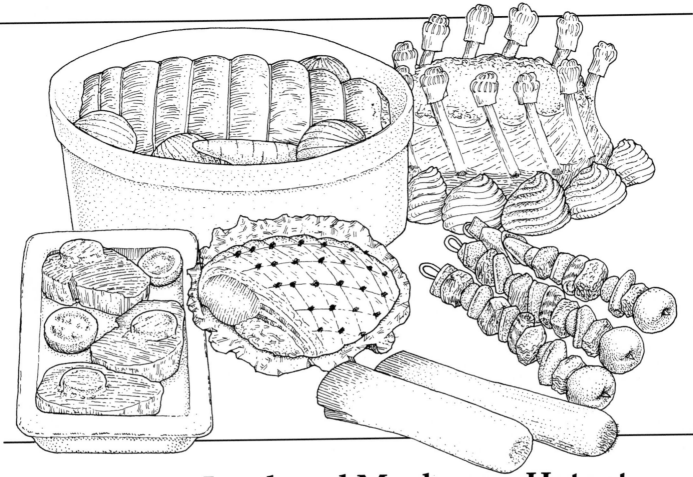

Lamb and Mushroom Hotpot

800 g/1¾ lb best end of neck of
    lamb
225 g/8 oz onions
2 large carrots, sliced
4 stalks celery, sliced
1 small turnip, finely diced
700 g/1½ lb potatoes, peeled and
    thinly sliced
225 g/8 oz mushrooms, sliced if
    large
15 ml/ 1 tbls tomato purée
275 ml/10 fl oz chicken or
    vegetable stock
salt and ground black pepper
25 g/1 oz polyunsaturated
    margarine
25 g/1 oz grated cheese

Trim any surplus fat from the meat and cut away any loose bone splinters. Wipe the meat with a clean, damp cloth.

Mix together the onions, carrots, celery and turnip. Make a layer of the vegetables in the base of a deep casserole.

Cover with a layer of the meat, then potatoes, then mushrooms, seasoning lightly between each layer with salt and pepper. Continue making layers, leaving enough potatoes to cover the top.

Mix the tomato purée to a thin paste with a little hot water, then stir in the stock. Pour over the casserole. Arrange the remaining potatoes in overlapping rings to cover the top completely and dot with pieces of the margarine.

Cover the casserole with the lid, or first with a piece of foil if the lid is not a good fit. Cook in the centre of the oven for 1¼-1½ hours. The exact time will depend on the quality of the meat.

Remove the lid and foil if used and sprinkle on the cheese. Continue cooking for 30 minutes, until the potatoes are golden brown. Serve at once, straight from the pot.

Serves 4
Calories 2911 (12226 kJ)
Protein 238 grams

Lamb with Red Wine Sauce

Mix together the ingredients for the marinade. Place the lamb joints in a large dish, pour over the marinade and cover with foil. Refrigerate for 1-2 days, turning the meat and basting it with the marinade occasionally.

Heat the oven to 180C/350F/gas 4.

Drain the meat, reserving the marinade, and place in a large roasting pan. Cook in the centre of the oven for 2 hours, or until both joints are tender. Test by piercing with a fine skewer or sharply-pointed knife.

While the meat is cooking, make the sauce. Strain the marinade into a pan and bring to the boil, stirring occasionally. Boil for 10 minutes, or until the sauce has reduced by about one-third. Beat together the butter and flour until it forms a smooth paste. Reduce the heat to low and stir this beurre manie, a little at a time, into the sauce. Cook for a further 2 minutes or until the sauce is smooth, thickened and glossy.

Transfer the meat to a warmed serving dish. Pour the sauce into a warmed jug and serve separately.

Onions roasted in the oven at the same time as the meat make a good accompaniment to this dish, but remember to count the extra calories.

Serves 4
Calories 7115 (29460 kJ)
Protein 323 grams

1.5-kg/3½-lb shoulder of lamb
900-g/2-lb breast of lamb
15 g/½ oz butter
15 ml/1 tbls flour

For the marinade
1 bottle red wine
125 ml/4 fl oz red wine vinegar
125 ml/4 fl oz olive oil
5 ml/1 tsp salt
3 garlic cloves, crushed
10 juniper berries, crushed
10 white or green peppercorns
4 bay leaves
4 stalks each of parsley and thyme
1 spring onion, chopped
2 stalks celery, sliced
2 medium-sized carrots, sliced

Roast Lamb Pilau

Mix together the ingredients for the marinade, stirring to amalgamate them.

Ask the butcher to remove the chine bone from the lamb. Score across the fat with a sharp knife to make deep diamond patterns. Put the lamb into a dish, pour over the marinade, cover and set aside at room temperature for at least 6 hours, or overnight. Turn the meat and baste it with the marinade once or twice.

Heat the oven to 190C/375F/gas 5.

Lift the joint from the marinade and reserve the liquid. Place the meat in a roasting tin, spoon over 30 ml/2 tbls of the marinade, cover with foil and cook in the centre of the oven for 1½ hours, basting occasionally.

While the meat is cooking, heat the oil in a frying-pan, stir in the rice and stir over a low heat for 2 minutes, to coat the rice thoroughly with oil. Pour on the marinade, bring to the boil and simmer over a low heat for 45-50 minutes, or until the rice is tender and has absorbed all the liquid. If it dries out too quickly, add a little chicken stock or water. Taste the rice and season with salt and pepper.

Transfer the meat to a warmed serving dish and spoon the rice round the outside. Toss the peaches in the juices in the roasting pan over a low heat until they are just heated through. Drain them and arrange them round the meat.

Serves 4
Calories 2995 (12455 kJ)
Protein 148 grams

900-g/2-lb joint loin of lamb
15 ml/1 tbls vegetable oil
75 g/3 oz brown long-grain rice
salt and ground black pepper
4 fresh peaches, skinned and
   quartered

For the marinade
1 onion, sliced
grated zest and juice of 1 orange
30 ml/2 tbls olive oil
75 ml/5 tbls dry sherry
15 ml/1 tbls soy sauce
15 ml/1 tbls molasses or black
   treacle
2.5 ml/½ tsp ground cinnamon

Spicy Meat Soup

450 g/1 lb beef brisket
100 g/4 oz peeled prawns
6 shallots
3 garlic cloves
30 ml/2 tbls vegetable oil
2.5 ml/½ tsp ground ginger
2.5 ml/½ tsp turmeric
salt
10 ml/2 tsp lemon juice

For the garnish
15 ml/1 tbls oil for frying
1 medium-sized onion
15 ml/1 tbls chopped parsley
1 lemon

Cover the meat with salted water and boil for 1 hour, skimming off any scum that rises to the surface.

Chop or finely mince together the prawns (thawed if frozen), shallots and garlic.

Drain the meat, reserving the cooking liquid. When the meat is cool enough to handle, cut it into 2.5 cm/1-in cubes.

Heat the oil in a pan and cook the prawn mixture for 1 minute over a moderate heat. Add the ginger, turmeric, salt and 225 ml/8 fl oz of the reserved liquid. Cover the pan and simmer for 7-8 minutes.

Put the meat into a clean saucepan, strain over the prawn mixture and discard the contents of the strainer. Simmer for 2 minutes, then add 350 ml/12 fl oz more of the meat stock. Bring slowly to the boil and simmer for 20 minutes. Add the lemon juice, taste the soup and adjust seasoning if necessary. Pour the soup into a heated serving dish and garnish with fried onion rings and parsley.

To make the garnish, heat the oil in a frying pan. Thinly slice the onion into rings and fry them, turning frequently, for 5 minutes, until just golden brown. Drain on crumpled kitchen paper.

Garnish with lemon wedges.

Serves 4
Calories 1640 (6810 kJ)
Protein 100 grams

Braised Beef

Heat the oven to 150C/300F/gas 2.

Cut the meat into chunks about 75 g/3 oz each. Heat the oil in a flameproof casserole and fry the pieces of meat a few at a time over moderate heat. Remove meat and fry the chopped onions until they are soft. Stir in the tomato purée and continue cooking for 5 minutes. Remove from the heat and cool for 10 minutes.

Wrap the strip of orange zest round the whole onion and secure it in place with the cloves. Add this to the casserole with the meat, carrots and whole garlic cloves. Split the calf's foot or pig's trotter in half, cut the bacon into strips and add them to the casserole with the bouquet garni.

With a spoon, ease the meat to the top. Pour on the wine and season with pepper.

Cover the dish with foil and then with the lid and bring slowly to the boil. Reduce the heat and simmer on top of the cooker for 10 minutes. Transfer to the oven and cook for about 6 hours, checking towards the end that the sauce is not drying out. If it is, top up with a little more wine. Turn the pieces of meat over once during cooking.

Taste the sauce, add salt, and adjust the seasoning . Discard the calf's foot or pig's trotter before serving.

Serves 6
Calories 3590 (14935 kJ)
Protein 272 grams

1.2 kg/2½ lb braising steak
60 ml/4 tbls olive oil
2 large onions, chopped
30 ml/2 tbls tomato purée
1 strip orange zest, 6 cloves and
*   1 medium-sized onion*
2 large carrots, halved
4 garlic cloves
1 calf's foot or pig's trotter
225 g/8 oz unsmoked streaky bacon
1 bouquet garni
575 ml/1 pt red wine
ground black pepper and salt

Grilled Steak Fingers

900g/2lb sirloin steak
3 spring onions, chopped
4 garlic cloves, crushed
75 ml/5 tbls soy sauce
30 ml/2 tbls sesame oil
50 g/2 oz sugar
30 ml/2 tbls medium-dry sherry
50 ml/2 fl oz beef stock
ground black pepper

Cut the steak across the grain into thin, finger-sized pieces removing all fat. Score a cross on top of each piece.

Mix the spring onions and garlic together, stir in the soy sauce, sesame oil, sugar, sherry and stock and season with pepper. Put the steak in to a shallow dish, pour over the marinade, cover and leave to marinate at room temperature for at least 2 hours, or overnight if more convenient.

Heat the grill to high.

Remove the steak fingers from the marinade, reserving the liquid. Grill the steak according to the way you like it cooked. Turn the pieces frequently and brush them with the marinade. Heat the remaining marinade and serve it separately.

This Korean dish, called Bulgogi, is served piping hot, with noodles.

Serves 4-6
Calories 1345 (5640 kJ)
Protein 148 grams

Spiced Brisket

1.5 kg/3½ lb beef brisket
25 g/1 oz soft brown sugar
15 g/½ oz saltpetre
50 g/2 oz sea salt
15 ml/1 tbls black peppercorns
15 ml/1 tbls juniper berries
5 ml/1 tsp allspice berries
5 ml/1 tsp mustard seed
2.5 ml/½ tsp coriander seed

Put the beef on to a large plate and, with the palm of your hand, rub the sugar firmly into the meat to coat it on all sides. Put the beef into a large casserole, cover with a piece of clean muslin or cheesecloth and put in the refrigerator or a cool place for 2 days.

Crush together the saltpetre, salt and spices. Use a pestle and mortar if you have one, or put the ingredients into a strong bag and hit them firmly with a wooden rolling pin. Stir or shake the ingredients together to mix well.

Rub the spice mixture into the beef, taking care to cover all surfaces. Cover, return it to the refrigerator and rub it with the mixture once each day for 8 days. After a few days you will find that the salt has drawn some of the moisture from the beef and you will be spooning the mixture on to the meat, rather like basting it.

Remove the beef from the casserole and scrape off any excess sugar and the spices sticking to the surface. Dry the meat with a pad of crumpled kitchen paper.

Heat the oven to 140C/275F/gas 1.

Place the beef in an ovenproof casserole with 225 ml/8 fl oz water. Cover the casserole closely with foil and then with the lid. Cook the meat for 3 hours without lifting the lid. Remove the casserole from the oven, and pierce the meat with a fine skewer or a sharp-pointed knife to check that it is cooked. Replace the foil and lid and set aside for 2 hours.

Reserving the stock for soup or a casserole, lift out the meat and wrap in foil. Put on a board with a heavy weight on top. Leave for 24 hours.

Serve the meat very thinly sliced.

Spiced Brisket is a traditional Christmas joint, delicious with crisp pickled vegetables. Because all the preparation is done well in advance, it is also suitable for a buffet party served, perhaps, with hot jacket potatoes and crisp green salad.

Serves 6
Calories 3690 (15300 kJ)
Protein 240 grams

Beef and Butter Bean Casserole

Heat the oven to 85C/180F/gas low.

Cut the meat into 4-cm/1½-in cubes. Put the flour, salt and pepper into a polythene bag and toss the meat cubes to coat them thoroughly.

Put the meat into an ovenproof casserole, add the prepared vegetables, including the garlic and drained beans, together with the sugar and the brown ale. Cook in the oven for 8 hours, then skim the fat from the top of the casserole. Taste and adjust the seasoning if necessary.

Serves 4-6
Calories 2320 (9550 kJ)
Protein 265 grams

1.2 kg/2½ lb stewing beef
45 ml/3 tbls flour
salt and ground black pepper
1 small onion, finely chopped
3 stalks celery, thinly sliced
2 medium carrots, thinly sliced
2 garlic cloves, crushed
75 g/3 oz butter beans, soaked
15 ml/1 tbls soft brown sugar
275 ml/10 fl oz brown ale

Liver with Sage and Apples

Cut the liver into thin slices. Season the flour with the dried oregano, salt and pepper. Toss the liver in the seasoned flour to coat it thoroughly.

Heat the butter and oil in a frying-pan, and fry the apples over a moderate heat for about 2 minutes on each side. Remove them and keep them warm. Add the sage leaves and fry the liver over a moderate heat for about 4 minutes on each side. Test to check that it is cooked just the way you like it.

Pour on the stock, and lemon juice, stir well to take up all the pan juices and bring to the boil. Simmer for 2-3 minutes. Remove the sage leaves. Check and adjust seasoning if necessary.

Transfer the meat and sauce to a warmed serving dish and garnish with the apple slices and sage sprigs.

Serves 4
Calories 1140 (4780 kJ)
Protein 94 grams

450 g/1 lb lamb's or calf's liver
15 ml/1 tbls flour
2.5 ml/½ tsp dried oregano
salt and ground black pepper
25 g/1 oz unsalted butter
15 ml/1 tbls olive oil
2 dessert apples, cored and sliced
6 sage leaves
90 ml/6 tbls beef stock
10 ml/2 tsp lemon juice
small sage sprigs

New England Boiled Dinner

Trim fat from beef, then put into a very large flameproof casserole or pan, cover with water and bring to the boil. Skim off any scum that rises. Cover and simmer over low heat for 2½ hours. Top up with more boiling water if necessary, so that the meat is always covered.

Peel and halve the potatoes, cut the cabbage into wedges, and add with the other vegetables. Season well with pepper. Bring back to the boil, cover and simmer for a further 30 minutes, or until the beef and vegetables are all tender.

Test the meat by piercing with a fine skewer or sharply-pointed knife.

Taste and adjust the seasoning if necessary.

Drain the meat, place it on a large, warmed serving plate and arrange the vegetables round it. Skim the fat from the top of the stock, reheat it and serve it separately.

Serves 6
Calories 2405 (10215 kJ)
Protein 271 grams

1.5 kg/3½ lb salt beef
6 medium-sized potatoes
1 small, firm head cabbage
1 small swede, peeled and diced
2 small turnips, peeled and diced
12 small onions
6 medium-sized carrots, sliced
ground black pepper

Healthy Fish Cooking

When you're trying to decide what to have for any meal through the day, fish can be the best catch of all – for a whole shoal of reasons. It is highly nutritious, rich in proteins, vitamins and minerals, and relatively low in calories. A 100-g/4-oz portion of cod or coley clocks up only 92 calories, against 120 calories for chicken and 104 for rabbit. And even the oily fish, higher in fat and therefore in calorific value, do not break the bank, with herring at 148 and trout at 152 (against similar portions of beef at 328 and lamb at 300).

Added to that, fish offers an almost bewildering variety of type, size, shape, flavour and cooking method – with dishes ranging from a whole bream baked in tangerine sauce, through a fish and vegetable-packed chowder with garlicky bread topping, to a hot fish salad or elegant dressed crab, could we ever exhaust all the possibilities?

Many types of fish are available frozen – whole trout, fillets of plaice and cod, smoked haddock and kippers. Already prepared and ready to cook, they are marvellously convenient for busy days and emergencies and can be dressed up with interesting flavour combinations to give them added personality. But to limit our repertoire to these convenience fish is to deny ourselves the delicate flavours and exciting bargains of other seasonal catches.

It is well worth getting to know a fishmonger (admittedly not easy in every town) who has a steady turnover and a good selection of fresh fish. And worth trying to overcome any qualms we might have about handling 'recognisable' fish. Most fishmongers will scale, gut and even fillet fish for you – it is after all an important part of their craft. But if for any reason they cannot, you will find it is not at all difficult – our step-by-step illustrations explain the tasks simply and clearly.

When buying fresh fish, look for those with bright, shiny scales and bright, clear eyes. Fillets and cutlets should be translucent, and not opaque, and smoked fish should have a dry, glossy shine and be firm and slightly dry – never slimy.

Calculating how much fish to buy can be rather tricky – the proportion of bone to flesh varies considerably in the different types, and of course the size of an 'average portion' varies with different appetites. Generally, for a main course it is reasonable to allow 150-175 g/5-6 oz of filleted fish per portion; 175-200 g/6-7 oz of a cutlet, a cod steak for example; 250-350 g/9-12 oz small whole fish, and at least 225 g/8 oz of a large whole fish which is to be cut into portions at the table.

The freshness of fish is all-important. It is definitely not something to buy at the weekend to cook in the middle of the week. As soon as you get home, wash fish under cold running water, pat it dry and wrap it loosely in foil or polythene. Put it on a tray just under the freezer compartment of the refrigerator, and cook within 24 hours, or 2-5 days for smoked fish. Seasoning fillets of fresh fish with salt, pepper and lemon juice before wrapping gives time for the flavours to penetrate.

Preparing

Whole, boned or filleted, fish can be cooked in a number of ways. Small whole fish can be grilled, poached, soused, steamed, baked or simmered. For frying, it can have added fibre with a jacket of oatmeal, rolled oats, wholewheat breadcrumbs, ground almonds, bran, wholewheat semolina, or kibbled wheat. And boned fish can have fibre-full stuffings of cereals perked up with herbs, spices and chopped fruit or vegetables. Large whole fish can be baked, poached or – deliciously – simmered in sauce. Fish to be served on the bone should not have thick, masking sauces – the bones should be readily seen and easily accessible.

Once fish is filleted it opens up yet more possibilities. Cut into chunks, fish makes unusual kebabs; thinly sliced and steamed in a marinade it takes on an Oriental flavour; in more homely ways, it can be poached in milk or stock, baked in a sauce or given a crisp and crumbly or gratinated topping. For fresh summer meals, serve salads of cooked, cooled fillets.

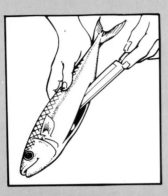

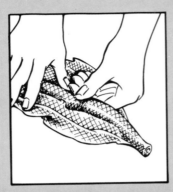

To clean round fish, slit down belly and scrape out all entrails.

To bone, cut off head and slit down to tail. Open out on board, skin side up.

Press hard on backbone through skin. Turn fish over; lift out bones in one piece.

To clean flat fish, cut into flesh just below gills. Scrape out entrails.

Grilling

Brush whole fish for grilling lightly with oil and cut diagonal slits to prevent splitting. Grill under high heat for 1-2 minutes on each side to crisp the skin and keep that healthy glow. Then grill fresh fish at medium heat, unthawed frozen fish at medium-low. Fish cooks so quickly that it is best to keep an eye on it – it's cooked as soon as the skin starts shrinking, or the flesh becomes opaque and comes cleanly away from the bone. With skinned fish you will notice a white creamy substance oozing out between the flakes when it is cooked.

Marinating white fish in a mixture of oil and wine, cider or vinegar with herbs and spices adds moisture the fish lacks. The acidity of the marinating ingredients, helps to offset the richness in oily fish.

Poaching

Not many households can lay hands on an old fish kettle these days, but an improvised trivet or rack in the base of the dish or pan is useful when poaching large whole fish – it is so much easier to lift it out without breaking. Smaller, one-portion size whole fish, cutlets and fillets, and smoked fish of all kinds can also be poached either on top of the cooker or in the oven. A little acid added to the water or fish stock improves the flavour – it can be lemon juice, vinegar or wine.

Whole fish should be cooked in liquid starting from cold to preserve the shape of the skin, but fillets and 'steaks' are best started in simmering liquid.

As the skin cannot be crisped attractively by this means of cooking, it is best to peel it off just before serving. Poached fish should be very well drained and then patted dry; the liquid can be reduced or stirred into a roux, to make an accompanying sauce.

Sousing

Sousing is poaching by another name. The fish is cooked in vinegar, or a 50-50 solution of vinegar and water, with peppercorns, onion, bay leaves, celery leaves, mace and other herbs and spices to taste. This is a perfect way to hive off some of the richness of oily fish. Sousing acts as a mild preservative; the cooked fish should be eaten within 3 days.

Steaming

Steaming whole fish, fillets or wafer-thin slices in a marinade is a quick and trouble-free way to cook them. Generally, the faster the cooking time, the

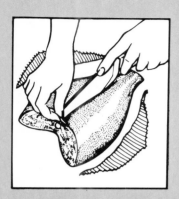

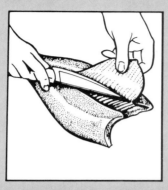

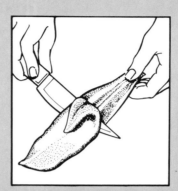

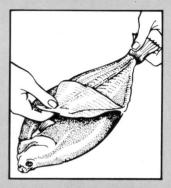

To fillet flat fish, cut off head in a V. Cut down centre of fish to bone.

Cut away fillet keeping knife against bones. Repeat with 3 remaining fillets.

To skin fillets, take hold of tail and cut along skin with a sawing motion.

To skin whole fish, cut through skin by tail. Pull skin sharply upwards.

greater the advantage there is to the initial blending and mellowing of flavours, however slight or subtle, that a marinade can give. The juices from steaming fish are too nutritious and delicious to be frittered away into the liquid in the base pan so the fish should be cooked on a heatproof plate set on a trivet, between two plates forming a lid to the pan, or sealed into greased foil or greaseproof paper parcels.

Baking
Baking fish is almost a chapter in itself, there are so many ways of doing it – in foil parcels, under foil in a shallow dish, in a covered casserole, with a savoury crumble or cheesey topping, or in a clay fish brick. Large whole fish may be stuffed and open-roasted, too, but possible dryness here is a slight hazard.

Onions, tomatoes, courgettes and other vegetables with a high moisture content make perfect partners for baked fish – as the fish juices blend you have a ready-made sauce with no additional liquid. Otherwise, a minimum of fish or vegetable stock, cider or dry white wine is added – any more, and the fish would poach! A low-medium temperature, about 180-190C/350-375F/gas 4-5, best preserves the shape and texture of the fish.

Whole fish up to 1.1-1.4 kg/2½-3 lb can be cooked in a clay fish brick at a temperature of 180C/350F/gas 4 for about 1 hour, or 1¼ hours if a stuffing is included. Smaller fish or portions are baked more quickly – in about 25-30 minutes at 230C/450F/gas 8.

Frying
In Britain 'fried fish' invariably conjures up the image of a piece of white fish – hake, cod, coley, plaice – puffed up in a rich, fat-laden batter, and served with delicious, fat-laden chips. But fried fish need not show up so badly under the microscope of healthy eating.

The main factor is the choice of frying medium. Opt for a polyunsaturated oil or margarine and you have eliminated most of the problem. Fresh herrings coated in oatmeal, a Scottish speciality, have the bonus of added fibre – you can almost feel your halo returning? – and coated in a mustard paste, or devilled, they scarcely seem 'fatty' at all. In many recipes the fish is quickly and lightly fried in oil to seal the exposed surfaces and trap the juices. After that, it can graduate to simmering in yoghurt, sweet and sour sauce, wine or fruit juice.

Whiting Pinwheels

2 whiting, 350-450 g/³/₄-1 lb
   each
salt and ground black pepper

For the stuffing
75 g/3 oz butter
40 g/ 1½ oz white breadcrumbs
30 ml/2 tbls chopped fresh herbs,
   parsley, chervil, oregano, mint
grated zest and juice of 1 lemon

Ask the fishmonger to clean and fillet the fish for you, or prepare them yourself, following the directions on pages 32 and 33. Skin each fillet by easing a knife under the skin and gently pulling the skin away. Cut each fillet in half lengthways, so that you have a total of 8 fillets.

Butter a shallow, flameproof dish. Heat the grill to medium.

To make the stuffing, beat the butter in a small bowl until it is smooth and creamy. Stir in the breadcrumbs, herbs and lemon zest. Season with salt and pepper and a few drops of the lemon juice. Add a little more lemon juice if necessary to give the stuffing a smooth, spreadable consistency.

Arrange the fillets on a working surface and, using a round-bladed knife, spread the stuffing over them. Roll up each fillet from the tail end and secure with a skewer or cocktail stick.

Arrange the rolled fish fillets in the dish and pour over the remaining lemon juice. Grill under medium heat for 5 minutes. Turn each fillet carefully, using a fish slice. Grill for a further 5-8 minutes, until the fish is cooked. Serve at once.

Serves 4
Calories 1140 (4755 kJ)
Protein 101 grams

Fish in Tangerine Sauce

Heat the oven to 200C/400F/gas 6.

Ask the fishmonger to gut the fish, or do it yourself, following the directions on page 32. Wash the fish thoroughly and dry it with kitchen paper. Season it inside and out with salt, pepper and lemon juice. Butter a shallow ovenproof baking dish just large enough to hold the fish. Place the bream in the dish and scatter the mushrooms, spring onion and parsley over it. Pour on the olive oil and butter and the wine and tangerine juice.

Bake the fish for 25-30 minutes, basting it from time to time with the juices, or until it is cooked. It should flake easily when tested with a fork.

To serve the fish, transfer it to a warmed serving dish, arrange the mushrooms round it and pour over the sauce.

If tangerines are not available, you can use the juice of satsumas or even orange juice, though naturally this will not have such a refreshingly original flavour.

Serves 4
Calories 1800 (7475 kJ)
Protein 155 grams

1.5 kg/3½ lbs bream, or similar
  fish
salt and ground black pepper
30 ml/2 tbls lemon juice
100 g/4 oz mushrooms, sliced
1 spring onion, chopped
15 ml/1 tbls chopped parsley
15 ml/1 tbls olive oil
15 ml/1 tbls melted butter
225 ml/8 fl oz white wine
150 ml/5 fl oz tangerine juice

Breton Chowder (Cotriade)

900 g/2 lb mixed fillet of fish, such
   as cod, haddock, mackerel,
   mullet, with some shellfish,
   such as shelled prawns,
   shrimps, mussels (see method)
25 g/1 oz butter
1 large onion, chopped
1 garlic clove, crushed
2 medium-sized carrots, chopped
1 stalk celery, sliced
1 large potato, peeled and diced
1 bouquet garni
salt and ground black pepper
15 ml/1 tbls tomato purée
juice of 1/2 lemon

To serve
1 small French loaf
2 large garlic cloves, crushed
30 ml/2 tbls olive oil
15 ml/1 tbls chopped parsley

The amount of fish called for is the filleted and shelled weight. Remember that 450 g/1 lb fresh mussels gives about 100 g/4 oz when shelled.

If you are using fresh mussels, prepare them as described on page 44. Shake them in a heavy-based pan over low heat for about 10 minutes, or until the shells open. Discard any that remain shut. Reserve the liquor to add to the soup.

Cut all the other fish into bite-sized chunks and set aside.

Melt the butter in a heavy-based pan over low heat. Cook the onion and garlic for about 4 minutes, or until soft. Pour on 1 L/2 pt cold water and add the carrot, celery, potato and bouquet garni. Bring to the boil and simmer for 15 minutes.

Add the fish, salt, pepper, tomato purée and lemon juice. Simmer for a further 15 minutes, or until the fish is cooked but still firm. Do not overcook it, or it will become tough. Taste the soup and adjust the seasoning if necessary.

Meanwhile, cut the French loaf into thick slices. Put half the oil and half the garlic into a frying-pan over medium heat. Fry the bread slices on both sides in batches, adding more oil and garlic as necessary.

Pour the soup into a warmed serving dish, float the bread slices on top, sprinkle with the parsley and serve.

Serves 6
Calories 1510 (6335 kJ)
Protein 171 grams

Sweet and Sour Fish

450 g/1 lb fillet of white fish,
   such as plaice, cod, halibut
10 ml/2 tsp salt
30 ml/2 tbls cornflour
1 large egg white, beaten
60 ml/t tbls vegetable oil
5 ml/1 tsp olive oil
3 spring onions, sliced
2 garlic cloves, thinly sliced

For the sauce
20 ml/4 tsp soy sauce
60 ml/4 tbls red wine vinegar
25 ml/5 tsp sugar
25 ml/5 tsp tomato purée
30 ml/2 tbls orange juice
30 ml/2 tbls dry sherry
25 ml/5 tsp cornflour blended with
   150 ml/5 fl oz water

Wash and thoroughly dry the fish. Cut it into strips measuring 5 x 2 cm/2 x 3/4-in, discarding any skin and bones. Rub with salt, toss in cornflour and dip in the beaten egg white.

Heat the oil in a frying-pan over moderate heat. Fry the fish in batches for 30 seconds on each side, then remove the fish from the pan and drain on kitchen paper. Pour off and discard the oil.

Blend all the ingredients for the sauce. Heat the olive oil in the pan, add the spring onion and garlic and stir over moderate heat for 1 minute. Pour in the sauce mixture and stir until it becomes translucent and softened.

Remove the pan from the heat and add the fish. Return the pan to the heat until the sauce bubbles, remove it from the heat again and carefully turn over each piece of fish. Cook for a further 30 seconds, shaking the pan gently.

Lift the fish on to a warmed serving dish, carefully pour over the sauce and serve at once.

Serves 4 as part of a larger meal
Calories 1135 (4745 kJ)
Protein 76 grams

Fish Steaks with Yoghurt

To stabilise the yoghurt and prevent it from curdling, mix the flour and a pinch of salt with a few drops of water to make a paste. Whisk the paste into the yoghurt, pour it into a small pan over low heat and stir in one direction for about 10 minutes, until the yoghurt begins to simmer. Remove the pan from the heat.

Wash and dry the fish thoroughly and sprinkle with the salt and 5 ml/1 tsp turmeric. Heat the oil in a frying-pan over moderate heat and cook the fish for 3-4 minutes on each side. Remove the fish from the pan and keep warm.

To clarify the butter, melt it in a small pan. Allow the foam to subside, then pour off the clear butter and discard the sediment.

Add the clarified butter to the frying-pan and reduce the heat. Add the chilli powder, grated ginger and onion, the remainder of the turmeric, cardamom, cloves, cinnamon and chillies to the pan. Cook for 5 minutes, stirring occasionally. If the spices begin to stick, add a few drops of water.

Add the yoghurt, 50 ml/2 fl oz water and the sugar to the pan. When the mixture begins to simmer, place the fish in the pan and continue cooking until the liquid thickens and the fish is cooked – about 5 minutes. Remove the chillies.

Serve the fish, hot or cold, in the yoghurt sauce, with rice.

Serves 4
Calories 1510 (6310 kJ)
Protein 171 grams

900 g/2 lb white fish, such as cod, halibut, in one piece
275 ml/10 fl oz natural yoghurt
10 ml/2 tsp flour
5 ml/1 tsp salt
10 ml/2 tsp turmeric
45 ml/3 tbls vegetable oil
30 ml/2 tbls butter, clarified, (see method)
2.5 ml/$\frac{1}{2}$ tsp chilli powder
2.5 cm/1 in piece fresh root ginger, grated
1 medium-sized onion, grated
6 cardamom pods, crushed
3 cloves
25 mm/1 in cinnamon stick
2 green chillies
15 ml/1 tbls sugar

Fish Stew

If possible, ask the fishmonger for the bones, heads and other trimmings from the fish and use them to make a fish stock. Put them in a pan with about 1 L/2 pt water, 1 small sliced onion and 1 bouquet garni. Bring to the boil, partly cover the pan and simmer for 40 minutes, then strain. If you have no time to make the fish stock, use water.

Skin the fish, remove any small bones and cut it into large chunks. Set aside.

Heat the oil in a large pan and fry the onions and garlic over low heat for 5 minutes. Add the tomatoes and bouquet garni, increase the heat and simmer for 20 minutes. Add 850 ml/1½ pt hot fish stock, or water. Bring to the boil, then simmer for 10 minutes. Season with salt and pepper, add the potatoes, strip of orange zest and the juice and simmer gently for 20 minutes.

Add the fish and simmer over low heat for 12-15 minutes, until the fish is just tender. Do not overcook, or it will become tough. Stir in the saffron, taste the sauce and adjust the seasoning if necessary. Discard the bouquet garni and orange zest. Pour into a warmed serving dish, sprinkle with parsley and serve.

If you like a stronger flavour of garlic, stir the extra garlic into the mayonnaise and stir a spoonful into each serving.

If you have a chance to make the stew a day in advance of serving, the flavour will be much more mellow and well blended. Store in the refrigerator covered for no more than 2 days.

Serves 6-8
Calories 1595 (6715 kJ)
Protein 160 grams

450 g/1 lb fillet of fresh white fish such as cod, haddock, whiting
450 g/1 lb fillet of smoked white fish such as cod, haddock
45 ml/3 tbls olive oil
2 large onions, sliced
3 garlic cloves, crushed
2 400-g/14-oz cans tomatoes
1 bouquet garni
salt and ground black pepper
450 g/1 lb potatoes
pared zest and juice of 1 orange
2.5 ml/$\frac{1}{2}$ tsp saffron
30 ml/2 tbls chopped parsley

To serve (optional)
60 ml/4 tbls mayonnaise
1-2 garlic cloves, crushed

Marinated Mackerel

4 fresh mackerel, weighing about
 350g/12 oz each

For the marinade
45 ml/3 tbls olive oil
45 ml/ 3 tbls lemon juice
5 ml/1 tsp salt
ground black pepper
1 bay leaf

For the garnish
2 seedless oranges, thinly sliced
50 g/2 oz black olives
watercress sprigs

Ask the fishmonger to gut the fish, or do it yourself, following the directions on page 32. Wash thoroughly.

Cut the fish open from the cavity to the tail end. Press along the backbone to open it without actually halving it. Working from the head end, ease away the backbone, and cut it free at the head and tail ends. Lift it out with as many bones as possible. Cut a few oblong slits along the body length. Arrange the fish in a flameproof dish.

Mix together all the marinade ingredients, pour over the fish and spoon into the cavities. Cover and set aside for 2 hours at room temperature turning and basting the fish occasionally.

Heat the grill to medium. Uncover the fish, baste them again with the marinade and place the dish under the grill. Cook for 6-8 minutes, depending on the thickness of the fish. Turn and cook for 6-8 minutes on the second side, basting occasionally with the marinade, until the fish is cooked.

Set the dish aside and leave until completely cold, basting occasionally.

Arrange the fish on a flat dish and spoon a little marinade over. Garnish with the oranges, olives and watercress.

Serves 4
Calories 2215 (9205 kJ)
Protein 149 grams

Salmon Steaks Florentine

Remove the stems and discard any discoloured leaves from the spinach. Wash thoroughly, drain off any excess water, pack into a large pan and cover.

Season the salmon steaks. Put them on the grill rack and dot with butter. Grill for 8-10 minutes on one side. Meanwhile, put the spinach pan over a fairly high heat. When it starts to sizzle, turn it with a wooden spoon and reduce the heat.

Turn the salmon steaks and cook for 8-10 minutes on the second side, basting with the juices. Stir spinach over and over and cook for a total of 10-12 minutes, until it is well reduced and tender.

Melt the butter for the sauce in a small pan, add the lemon juice and season with salt, pepper and cayenne.

Turn the cooked spinach into a colander and press it with a spoon to extract any remaining moisture. Return to the pan and add the cream, salt and pepper. Heat through, then transfer to a warmed serving dish.

Arrange the salmon steaks on the spinach and pour over the sauce.

*The sauce is very rich – full of fat and calories. Serve the fish without it if you are very health conscious.

Serves 4
Calories 2380 (9855 kJ)
Protein 115 grams

4 salmon steaks about 2.5 cm/1 in thick
900 g/2 lb spinach
salt and ground black pepper
50 g/2 oz unsalted butter
50 ml/2 fl oz thick cream

For the sauce
100 g/4 oz unsalted butter
juice of ½ lemon
cayenne pepper

Chinese-style Steamed Trout

4 fresh trout, weighing about
   350 g/12 oz each
12 thin slices fresh root ginger
12 button mushrooms, thinly
   sliced
8 spring onions, thinly sliced

For the sauce
45 ml/3 tbls dry sherry or sake
10 ml/2 tsp sugar
30 ml/2 tbls soy sauce
20 ml/4 tsp cornflour

Ask the fishmonger to clean and gut the fish, or do it yourself, following the directions on page 32. Wash the fish thoroughly and dry. Place them side by side in a shallow oval ovenproof dish just large enough to hold them.

Mix together the sauce ingredients and pour over the fish, basting them well and spooning the liquid into the cavities.

Cut the ginger into narrow strips and scatter over the fish with the mushroom and spring onion slices.

Place the dish in a steamer basket, or stand it on a trivet in the base of a large pan or flameproof casserole containing 5 cm/2 in of rapidly-boiling water. Cover the pan or casserole and steam for 15-20 minutes. It is important to keep the water at a good, steady boil, otherwise there will not be enough steam or heat to cook the fish thoroughly. Serve at once. Rice is a good accompaniment.

Serves 4
Calories 1135 (4775 kJ)
Protein 180 grams

Fish Provençal

1 whole grey or red mullet
   weighing about 1 kg/2 lb, or
   codling
60 ml/4 tbls olive oil
2 medium-sized onions, finely
   chopped
700 g/1½ lb tomatoes, skinned and
   sliced, or canned ones, drained
100 g/4 oz mushrooms, thinly
   sliced
50 g/2 oz blanched almonds,
   chopped
30 ml/2 tbls mixed fresh herbs,
   such as parsley, chervil, fennel,
   or 10 ml/2 tsp dried herbs
275 ml/10 fl oz red wine
12 black olives
salt and ground black pepper

Ask the fishmonger to clean and gut the fish, or do it yourself, following the directions on page 32. Thoroughly wash and dry it using absorbent kitchen paper.

Heat the oil in a large frying-pan and fry the fish over a low-moderate heat for about 8 minutes on the first side. Turn it over very carefully, using two fish slices so that you do not pierce or tear the skin. Cook for a further 8 minutes on the second side. Carefully lift the fish on to a warmed dish, cover it with foil and keep warm while you make the sauce.

Fry the onions in the pan over low heat for about 4 minutes, stirring occasionally, then add the tomatoes and mushrooms, stir well, increasing the heat to moderate, and cook for 5 minutes, or until slightly thickened.

Add the almonds, herbs, wine and olives and season with salt and pepper. Bring the sauce to the boil and simmer for 10-15 minutes, or until it is cooked. Taste the sauce and adjust the seasoning if necessary.

Lift the fish on to a warmed serving dish and carefully pour the sauce round it. Serve at once.

Small new potatoes, or potatoes boiled in their skins, and a green salad make good accompaniments.

Serves 4
Calories 1605 (6675 kJ)
Protein 132 grams

Mackerel and Grapefruit Kebabs

Ask the fishmonger to clean, gut and fillet the fish, or do it yourself, following the directions on pages 32 and 33. Wash well and cut each mackerel fillet into 4 or 5 pieces. Skin the onions and blanch them in boiling water for 1 minute, then drain, and refresh under cold water.

Thread a tomato on to each of 4 kebab sticks, then alternate with pieces of mackerel, onions, mushrooms, pepper and grapefruit segments. Finish with the remaining tomatoes. Put the kebabs into a shallow dish.

Mix together the ingredients for the marinade and pour it over the kebabs. Cover and set aside at room temperature for at least 2 hours, turning and basting the kebabs occasionally.

Heat the grill to high. Cook the kebabs for about 12 minutes, turning them frequently and basting them with the remaining marinade, or until the mackerel is cooked and the grapefruit well browned.

Serve the kebabs hot, on a bed of rice.

Serves 4
Calories 1975 (8190 kJ)
Protein 107 grams

2 large mackerel, weighing about 450g/1 lb each
8 button onions
8 small tomatoes, skinned
225 g/8oz mushrooms, halved
1 large green pepper, de-seeded and cut into 2.5-cm/1-in squares
2 small grapefruits, peeled and divided into segments

For the marinade
75 ml/5 tbls olive oil
30 ml/2 tbls orange juice
15 ml/1 tbls medium sherry
5 ml/1 tsp brown sugar
15 ml/1 tbls chopped thyme
15 ml/1 tbls chopped parsley
a pinch of cayenne pepper

Humberside Smoked Haddock

Heat the oven to 190C/375F/gas 5. Wash the haddock and cut it into 4 portions. Place the fish in a shallow ovenproof dish, pour over just enough boiling water to cover, allow to stand for 1 minute, then drain off the water.

Pour the milk over the fish and sprinkle with a few grindings of black pepper. Mix together the tomatoes and mushrooms and spread them over the fish. Dot with half of the butter. Cover the dish with greased foil and bake for 25 minutes, until the fish is tender.

Melt the remaining butter in a small pan and stir in the flour. Cook for 1 minute. Strain off the liquid from the baking dish and reserve. Keep the fish warm. Stir the reserved liquid gradually into the butter and flour mixture. Stir over a moderate heat until sauce boils and thickens. Lower the heat and simmer for 2-3 minutes.

Arrange the fish portions on a warmed serving dish and pipe the mashed potato round to form a border. Pour a little of the sauce over the fish and serve the rest separately. Garnish the dish with the parsley sprigs and serve at once.

Serves 4
Calories 2020 (8465 kJ)
Protein 141 grams

700 g/1½ lb fillet smoked haddock
450 ml/15 fl oz milk
ground black pepper
6 large tomatoes, skinned, de-seeded and sliced
225g/8 oz mushrooms, sliced
50 g/2 oz butter
25 g/1 oz flour
700 g/1½ lb hot mashed potatoes
parsley sprigs

Coral Reef Prawns

225 g/8 oz brown long-grain rice
100 g/4 oz butter
15 ml/1 tbls olive oil
2 shallots
16 king prawns, boiled and peeled
60 ml/4 tbls brandy
5 ml/1 tsp lemon juice
salt and ground black pepper
275 ml/10 fl oz thick cream
30 ml/2 tbls each chopped parsley,
    fennel and chives
paprika
1 lemon

Boil the rice in a large pan of salted water for 30-35 minutes, until just tender. Drain and keep it warm in a covered bowl over a pan of simmering water.

Heat 50 g/2 oz of the butter and the oil in a large, heavy based frying-pan and cook the shallots over a low heat for 2 minutes. Add the prawns, stir and cook very gently for a further minute. Add the brandy and heat through for 1 minute, then set the contents of the pan alight and shake gently to distribute the flames.

When the flames die down, add the lemon juice and season with salt and plenty of pepper. Stir and heat through gently for 1 minute. Add the cream and stir to thicken over low heat for about 3 minutes. Check seasoning.

Fork the remaining butter into the rice and when it has melted stir in the herbs. Spread the rice on a warmed serving dish, spoon the creamed prawns into the centre and sprinkle generously with paprika. Garnish with lemon wedges.

Serves 4
Calories 3455 (14390 kJ)
Protein 125 grams

Hot Seafood and Vegetable Salad

In a shallow, ovenproof dish large enough to hold the fish slices in one layer, combine the olive oil, chilli powder, parsley, thyme, bay leaf and garlic. Cut the fish into 6 pieces, place them in the marinade, cover the dish and leave at room temperature for 1 hour, basting and turning occasionally.

Heat the oven to 190C/375F/gas 5. Cover the dish with foil and bake for 15 minutes, until the fish is tender.

Cut the pimentos into strips. Add them with the petits pois and mussels to the dish. Bake it, uncovered, for a further 5-10 minutes, or until the fish flakes easily when tested with a fork. Discard the bay leaf.

Garnish the dish with croûtons and slices of hard-boiled egg and serve at once.

*For details of how to prepare see page 44.

Serves 4-6
Calories 2225 (9245 kJ)
Protein 144 grams

700 g/1½ lb hake
3 canned red pimentos
100 g/4 oz petits pois, cooked
24 mussels, scrubbed and steamed*
8-12 croûtons
2 hard-boiled eggs, quartered

For the marinade
125 ml/4 fl oz olive oil
1.5 ml/¼ tsp hot chilli powder
30 ml/2 tbls chopped parsley
1.5 ml/¼ tsp dried thyme
1 bay leaf
2 garlic cloves, crushed

Moules à la Marinière

1.2 L/1¾ pt mussels
40 g/1½ oz butter
1 medium-sized onion, finely chopped
1 garlic clove, finely chopped
1 shallot, or 3 spring onion bulbs, finely chopped
4 parsley stalks
1 sprig of thyme or 2.5 ml/½ tsp dried thyme
200 ml/7 fl oz dry white wine or dry cider
salt and ground black pepper
30 ml/2 tbls chopped parsley

Clean and prepare the mussels, following the directions below very carefully.

Melt the butter in a large saucepan over low heat. Add the vegetables, cover and sweat for 10 minutes.

Tie the parsley stalks and sprig of thyme together with fine string. Or if you use dried thyme, put the herbs in a small piece of muslin or cheesecloth and tie it up to enclose them.

Add the herbs, wine or cider and 75 ml/5 tbls water to the pan. Heat through slowly until the liquid is almost boiling.

Add the mussels, cover and shake the pan gently over fierce heat for 2 minutes, to open the shells. Reduce the heat and cook for a further 3 minutes, until the mussels are cooked.

Strain the liquor through a colander into a second saucepan and discard the herbs.

Discard any mussels that have not opened – this is most important and if you are in any doubt at all, have no hesitation in discarding them.

Remove one half of the shell from each cooked and opened mussel. Return these mussels in the half-shells to the liquor in the pan. Reheat gently and season to taste.

Ladle the soup into a warmed tureen or individual bowls, heaping up the mussels in the centre. Garnish with the chopped parsley.

Serve hot, with hot French bread or granary rolls.

Serves 4 as a first course
Calories 430 (1785 kJ)
Protein 21 grams

Choosing and Preparing Fresh Mussels

Pull away seaweed 'beards'.

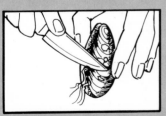

Scrape shell clean.

The success of this classic French dish depends on the freshness of the mussels and the care with which they are cleaned. As the fish, when in season, are relatively inexpensive yet the dish has such an air of luxury, it is worth taking the trouble to prepare it to perfection.

The mussels must be live when you buy and cook them. Live mussels usually keep their shells closed out of water. And so look carefully at those on a fishmonger's slab. If the shells are open, or broken, do not buy them. Tap any open shells you find in your purchase. They should snap shut at once. If they don't, discard them.

If possible, eat mussels on the day you buy them. If you have to leave them overnight, put them in a bucket of salted water. You can also, if you like, add a little flour or oatmeal to feed the shellfish and fatten them up. Cover the bucket with a cloth and leave it in a cool place.

To clean the mussels, pull away the seaweed 'beards', left top. Scrub the mussels under cold running water and scrape away any encrustations, left bottom.

Keep the mussels immersed in cold water until ready to cook. Change the water several times, then drain them just before cooking.

Make it as easy as possible for your guests to enjoy the dish. Put an empty plate in the centre of the table for the discarded half-shells, and provide a spoon for the delicious wine-flavoured liquor. Provide large napkins – or old-fashioned finger-bowls, which were an excellent idea – to clean sticky fingers.

Dressed Crab

Clean and prepare the crab, following the directions below very carefully.

Add the breadcrumbs and lemon juice to the brown meat and season it with salt and pepper. Pack the mixture neatly into the centre of the shell, leaving room for the white meat on either side.

Season the white meat with 5 ml/1 tsp lemon juice, salt and pepper and the mayonnaise, if you use it. Pile this mixture into the shell at each side, keeping neat divisions between the two types of meat.

Finely chop the white of the egg and sieve the yolk. Using a knife as a guide, use the chopped parsley, chopped egg white and seived egg yolk to make dividing lines, with the yolk close to the white meat, the parsley in the centre and the egg white next to the brown meat.

Sprinkle thin diagonal lines of paprika pepper in a diamond pattern across the white meat, or lay very thin strips of canned pimento in a diagonal pattern.

Line a serving dish with lettuce leaves and place the dressed crab in the centre, and, if you like, arrange extra hard-boiled eggs round the dish. Serve with a crisp green salad, and, traditionally, brown bread and butter, or crusty wholewheat rolls.

1 large boiled crab, 900 g/2 lb
30 ml/2 tbls fresh brown breadcrumbs
10 ml/2 tsp lemon juice
salt and ground black pepper
15 ml/1 tbls mayonnaise
1 hard-boiled egg
10 ml/2 tsp finely chopped parsley
paprika pepper, or small can red pimentos, drained

Serves 4
Calories 680 (2840 kJ)
Protein 79 grams

Choosing and Preparing Crab

Ask the fishmonger to pull the cooked crab slightly open so that you can see how much meat there is inside – there are both lean and fat crabs, so take care to choose one that is full of meat. A large 1-kg/2-lb crab should yield about 350g/12 oz of meat.

To prepare the crab, put it on its back on a wooden board. Using your fingers, twist off the legs and claws – they should come away without any pressure.

With your thumbs against the back shell, close to the tail, prise the soft central body section away from the hard shell, right.

Remove and discard the small grey stomach sack from the body section, and all the long greyish-white and pointed 'dead man's fingers', right bottom.

Use two bowls to keep the white and dark meat separate. Crack the claws and legs with a pair of nutcrackers or a hammer and, with a skewer, scrape out all the meat.

Scrape out all the white meat from the body shell, not forgetting to poke out all the crevices with a skewer. With a teaspoon, scrape the meat away from the hard back shell.

Break off the rim round the back shell so that the edge is smooth and neatened. Wash and dry the shell and rub the inside with a small pad of kitchen paper moistened with olive oil.

Season the meat and arrange it in the shell as described in the recipe. This is the traditional way to serve dressed crab. Having cooked and prepared the crab as described above, you can of course use the meat in a variety of ways and recipes.

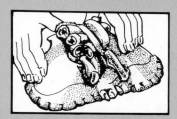
Push body out of shell.

Discard intestines (see text).

Healthy Vegetable Cooking

Probably not very many people raise up a dish of freshly-picked, tender young vegetables and say, 'Cheers', or 'Good health', but the sentiment would be highly appropriate if they did. For vegetables are rich in vitamins B and C, and also an invaluable source of dietary fibre. Many more vegetables than we suppose can be eaten raw – matchsticks of parsnips and green peppers in a selection of crudités, Brussels sprouts with nuts and seeds in salad, and examples galore in Chapter 5 – and we should make more room for them in our menus. For a raw vegetable is a healthy vegetable. Cooking destroys Vitamin C and much of the Vitamin B complex; Vitamin C and the B complex are water-soluble. And so vegetables that have been lying around in the shops, put in soak before cooking, long overcooked and then kept waiting before serving are about as nutritious – and tasty – as a sheet of blotting paper.

Speed is the answer. Pick, dig or buy your vegetables in small quantities just before you need them. Prepare them just before you cook them, and cook them as quickly and for as short a time as possible. Then pretend that the cooked vegetables are a soufflé and will collapse if they are not served at once. The vitamins will, anyway!

Preparing

Many of us have been wasting our time peeling vegetables quite unnecessarily for years. Wasting the 'goodness' too, for most of the nutrients in root vegetables are just beneath the skin. Wash all vegetables thoroughly, root vegetables by brushing vigorously with a brush kept just for the purpose, and leaf vegetables one leaf at a time under cold, running water. When root vegetables are old and tough or have to be peeled, pare off the thinnest possible layer – a swivel peeler is ideal – and save the peelings for soup or stock. They're too good to throw away! Trim off very tough stalks from leaf vegetables. You can use these, too, for soup, or finely chop or shred them into salads. Cabbage stalk soup is super!

Vegetables can be cooked in many more ways than most of us imagine as well as playing a vital but supporting role to other ingredients in soups, stews, casseroles and gratinated dishes. Brush up on your vegetable versatility and enjoy these valuable fruits of the soil in all their crisp and colourful variety.

Baking
Prick skins of root vegetables to prevent them from bursting and insert a few slivers of garlic into slits – aubergines take well to this trick, too. Brush sweetcorn and globe artichokes with oil and wrap in foil before putting in oven.

Season spinach and other young leaves, brush each one with oil and roll up several together into a sausage shape. Bake in a hot oven until the outsides are crisp, the insides meltingly soft.

Boiling
Not considered one of the finest arts of vegetable cookery, but certainly useful for partly cooking hard vegetables to be stir-fried and stir-braised, and for soft-cooking those for purée. Always save the water for soup stock.

Braising and simmering
A refinement of boiling which can be carried out in the oven or on top of the stove, whichever is more economical. Vegetables with a high liquid content, courgettes, spinach, marrow, mushrooms – can be cooked with little or no added liquid, though seasoning and a dash of chopped onion or garlic, herbs or spices are a definite advantage. Other vegetables need very little liquid – about 150 ml/5 fl oz of stock with orange or lemon juice, cider or wine added or, at a pinch, just water, is enough for each 450 g/1 lb of vegetables. Add a knob of polyunsaturated margarine or 15 ml/1 tbls vegetable oil so that the vegetables are glazed as the liquid evaporates. Cover the pan or dish closely and set the oven at about 190C/375F/gas 5. Toss braised vegetables with chopped herbs, in yoghurt or soured cream before serving.

Grilling
This method is suitable only for the high-moisture category – aubergines, courgettes, mushrooms, tomatoes – though parboiled vegetables can be finished off under the grill. Brush vegetables with oil and sprinkle them with herbs, garlic or cheese.

Halve aubergines and courgettes and degorge them with salt first, then season them well. Prick tomato skins if grilling them whole.

Parcels

Just like parcels of meat or fish, vegetable parcels can be baked, boiled or steamed – choose the method that fits in best with the rest of the meal. It's a marvellous opportunity to mix and mingle shapes and flavours – small whole celery hearts sprinkled with onion rings, mushroom slices and thyme leaves; mushroom caps stuffed with pea and mint purée; partly-cooked carrots, swedes and potatoes tossed with sliced onion and leeks – broccoli flowerets with sliced carrots and grated orange zest – you really can't go wrong. Add 15 ml/1 tbls of vegetable oil and 30 ml/2 tbls of stock to each 450 g/1 lb of root vegetables and be lavish with the herbs. Make sure vegetables are well wrapped in double-thickness foil, particularly if the parcels are to be boiled.

Purée

Cook root vegetables until they are really tender, then sieve, mash, liquidize or put them through a food mill. (Stringy vegetables will need sieving after mashing or liquidizing.) It's a spectacular way to serve humble root vegetables, and a clever way to rescue overcooked ones. 'Cream' them with polyunsaturated margarine and yoghurt, add plenty of seasoning and a generous pinch of nutmeg or allspice. Root vegetable purée can be piped into whirls, rosettes or topping – an

appropriate crown for a vegetable pie. Extend the range by blending the puréed vegetables with the roots – pea and potato, pumpkin and carrot, parsnip and tomato. Purées that are not stiff enough to hold a shape can be piled into a mound on a serving dish, brushed with oil and finished in the oven or under the grill. Re-heat piped vegetable decorations – duchesse potatoes, for example – on a greased baking sheet for 5-10 minutes at 220C/425F/gas 7. Purées of vegetables freeze well. Thaw at room temperature.

Steaming

Steaming does for vegetables what boiling often fails to do – presents them crisp and dry and proud of their appearance. Open steam them on a steaming 'fan' or close-steam them in a dish – this way you trap all the juices. This is another perfect way to cook a medley of vegetables in one container, though this time they retain their separate identities. Steaming takes longer than boiling. If this is a problem, parboil root vegetables first, then finish them off in the steamer alongside quickie-cook bean shoots, sprouts or tiny cauliflower flowerets and young French beans.

Steam-heat can be deceptive – be on the look-out and remove vegetables from the heat as soon as

they are just tender, then serve them, at once. Otherwise they just go on cooking – and spoiling. If steamed vegetables are to be served cold, dunk them straight into iced water. Drain when they are cool. Cover and keep in the refrigerator until ready to serve.

Stir-frying and stir-braising
Have all the vegetables absolutely ready before you start – washed, trimmed, dried and cut into small, neat, even-sized pieces. Diagonal slicing is the Chinese way – and they should know! Heat the oil – peanut, ground-nut, sunflower or sesame, usually – in a Chinese wok or heavy-based pan, add the salt and any initial flavouring – ginger or garlic, then the vegetables. If you are stir-frying more than one type, add them in sequence, the longest-cooking ones first, the 'quickies' last. Or parboil root vegetables to bring them into line.

Have the sauce ready mixed – it can be a three or four ingredient combination of soy sauce with sake or sherry, wine, cider, stock, tomato purée, sugar, honey or lemon juice. Pour it over the vegetables and bring it quickly to the boil to reduce it rapidly and almost totally – see individual recipes for actual times.

Longer-cooking vegetables can be stir-braised in the sauce at intervals for 5-10 minutes. Meanwhile, the heat is lowered to moderate and the pan covered. Stir-braising takes practice, though – it's important to reduce the sauce quickly to a minimum before the vegetables lose their crispness and bright, fresh colour.

Stuffed Vegetables
Aubergines, cabbages, courgettes, cucumbers, marrows, onions, peppers, tomatoes and mushroom caps make perfect containers for high-fibre fillings of cooked brown rice, lentils or wholewheat breadcrumbs tossed with cheese, herbs or small amounts of meat or sometimes fish. It's a healthy way of majoring on the vegetables and letting other ingredients take second place. Cabbage or vine leaves can be used as the wrapping device for little parcels, Balkan-style. Stuffed whole vegetables are usually baked in a moderate oven, either just in a well-greased dish or in a little stock or well-flavoured tomato sauce. Cold stuffed vegetables, often with a herb-scented sausage meat stuffing, are a favourite Italian antipasto dish. Experiment to add variety to your vegetable starters.

Cold cooked vegetables
Perhaps it should be emphasized that raw vegetables in salads are healthier than cooked ones; but there again a separate course of a cold, cooked vegetable is a great deal healthier than some foods we could mention! Cook vegetables that are to be served cold until they are only just tender, so as to preserve their crispness. Drain them quickly and thoroughly. A cold vegetable dish makes a refreshing and interesting 'starter', or can be served alone after the main dish as a 'palate freshener'.

Vegetable Couscous

450 g/1 lb couscous grains
salt
225 g/8 oz dried chick peas, soaked overnight
45 ml/3 tbls peanut oil
225 g/8 oz sliced onions
2 large garlic cloves, crushed
2 green peppers, de-seeded and chopped
2 large carrots, sliced
2 medium-sized courgettes, sliced
3 medium-sized potatoes, peeled and quartered
225 g/8 oz pumpkin, cubed (optional)
100 g/4 oz sultanas
400 g/14 oz canned okra, drained
5 ml/1 tsp cayenne pepper
10 ml/2 tsp ground cumin
5 ml/1 tsp paprika
ground black pepper
150 g/5 oz harissa sauce
40 g/1½ oz butter
150 g/5 oz ripe tomatoes, skinned and quartered
3 hard-boiled eggs, quartered

First make the couscous. Put the grains into a bowl and pour over about 275 ml/10 fl oz lukewarm salted water. Stir until blended then set aside for 30 minutes to allow the grains to swell. Repeat at least once more.

Meanwhile, put the chick peas and their soaking liquid into a large saucepan, adding more water if necessary to cover them. Bring quickly to the boil, cover the pan and simmer for about 2 hours, or until the peas are tender. Drain and set aside.

Heat the oil in a large, deep pan with a heavy base. Add the onions, garlic, peppers and carrots and fry gently until the onions are soft. Stir in the courgettes, potatoes and pumpkin, if using, and pour on 850 ml/1½ pt water. Bring to the boil, cover the pan and simmer for 20 minutes, until vegetables are tender.

Stir in the cooked chick peas, the sultanas, okra, cayenne, cumin and paprika and season with salt and pepper. Add about 15 ml/1 tbls of the harissa sauce and bring to the boil again.

Line a colander with scalded muslin or cheesecloth and set it over the pan containing the vegetables, or over a separate pan of simmering water. Seal the space between the colander and pan, if necessary, with a rolled-up teacloth. Put the couscous grains into the colander, cover tightly and cook the couscous and vegetable mixture over low heat for 15 minutes or so.

Remove the colander and stir the butter gently into the grains. Add the tomatoes and eggs to the vegetables. Return the colander to the pan, cover it again and cook both grains and vegetables for a final 5 minutes.

Spread the couscous on a large, deep serving dish. Spoon over the vegetable mixture with some of the cooking liquid and hand the rest of the harissa sauce separately. If you wish, you can thin the sauce a little by stirring in some of the remaining vegetable stock from the pan.

Serves 4-6
Calories 3935 (16680 kJ)
Protein 145 grams

Spinach with Yoghurt

900 g/2 lb fresh spinach leaves
25 g/1 oz butter
salt and ground black pepper
30 ml/2 tbls lemon juice
150 ml/5 fl oz natural yoghurt
1 lemon, quartered

Thoroughly wash the spinach in several changes of water. Discard any damaged, wilted or discoloured leaves. Strip off and discard the tough stalks. Drain.

Put the butter in a large, heavy-based saucepan, melt it over low heat and season well with salt and pepper. Add the spinach leaves and stir them, turning them over and over so that they all wilt as they come into contact with the heat.

Stir the lemon juice into the yoghurt. As soon as the spinach has collapsed and is tender, stir in the yoghurt mixture. Stir over very low heat, just to heat the yoghurt through.

Turn the spinach into a warmed serving dish and garnish with the lemon quarters. Serve hot.

Serves 4
Calories 410 (1710 kJ)
Protein 30 grams

Spinach Crêpes

50 g/2 oz flour
2.5 ml/½ tsp salt
2 medium-sized eggs, beaten
75 ml/5 tbls melted butter
150 ml/5 fl oz milk
225 g/8 oz frozen spinach, thawed
   and finely chopped
15 ml/1 tbls chopped sorrel or mint
oil for frying
60 ml/4 tbls grated Parmesan
   cheese

For the filling
450g/1 lb cottage cheese, sieved
60 ml/4 tbls natural yoghurt
1 egg, beaten
30 ml/2 tbls grated Parmesan
   cheese
2 medium-sized carrots, finely
   diced and cooked
6 asparagus spears, cooked and
   chopped

Sift the flour and salt into a bowl and stir in the beaten eggs. Gradually add 30ml/2 tbls of the melted butter, the milk and 75 ml/5 tbls water. Stir until the batter is smooth and completely lump free.

Strain the batter through a fine sieve and stir in the chopped spinach and herb. Add a little more water, if necessary, to make the batter the consistency of thin cream. Leave to rest for about 2 hours in a cool place.

Heat a small non-stick pan and when it is hot rub it with a wad of kitchen paper soaked in vegetable oil. Pour in about 30 ml/2 tbls of the crêpe mixture, tilt the pan so that it covers the base and cook over a moderate-high heat until the crêpe bubbles. Toss or flip the crêpe over and cook for a few moments on the other side. Stack the cooked crêpes on a plate put over a pan of hot water and cover them with a cloth to keep them warm while

you cook the remaining batter.

Heat the oven to 180C/350F/gas 4. Stir together the sieved cottage cheese, the yoghurt, beaten egg and grated cheese and season with salt and pepper. Stir in the vegetables.

Divide the filling mixture between the crêpes, spooning it into the centre. Roll them up loosely. Arrange the crêpes in a greased shallow ovenproof dish and brush them with the remaining melted butter. Sprinkle them with the grated cheese and bake for 20 minutes, until they are heated through.

Serves 4-6
Calories 1880 (7840 kJ)
Protein 128 grams

Skirlie-Mirlie

450 g/1 lb turnips, peeled and
   thickly sliced
450 g/1 lb old potatoes, peeled and
   thickly sliced
salt
60 ml/4 tbls top of milk or thin
   cream
25 g/1 oz butter
ground black pepper
15 ml/1 tbls chopped parsley

Put the turnips into a pan of boiling, salted water, cover and simmer for 15 minutes. Add the potatoes, cover, bring back to the boil and simmer for a further 15 minutes, or until both vegetables are tender. Drain well and mash thoroughly.

Add the milk or cream and butter and season well with salt and pepper. Return the pan to a low heat just to heat the ingredients through.

Pile the vegetable mixture on to a warmed serving dish and sprinkle with the parsley to garnish.

*For a quick, filling snack dish, you can push holes in the dish of vegetables with the back of a large spoon and slide a lightly-poached egg into each one.

Serves 4-6
Calories 715 (3015 kJ)
Protein 13 grams

Curried Cabbage and Potatoes

Heat the oil and clarified butter in a frying-pan over low heat. Add the spice seeds and stir until they begin to crackle. Add the onion, ginger, chilli, cardamom, cumin, clove and cinnamon, and stir well.

Dry the potato cubes on absorbent kitchen paper and add them to the pan. Stir for 4 minutes.

Add the shredded cabbage, peas and salt and sugar to taste. Stir for 5 minutes, then add 125 ml/4 fl oz hot water. Slightly increase the heat until the mixture boils, then reduce the heat again and simmer gently until the vegetables are tender. If the mixture dries out before the vegetables are cooked, stir in a little more hot water.

Turn on to a warmed serving dish and remove the chilli. Serve with rice.

Serves 4
Calories 890 (3760 kJ)
Protein 24 grams

1 small cabbage, shredded
4 medium-sized potatoes, cut into
   2.5-cm/1-in cubes
15 ml/1 tbls vegetable oil
10 ml/2 tsp clarified butter
2.5 ml/½ tsp mixed anise,
   fenugreek, onion and black and
   white mustard seeds
1 medium-sized onion, chopped
2.5-cm/1-in piece fresh root
   ginger, chopped
1 green chilli, slit
2 cardamom pods, crushed
5 ml/1 tsp cumin seeds
1 clove
25 mm/1 in cinnamon stick
30 ml/2 tbls peas
salt
sugar

Orange Sugared Carrots

Trim the carrots, scrape or peel them and slice them thinly. Put them into a small pan with the sugar, chicken stock and butter and season with salt and pepper.

Squeeze the juice from one orange. Grate the zest of one half and add both juice and zest to the carrots in the pan. Cover the pan, bring to the boil and simmer gently for 25-30 minutes or until the liquid has almost evaporated and the carrots are just tender. Check from time to time that the carrots are not drying out before they are cooked – they will if the heat is too high.

Meanwhile, thinly pare the zest from the second half of the orange and cut it into very fine matchstick strips. Put them in a small pan, cover with water, bring to the boil and simmer for 20 minutes. Drain and toss the orange strips on kitchen paper to dry them. Cut the remaining orange into thin slices.

When the carrots are just tender and glazed with the orange syrup, turn them on to a warmed serving dish. Arrange the orange slices around the edge and scatter the carrots with the parsley and orange strips to garnish.

Serves 4
Calories 570 (2415 kJ)
Protein 9 grams

750 g/1½ lb carrots
30 ml/2 tbls brown sugar
150 ml/5 fl oz chicken stock
25 g/1 oz butter
salt and ground black pepper
2 oranges
15 ml/1 tbls chopped parsley

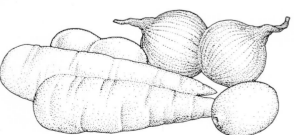

Stuffed Artichokes

4 medium-sized artichokes
100 g/4 oz dried breadcrumbs
2 garlic cloves, finely chopped
10 ml/2 tsp mint leaves, finely
  chopped
1.5 ml/¼ tsp nutmeg, finely
  grated
2.5 ml/½ tsp salt
2.5 ml/½ tsp ground black pepper
125 ml/4 fl oz olive oil

Heat the oven to 180C/350F/gas 4. To prepare the artichokes, hold each one upside-down and strike it firmly against a table top to make the leaves open easily. Cut off the stems evenly at the base so that the artichokes will stand upright. Cut off the tough outer leaves. Trim 2.5 cm/1 in from the tips of the remaining leaves to level the tops. Pull the outer leaves back and cut away the inner purple leaves. Remove the prickly centre choke with a teaspoon.

Mix together the breadcrumbs, garlic, mint, nutmeg, salt, pepper and oil. Spoon this mixture into the centre of the artichokes and reshape them.

Place the artichokes in a casserole that just fits them, so that they stand upright. Pour in water taking care not to spill it into the artichokes centres, to come 2.5 cm/1 in up the sides of the dish. Cover the dish and bake for 1 hour, or until the artichokes are tender. Test by piercing a fine skewer down through the centre.
*As artichokes are slightly messy vegetables to eat provide plenty of napkins and, if possible, finger-bowls, too.

Serves 4
Calories 1220 (5060 kJ)
Protein 16 grams

Runner Beans à la Grècque

Place all the ingredients except the runner beans, chopped herbs and lemon in a medium-sized saucepan and cover with 400 ml/14 fl oz water. Bring to the boil, cover the pan and simmer for 15 minutes or so.

Top and tail the beans, remove any strings and cut them into 2.5 cm/1-in lengths. Add the beans to the pan and stir them into the liquid. Bring back to the boil, cover the pan and continue simmering for 7-10 minutes, or until the beans are just tender. It is important not to overcook them.

Using a slotted spoon, transfer the beans and onions to a dish and cover them. Put on one side.

Boil the cooking liquor rapidly for about 15 minutes until it is reduced to about 150 ml/5 fl oz. Strain it over the beans and leave to cool.

Serve the dish tepid or slightly chilled garnished with the chopped herbs and slices of lemon.

*This dish makes an unusual and refreshing first course, served with wholemeal bread rolls.

Serves 4
Calories 620 (2585 kJ)
Protein 11 grams

1 small onion, finely chopped
60 ml/4 tbls olive oil
60 ml/4 tbls dry white wine or lemon juice
6 parsley sprigs
1 stalk celery
1 bay leaf
1.5 ml/¼ tsp dried thyme
6 black peppercorns, crushed
6 coriander seeds, crushed
1.5 ml/¼ tsp salt
450 g/1 lb runner beans
30 ml/2 tbls chopped mixed herbs
1 lemon, quartered

Vegetable Risotto

15 ml/1 tbls vegetable oil
50 g/2 oz butter
1 medium-sized onion, finely
  chopped
1 garlic clove, crushed
225 g/8 oz brown long-grain rice
about 1 L/1¾ pt chicken stock,
  hot (see method)
1 medium-sized carrot, finely
  diced
2 celery stalks, finely sliced
100 g/4 oz French beans, cut into
  15-mm/½-in pieces
100 g/4 oz frozen peas, thawed
1 medium-sized courgette, finely
  diced
2 large tomatoes, skinned,
  de-seeded and diced
10 ml/2 tsp fresh thyme leaves or
  5 ml/1 tsp dried thyme
salt and ground black pepper
75 g/3oz grated Parmesan cheese

Heat the oil and butter in a heavy-based pan over low heat and sauté the onion and garlic until the onion is translucent and golden brown. Stir in the rice to coat it thoroughly. Pour on about 200 ml/7 fl oz of the hot stock and stir the rice to separate all the grains. When the rice has absorbed the stock pour on another 150 ml/5 fl oz and stir until this has been absorbed too.

Add the carrot, celery and beans and another 150 ml/5 fl oz of hot stock. Stir well and leave over low heat for 10 minutes. Add the thawed peas, the courgette, tomatoes and thyme and another 150 ml/5 fl oz of hot stock. Continue stirring and adding more stock until the rice is tender; it takes about 45 minutes in all to cook.

Season well with salt and pepper and add 50 g/2 oz of the grated cheese.

Cover the pan and leave it in a warm place to sweat for 5 minutes.

Turn the rice into a warmed serving dish and sprinkle with the remaining cheese. Serve at once.

Serves 4
Calories 1834 (7703 kJ)
Protein 53 grams

Broad Beans with Lettuce

450 g/1 lb fresh shelled or frozen
  broad beans, thawed
salt
15 g/½ oz butter
2 small onions, quartered
1 garlic clove, crushed
1 small head lettuce, washed and
  drained
2.5 ml/½ tsp savory or 1.5 ml/¼
  tsp dried savory
5 ml/1 tsp chopped parsley
2.5 ml/½ tsp sugar
ground black pepper
60 ml/4 tbls strong chicken stock
15 ml/1 tbls medium sherry
4 watercress sprigs

Boil fresh beans in boiling, salted water for 5 minutes, thawed frozen ones for 2 minutes. Drain them.

. Melt the butter in a pan and fry the onion and garlic over moderate heat for 3 minutes until transparent.

Shred the lettuce and add it to the pan with the beans, savory and parsley and the sugar. Season with salt and pepper, pour on the stock and sherry and bring just to the boil.

Cut 4 large pieces of double-thickness foil, large enough to enclose one portion of the vegetables in a loose parcel.

Divide the vegetables between the foil parcels, draw up the sides to make a dish shape and spoon on the liquid. Bring over the sides and seal them with a double seam all round.

Drop the foil parcels into a large pan of boiling water, cover the pan and boil rapidly for 20 minutes for fresh beans, 10 minutes for frozen ones.

Arrange the foil parcels on a warmed serving plate. Just as you serve them, slit a cross in the tops with a knife and pop a watercress sprig in each. Serve at once.

Serves 4
Calories 390 (1645 kJ)
Protein 23 grams

Stir-Fried Mixed Vegetables

Prepare the vegetables according to type. Cut carrots into thin slices and then, if you like, into flower shapes, using an ordinary petits fours cutter. Divide broccoli into small spears. Trim French beans and, if they are very young and tender, leave them whole, otherwise slice them. Trim and slice courgettes. Trim red peppers, remove the seeds and white pith and cut the flesh into thin strips. Thinly slice celery.

Put a colander over a large pan of boiling water, or use a steamer if you have one. Steam the vegetables, starting with those that require the longest cooking time first, and adding last the ones that cook most quickly. Allow about 8 minutes for carrots and broccoli, 5 minutes for French beans, 4 minutes for courgettes, red peppers and celery. Or,

if you prefer, cook the vegetables in a large pan of boiling, salted water, adding the quicker-cooking ones last. Cook them until they are barely tender. Drain the vegetables thoroughly.

Heat the oil in a Chinese wok or a large, heavy-based pan, add the salt and stir-fry for 2 minutes. Add 200 ml/7 fl oz water and continue stirring over high heat for 3 minutes. Mix together the soy sauce, sake or sherry and sugar and pour it into the pan. Stir for 1 further minute.

Turn the vegetables into a warmed serving dish and serve at once.

Serves 4
Calories 540 (2250 kJ)
Protein 9 grams

700 g/1½ lb mixed vegetables, such as carrots, broccoli, French beans, courgettes, red peppers, young tender celery
45 ml/3 tbls vegetable oil
2.5 ml/½ tsp salt
1 small onion, or 3 spring onion bulbs, finely chopped
15 ml/1 tbls soy sauce
30 ml/2 tbls sake or dry sherry
2.5 ml/½ tsp brown sugar

Purée Clamart

Put the peas into a pan, cover with cold water and bring to the boil. Strain in a colander, return the peas to the pan and add the butter, chicken stock and onion. Season to taste with salt and pepper. Bring to the boil, cover the pan and simmer for 10-15 minutes, until the peas and onion are tender and have absorbed most of the liquid. Purée the peas and any remaining liquid in an electric blender or a vegetable mouli.

Meanwhile cook the potatoes in boiling, salted water until they are tender. Drain them thoroughly and purée them in a vegetable mill.

Put the potato purée into a bowl and gradually beat in the pea purée, a little at

a time. Taste and adjust the seasoning if necessary. Stir in 15 ml/1 tbls of the chopped mint. Spoon the purée into a warmed serving dish and sprinkle with the remaining mint.
*A very attractive and festive way to serve the pea purée is to pile it into tiny pastry cases which have been just heated through, then sprinkle them with a pinch of chopped mint to garnish. Otherwise the purée can be served from a vegetable dish.

Serves 4
Calories 820 (3450 kJ)
Protein 33 grams

450g/1 lb frozen peas
50 g/2 oz butter
125 ml/4 fl oz strong chicken stock
1 small onion, finely chopped
salt and ground black pepper
225 g/8 oz old potatoes, peeled and thinly sliced
20 ml/4 tsp chopped mint

Stir-Fried Mushrooms with Mange-tout Peas and Cashews

225 g/8 oz mange-tout peas
salt
225 g/8 oz button mushrooms
1 small red pepper
15 ml/1 tbls soy sauce
15 ml/1 tbls dry sherry
5 ml/1 tsp clear honey
60 ml/4 tbls sunflower oil
1 garlic clove, chopped
50 g/2 oz cashews

Top and tail the mange-tout peas, remove any strings and cut them into 2.5 cm/1-in pieces. Blanch them in a large pan of boiling, salted water for 1½ minutes. Drain them and refresh them in cold water. Drain thoroughly again.

Trim, wipe and slice the mushrooms. Core and seed the red pepper and cut the flesh into matchstick strips.

In a small bowl, combine the soy sauce, sherry and honey.

Heat the oil and garlic in a Chinese wok or large heavy-based frying-pan over a moderate heat. When the garlic begins to sizzle, add the sliced mushrooms and strips of pepper and stir-fry for 2 minutes. Add the cashews and stir-fry for 1 minute more.

Add a good pinch of salt and 60 ml/4 tbls water and boil over high heat until the liquid has almost evaporated.

Stir the soy sauce mixture and pour it into the pan. Toss the vegetables and nuts in the sauce, add the mange-tout peas and stir-fry for 1 minute, or until the peas are tender.

Turn into a warmed serving dish and serve at once.

Serves 4
Calories 970 (4007 kJ)
Protein 21 grams

Aubergines Gratinées

Cut the aubergines into 6-mm/¼-in slices, put them in a colander and sprinkle them with the salt. Leave them for 30 minutes, then rinse them under running water. Drain them well and pat dry with kitchen paper. Toss the slices in flour to coat them.

Meanwhile, make the sauce. Melt the butter in a small pan, add the onion and fry over moderate heat, stirring occasionally, until it is soft. Add the flour and cook for 1 minute. Strain the liquid from the can of tomatoes into the pan, stir well and cook for 1 minute. Add the tomatoes, tomato purée, sugar, basil, salt and pepper and bring to the boil, stirring. Lower the heat, cover the pan and simmer for 15-20 minutes.

Heat the oven to 180C/350F/gas 4. Heat the oil in a large, heavy-based frying-pan over high heat. When it is very hot put in the aubergine slices, a few at a time. After a few seconds, turn them over. Drain them on kitchen paper and keep them hot while you fry the remaining slices, adding more oil if necessary.

Spoon a layer of tomato sauce into a medium-sized ovenproof casserole. Sprinkle with some of the cheese and put a layer of aubergine slices on top. Continue layers, finishing with tomato sauce. Mix the remaining cheese with breadcrumbs, sprinkle evenly over the dish and dot with butter. Top with tomato slices.

Stand the dish on a baking tray and bake for 25 minutes.

Serves 4
Calories 2190 (9130 kJ)
Protein 59 grams

4 medium-sized aubergines
15 ml/1 tbls salt
flour
75 ml/5 tbls vegetable oil
150 g/5 oz cheese, grated
25 g/1 oz white breadcrumbs
25 g/1 oz butter
2 medium-sized tomatoes

For the sauce
40 g/1½ oz butter
1 small onion, finely chopped
40 g/1½ oz flour
350 g/12 oz canned tomatoes
10 ml/2 tsp tomato purée
2.5 ml/½ tsp brown sugar
2.5 ml/½ tsp dried basil
salt and ground black pepper

Vegetable Kebabs

1 large aubergine
3 medium-sized courgettes
15 ml/1 tbls salt
12 small white onions
1 large green pepper
1 large red pepper
12 button mushrooms
8 small, firm tomatoes
45 ml/3 tbls melted butter

For the marinade
1 small onion, finely chopped
75 ml/5 tbls olive oil
30 ml/2 tbls red wine
15 ml/1 tbls chopped parsley
salt and ground black pepper

Cut the aubergine into 2.5 cm/1-in-thick slices, then halve or quarter them. Cut the courgettes into 2.5 cm/1-in slices. Put the vegetables into a colander, sprinkle them with the salt and leave them to drain for 30 minutes. Rinse them under cold water and drain them thoroughly.

Blanch the onions in salted water for 1½ minutes, then drain them thoroughly.

Trim the green and red peppers, remove the seeds and cut the flesh into 25-mm/1-in squares. Trim the mushroom stalks level with the caps.

Thread all the vegetables on to 4 skewers, alternating them for colours, shape and size and beginning and ending each skewer with a tomato. Lay the kebabs on a large flat dish, so they lie flat.

Mix together the ingredients for the marinade, pour it over the skewers and turn them to coat them thoroughly. Cover the dish loosely and leave it at room temperature for about 2 hours, turning the skewers occasionally.

Heat the grill to moderate. Brush the skewers with the melted butter. Grill them for 6-8 minutes, turning them often. Serve the kebabs very hot, on a bed of rice.

Serves 4
Calories 1270 (5290 kJ)
Protein 18 grams

Braised Vegetable Medley

45 ml/3 tbls vegetable oil
2 small turnips, peeled and diced
2 medium-sized carrots, peeled or
  scraped and diced
6 stalks celery, thinly sliced
1 green pepper, de-seeded and
  thinly sliced
1 red pepper, de-seeded and thinly
  sliced
175 g/6 oz frozen peas, thawed
175 g/6 oz frozen French beans,
  thawed
30 ml/2 tbls wholewheat flour
575 ml/1 pt chicken stock, hot
1 garlic clove, crushed
400 g/14 oz shredded white
  cabbage
salt and ground black pepper
a pinch of ground nutmeg
175 g/6 oz spinach
50 g/2 oz grated cheese

Heat the oil in a heavy-based frying-pan, add the turnips and carrots and stir-fry for about 4 minutes over a moderate heat until they are beginning to brown. Add the celery and cook, stirring frequently, for 4 minutes, then the peppers and cook for another 5 minutes, stirring often. Remove the vegetables with a slotted spoon and put them into a shallow oven-proof dish.

Heat the oven to 220C/425F/gas 7.

Add the peas and beans to the oil remaining in the pan and cook them over low heat for about 3 minutes, stirring often. Transfer them to the dish. Stir the flour into the pan, adding a very little more oil if necessary to form a smooth paste. Gradually pour on the stock, stirring, add the crushed garlic, season well with salt and pepper and nutmeg and

stir until the sauce thickens. Add the cabbage, bring back to the boil and pour over the dish of vegetables.

Wash the spinach leaves well and strip off and discard the tough central stems. Blanch the leaves in boiling, salted water for 1 minute. Drain them thoroughly and arrange them in overlapping rows over the vegetables to cover the top of the dish completely. Brush them with a very little oil. Sprinkle the grated cheese over the dish and bake for 20 minutes.

Serve very hot, with brown rice or pulses.

Serves 4
Calories 1090 (4585 kJ)
Protein 53 grams

Carrot Cake

Cook the carrots in a little boiling, salted water for 10-15 minutes, or until they are tender. Add the chopped onion for the last 1 minute. Drain thoroughly.

Heat the oven to 200C/400F/gas 5.

Put the eggs, yoghurt, thyme, lemon juice and rind into a blender with the cooked carrots and onion, season with salt and pepper and blend to a smooth purée. Without a blender, rub the carrots through a sieve or vegetable mouli and mix them thoroughly with the remaining ingredients. Taste the purée and adjust the seasoning if necessary.

Well grease an 18-cm/7-in diameter cake tin, turn the carrot mixture into it and smooth the top. Stand the tin on a baking sheet and bake for 30 minutes until the cake is slightly risen and firm.

Remove the cake from the oven, leave it to rest for about 3 minutes, then run a knife round the edge of the tin. Turn the cake out on to a heated serving dish and serve warm.

*A dish of crunchy celery and spring onion curls and a green salad makes a colourful accompaniment.

Cut celery stalks into thin strips about 7.5 cm/3in long and, using a sharp knife, cut slits from the top and bottom, almost but not quite meeting in the centre. Trim the spring onions, cut off most of the green tips and cut slits down from the top almost to the thick white bulb part. Put the celery and onions into a bowl of iced water and leave for at least 45 minutes for the tops to frill out.

Serves 4
Calories 370 (1545 kJ)
Protein 25 grams

450 g/1 lb young carrots, scrubbed
1 small onion, finely chopped
2 eggs
150 ml/5 fl oz natural yoghurt
2.5 ml/1/2 tsp chopped thyme or
    1.5 ml/1/4 tsp dried thyme
juice and grated rind of 1/2 lemon
salt and ground black pepper
celery and spring onion 'curls'
    (optional)*

Ratatouille

Cut the aubergines and courgettes into 20-mm/3/4-in-thick slices, put them into a colander and sprinkle them with salt. Set them aside for 30 minutes to drain. Rinse them under cold, running water, drain well and dry on absorbent kitchen paper.

Heat the oil in a large, heavy-based pan and cook the onions over low heat until they are transparent. Stir in the tomato purée and cook, stirring occasionally, for 3-4 minutes.

Add the aubergines and courgettes and stir well. Add the garlic and peppers, stir again, cover and simmer very gently for 20 minutes.

Add the tomatoes, coriander, cinnamon and basil and season with salt and pepper. Continue simmering for about 30 minutes. Uncover the pan, stir well and simmer for a further 10 minutes to allow any excess moisture to evaporate, if necessary. Taste and adjust the seasoning. The vegetables should be tender but retain their shape, without becoming mushy.

Serve hot or allow to cool, then chill and serve as a first course or salad accompaniment.

Serves 4
Calories 515 (2175 kJ)
Protein 15 grams

2 medium-sized aubergines,
    halved lengthways
2 medium-sized courgettes, halved
    lengthways
30 ml/2 tbls salt
30 ml/2 tbls olive oil
2 medium-sized onions, sliced into
    thin rings
30 ml/2 tbls tomato purée
3 garlic cloves, finely chopped
1 large green pepper, de-seeded
    and cut into thin strips
1 large red pepper, de-seeded and
    cut into thin strips
3 large tomatoes, skinned and
    chopped
a pinch of ground coriander
a pinch of cinnamon
1.5 ml/1/4 tsp dried basil
salt and ground black pepper

Gironde Onion Soup

6 large or 12 medium-sized onions
50 g/2 oz polyunsaturated
  margarine
a large pinch of dried thyme
5 ml/1 tsp salt
1.5 ml/¼ tsp ground black pepper
1.5 L/2½ pt chicken or veal stock
3 medium-sized egg yolks
2.5 ml/½ tsp white wine vinegar
6 slices French bread
½ garlic clove

Slice the onions into thin rounds. Melt the margarine in a saucepan and soften the onions over very low heat for 15-20 minutes, stirring occasionally. Do not allow them to brown. When they are soft and translucent, add the thyme, salt and pepper. Shake the pan, add the stock and bring to the boil. Lower the heat, cover the pan and simmer very gently for 15-20 minutes.

In a medium-sized bowl beat the egg yolks until smooth and pale, add the vinegar and beat again. Gradually whisk in a small cup of the hot soup.

Remove the saucepan from the heat and stir in the egg misture. Keep the soup hot without boiling again – otherwise the egg yolks will scramble. Check the seasoning and adjust if necessary.

When the soup is nearly ready, rub the bread slices with the garlic. Put them on a baking tray in a moderate oven until they are crisp. Float a slice of bread on each portion of the soup just before serving.

Serves 6
Calories 1290 (5415 kJ)
Protein 40 grams

Minestrone

Drain the soaked beans, put them in a saucepan and cover generously with fresh cold water. Bring slowly to the boil, cover the pan and simmer for about 1½ hours, or until the beans are tender.

Heat the oil in a large, flameproof casserole over low heat. Add the onion, garlic and leek and stir well. Cover the dish and cook gently for 5 minutes, shaking occasionally to prevent sticking.

Drain the cooked beans and add to the pan. Pour in the stock and bring to the boil. Add the bouquet garni, carrot and celery and stir well. Cover the pan and simmer for 15 minutes. Stir in the tomato purée and cabbage and simmer, covered, for a further 10 minutes.

While the vegetables are cooking, cut the bacon into strips; fry them gently until cooked, drain them with a slotted spoon and add to the soup. Bring back to the boil and add the pasta. Reduce the heat and simmer, uncovered, for about 8 minutes, or until the pasta is just tender.

Discard the bouquet garni. Stir in the 30 ml/2 tbls Parmesan cheese and season with salt and pepper. Just before serving, stir in the chopped parsley. Serve the soup with the extra cheese handed round separately.

Serves 4
Calories 1070 (4480 kJ)
Protein 47 grams

40 g/1½ oz dried haricot beans, soaked
30 ml/2 tbls olive oil
1 medium-sized onion, chopped
1 garlic clove, chopped
1 small leek, trimmed, washed and sliced
1 L/1¾ pt brown stock or strong chicken stock
1 bouquet garni
1 medium-sized carrot, sliced
2 stalks celery, sliced
10 ml/2 tsp tomato purée
¼ small white cabbage, shredded
2 slices bacon, rind removed
40 g/1½ oz miniature pasta shapes
30 ml/2 tbls grated Parmesan cheese
30 ml/2 tbls chopped parsley
extra grated Parmesan cheese

Provençal Vegetable Soup

1 large potato, peeled and diced
1 large onion, chopped
1 celery stalk, finely sliced
2 medium-sized carrots, scraped
   and sliced
salt
1 bouquet garni
225 g/8 oz French beans
225 g/8 oz runner beans
2 courgettes, thickly sliced
100 g/4 oz pasta shapes or
   short-cut macaroni

For the pistou sauce
3-4 large garlic cloves
60 ml/4 tbls chopped sweet basil
   leaves
ground black pepper
50 g/2 oz grated Parmesan cheese
2 medium-sized tomatoes,
   skinned, de-seeded and coarsely
   chopped
60 ml/4 tbls olive oil

Put the potato, onion, celery and carrots into a large flameproof casserole with 5 ml/1 tsp salt and the bouquet garni. Cover with 1.7 L/3 pt water, bring to the boil and cover the pan. Simmer for 10 minutes or so.

Top and tail the beans and remove any strings. Slice the French beans in half, cut the runner beans into 15-mm/½-in lengths. Add the beans, courgette and pasta to the casserole and simmer, uncovered, for 10-15 minutes, until they are all just tender.

While the soup is cooking, prepare the pistou. Pound the garlic and basil to a paste, using a mortar and pestle. Add salt and pepper to taste. Gradually work in the cheese and tomatoes alternately. Then slowly work in the olive oil, a few drops at a time to start with, to make a thick sauce.

Discard the bouquet garni from the soup. Blend 60 ml/4 tbls of the hot soup into the sauce, then stir the mixture into the soup. Taste and season with salt and pepper, and serve at once.

Serves 4-6
Calories 1460 (6150 kJ)
Protein 56 grams

Braised Fennel

4 large bulbs of fennel
10 ml/2 tsp lemon juice
25 g/1 oz butter
150 ml/5 fl oz chicken stock
salt and ground black pepper
15 ml/1 tbls chopped parsley

For the beurre manié
10 ml/2 tsp softened butter
10 ml/2 tsp flour

Heat the oven to 190C/375F/gas 5.

Wash and trim the fennel bulbs. Strip off the tough outer leaf from each one – you can use this to flavour a vegetable soup. Cut each bulb in half lengthways.

Arrange the fennel halves in a flameproof dish. Add the lemon juice, butter and chicken stock and season with salt and pepper. Put the dish over a low heat and bring just to simmering point. Cover the dish with a lid or foil and cook in the oven for 45 minutes.

Make the beurre manié by blending the softened butter with the flour to make a smooth paste.

Remove the fennel from the dish and keep it warm. Put the dish over a moderate heat, bring it just to a simmer again, then gradually stir in small pieces of the paste. Stir until the sauce has thickened. Return the fennel to the sauce and allow to heat through. Sprinkle with the parsley and serve hot.

Serves 4
Calories 570 (2360 kJ)
Protein 31 grams

Mushroom and Barley Casserole

Put the barley into a sieve and wash it thoroughly under cold, running water to release the starch. Then put it in a bowl of cold water and leave it to soak for about 4 hours. Drain.

Put 15 g/½ oz butter in a pan with 275 ml/10 fl oz water and salt and bring to the boil. Add the barley, cover the pan and simmer very gently for about 30 minutes, or until the barley is soft but still holds its shape. It should just have absorbed the water by then.

Heat the oven to 170C/325F/gas 3.

Melt the remaining butter in a frying-pan and sauté the onion and garlic until the onion is soft and translucent. Add the mushrooms, shake the pan and cook for about 3-4 minutes. Season with salt and pepper, add the stock, cover the pan and simmer for 10 minutes. Stir in half the chopped parsley.

Spread half the barley to cover the base of a greased 1-L/2-pt ovenproof dish. Cover with the mushroom mixture and spread the remaining barley over the top.

Mix together the egg, yoghurt and cheese and season well with salt and pepper. Pour the topping carefully over the barley.

Bake for 20 minutes, until the custard topping has set. If you like a well-browned top, put the cooked dish under a hot grill for 2-3 minutes. Sprinkle with the remaining parsley to garnish.

Serves 4
Calories 1160 (4860 kJ)
Protein 48 grams

150 g/5 oz pearl barley
25 g/1 oz butter
1 small onion, finely chopped
1 garlic clove, crushed
350 g/12 oz mushrooms, thinly
  sliced
salt and ground black pepper
45 ml/3 tbls chicken stock
30 ml/2 tbls chopped parsley
1 medium-sized egg, beaten
150 ml/4 fl oz natural yoghurt
50 g/2 oz cheese, grated

Leeks in Red Wine

Heat the oven to 190C/375F/gas 5.

Wash the leeks thoroughly. Trim off the roots, strip off the tough and discoloured outer leaves and cut off most of the green tops, to within 2.5 cm/1 in of the white part. You can use the green tops to make a robust leek soup or to flavour a meat or vegetable soup. Split the leeks down one side from the top almost to the root, gently open them out and hold them, tops down, under cold, running water.

Sauté the chopped bacon in a small, non-stick frying-pan until it is crisp. Remove with a slotted spoon and reserve for the garnish.

Sauté the chopped onion in the bacon fat until it is soft. Remove from the pan with a slotted spoon.

Arrange the leeks in a shallow flameproof dish and dot them with the butter.

Pour over the chicken stock and red wine and sprinkle with the sautéed onion. Season with salt and pepper and push the thyme sprigs into the liquor.

Put the dish over moderate heat and bring the liquor to a simmer. Cover the dish with foil and braise the leeks in the oven for 20 minutes, or until they are just tender.

Transfer the leeks to a heated serving dish, cover with foil and keep them warm. Place the flameproof dish over a moderate-high heat and boil the liquor until it is reduced to about 75 ml/5 tbls. Remove the thyme sprigs. Spoon this glaze over the leeks, garnish with the bacon and parsley and serve at once.

Serves 4
Calories 1070 (4405 kJ)
Protein 34 grams

16 small leeks
4 slices back bacon, rinds removed,
  finely diced
1 small onion, finely chopped
40 g/1½ oz butter
275 ml/10 fl oz strong chicken
  stock
150 ml/5 fl oz red wine
salt and ground black pepper
3 thyme sprigs, tied together
15 ml/1 tbls chopped parsley

Healthy Desserts

Desserts can be demons. After a carefully balanced meal it is all too easy to let your halo slip out of sight and blow your good intentions on an airy-fairy pudding full of 'empty' calories and fat-laden creaminess. Which is quite unnecessary, because the dessert hasn't been invented yet that looks as beautiful, or is as nutritious as a bowl of fresh fruit or a fruit salad. All the glorious colours from the coolest green to the deepest purple, and all the beautiful shapes, from cascading bunches of grapes to glowing golden-skinned oranges – what perfect packaging!

Fruit contains vitamins A and C, sucrose and dietary fibre – the 'roughage' that we now realise we need for healthy living. Choose top-quality dessert varieties and they are delicious just as they are, or served with a snowy-white bowl of low-fat yoghurt – much more halo-making, of course, than the equivalent amount of cream. Fresh fruit salads – an art form in themselves – fruit moulded in jelly made from unsweetened fruit juice and softened gelatine; raw fruit purée poured as a sauce, lifted high with egg whites, refreshingly frozen as granitas or sorbets, or stirred into yoghurt for traditional-style fruit fools – with so many fruits and such delicious variety there is scarcely any need to cook fruit at all.

It is when we do choose the cooking varieties or types of fruit, apples, plums, damsons, gooseberries, rhubarb and so on, we have to try to keep the sugar tin under lock and key, for it is all too easy to go on tipping in valueless refined sugar to bring the fruit to a palatable degree of sweetness. There are ways round this – by blending tart fruits with sweeter dessert ones, or with dried fruits which are packed full of both sucrose and fibre; by choosing unrefined sweeteners, discussed more fully in Chapter 8, or by cooking the fruits in unsweetened fruit juice – containing plenty of the natural sugars extracted from the fruit – pepped up, perhaps, with a dash of sweet sherry or other wine.

Preparing fruit

Fresh fruit should have the minimum of handling and be served slightly chilled. A bowl of fruit left on the sideboard looks decorative but is wasteful – the fruit will stay in peak condition longer in the refrigerator. Store stone fruits, such as peaches, apricots, nectarines, cherries and plums in a paper bag in the salad drawer, and currants and berries in a covered container, for up to three days, strawberries in a lidded box for only two days.

Wash berry fruits only if you really must, and never under cold, running water, which could bruise them. Put the fruit in a colander and lightly jump it up and down in a bowl of water. To serve the berries for dessert, tip them on to several layers of kitchen paper so that they dry without crushing.

You need only a large fork with long, widely-spaced tines to strip black, red or white currants from their stalks, and only a small, sharp-pointed knife to cut through into the centre of grapes and prise out the seeds. Stoning cherries is a thankless task without a special little gadget which punches

the stone neatly through the fruit and out at one side. Unless gooseberries are destined for sieving, as in a cooked purée, they should be topped and tailed; a little pair of clippers, like miniature pincers, does it in a twinkling.

Apples, pears, peaches and bananas discolour most unattractively – though quite harmlessly – as soon as the cut surfaces are exposed to the air. Squeeze the juice of one or two lemons into a bowl before preparing the fruits, slice them into the juice, toss them thoroughly to coat them on all sides and lift them out with a slotted spoon to make way for the next batch. If you are slicing only one or two fruits, you can brush the juice on to the slices with a soft pastry brush.

To peel or not to peel some fruits can be a vexing question. Whenever possible, it is best to leave on the skin, retaining as much as possible of the natural fibre. But this must be a personal choice, for some people find the skin of grapes, peaches or apples for example, so unacceptable that it completely spoils their enjoyment of the fruits.

Dipping fleshy fruits – large dessert grapes, peaches, apricots and nectarines – briefly into boiling water stretches the skin so that it can easily

be peeled off. Dunking in hot water also helps to separate the peel of citrus fruits and make the juice run more freely, so it's a trick worth remembering.

Oranges for fruit salad must be peeled meticulously to remove every scrap of the bitter white pith – a rotary potato peeler seems made for the task. Then they can be either segmented, the flesh cut cleanly away on both sides from the membrane (see the step-by-step directions on page 140) or thinly sliced. Anyone with an electric carving knife can really score points here – oranges never taste more delicious than when they are sliced to an almost translucent thinness.

For fruit salad, a few of the more unusual fruits, such as fresh mangoes, green or black figs or kiwi fruits, make stunning contrasts. Mangoes thinly peeled and sliced or diced reveal a sunrise-coloured blush of soft, fleshy fruit; figs sliced from top to bottom display a fascinating seed pattern excelled, though, by the cross-section of kiwi fruits. Peel them thinly and slice them crossways into 6-mm/¼-in slices for a dramatic black and cool green kaleidoscopic effect.

Larger fruits such as melons and pineapples have triple personalities. They can be served in single-portion slices, cut into cubes or (melons only) small balls to mix with other fruits, or hollowed out and used as decorative containers.

To prepare a melon slice, cut the fruit in half and scoop out the seeds and fleshy membrane. Cut honeydew or cantaloup melons into four or six slices, according to size, cut the flesh away from the skin, then cut it downwards, into bite-sized slices or cubes. Thin slivers of crystallized or preserved ginger pushed between the slices, thin slices of peeled orange or grapefruit all give an interesting flavour contrast.

Contrast in both shape and flavour can be the key to a successful fruit salad – cut balls of melon with a parisienne cutter if the salad has chopped apple or diced mango, or cut melon and pineapple, too, into neat-sided cubes if there are grapes and cherries in the medley.

To make decorative containers, cut a thin slice lengthways from a whole pineapple or a melon and carefully ease away the flesh to make space for a colourful cascade of fruits. With a little more time, you can sculpt a melon basket, complete with handle (see the directions right). Chill these containers or simpler individual ones, orange, grapefruit or large lemon shells, for a tinglingly fresh 'salad bowl'.

The salad dressing
Simple is beautiful when it comes to dressing fresh fruits, whether they are served alone or in a medley of several kinds. Whole or sliced strawberries tossed in the juice of sweet summer oranges, with perhaps a dash of orange liqueur to celebrate, sweet raspberries lightly crushed and stirred into thickened yoghurt, dessert apricots macerated in unsweetened pineapple juice are all cheatingly effective.

Bottled unsweetened fruit juices make a good basic dressing for fruit salads. Apple, pineapple and orange juices are often sweet enough used alone, though more memorable with a dash of red or white wine or liqueur. Dissolve 30 ml/2 tbls of clear honey in each 275 ml/10 fl oz of the fruit juice if you like it sweeter, or make a syrup by bringing the same amount of honey and water to the boil and boiling for 2 minutes. Spice the syrup if you like by adding a small stick of cinnamon, a piece of peeled root ginger, a few cloves – good with apples, pears and plums – or a vanilla pod. Remove the spices and cool the syrup before pouring it on to the fruits.

Raw fruit purée
Uncooked fruits make a purée that is pure nectar as a sauce for other fruits – and they retain all their vital vitamin content, too. Prepare the fruits according to type. Halve and stone apricots, very ripe cherries, peaches and nectarines and purée them in a liquidizer or sieve. Add a little lemon juice to bring out the flavour and preserve the colour. Hull berry fruits and sieve or liquidize them – pippy ones like blackberries will need

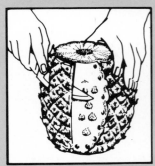

To prepare pineapple: cut off ends. Cut away peel with sawing motion.

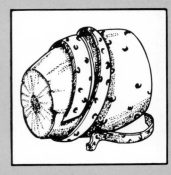

Cut out prickly dots in a spiral. Cut across flesh in thick slices. Cut our core.

To make container; cut round fruit between flesh and peel.

Lift out central flesh and prepare as above. Use container for fruit salad etc.

sieving anyway – and sweeten the purée (if really necessary) with a little honey. You will get about 275 ml/10 fl oz purée from each 450 g/1 lb of fruit.

Fresh raspberries tossed in the raspberry sauce, sliced dessert apples in blackberry purée, melon cubes in cherry sauce – discover your own talking-point combinations.

Use the purée in milk shakes, about 60 ml/4 tbls of the fruit to 275 ml/10 fl oz of milk; to flavour natural yoghurt for an instant dessert – 30 ml/2 tbls

To make melon basket; cut
through skin along lines
shown using a sharp knife.

Lift out segments. Scoop out
seeds from melon, and spoon
out flesh.

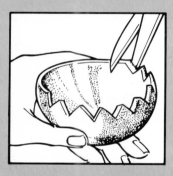

To vandyke empty citrus
fruit halves, cut V shapes
round top with scissors.

To make chrysanthemums,
score deep cuts almost to
ends. Pull apart.

whisked egg whites when partly frozen, beating
the purée first to eliminate the crystals.

Cooking with fruit
Whoops! Watch the sweetening! Fruit can be fast-cooked under the grill – whole apples and
bananas, halved oranges, grapefruit, peaches and
pineapple rings lightly dusted with brown sugar,
brushed with melted honey or dribbled with sweet
sherry or marsala are instant delight. Apple and
pineapple rings tossed in brown sugar can be
quickly fried in the minimum of butter – try
serving them very hot on top of chilled yoghurt
cheese (see page 89). The impact is rather like hot
chocolate sauce on ice cream. Bananas can be
baked whole in their skins in a moderate oven.
Unzip them quickly and scatter them with seedless
raisins or sultanas soaked in sherry. Or peel the
bananas first, dribble them with honey and dried
fruits and bake them to oozing perfection in about
25 minutes. Knowing that they are high in fibre
drives away some of the guilt! Bake peach or
apricot halves filled with yoghurt cheese and
ground almonds, apples filled with high-fibre
dried fruits, or orchard fruits like plums under a
high-fibre wholewheat flour and oat crumble
topping for a deliciously crunchy texture.

Poach fruit on top of the stove or in the oven in a
honey and water syrup. To every 275 ml/10 fl oz of
water, add 15-22 ml/1-1½ tbls of honey. Boil it for
2 minutes, then add the fruit and simmer or bake
in a covered dish only until the fruit is tender.
Once it collapses it loses its identity – and its looks!
Pears poached in red wine gain a pretty blush, as
they do when partnered with cranberries or
simmered in redcurrant or blackberry juice.
Gooseberries get really stylish if you add a head of
elderflower to the poaching liquor, and apples,
pears, quinces and rhubarb like a touch of spice –
try crushed allspice or juniper berries tied in
muslin as a change from ginger and cloves. Use
the minimum of liquid for poaching and it will
have the maximum of natural sweetness from the
fruit. Drown the fruit in water and the temptation
is there to pile on the sugar.

of fruit to 150 ml/5 fl oz of yoghurt – or lift it up
into a low-cholesterol fruit 'snow'. For this
deceptively impressive-looking dessert simply
whisk 2 large egg whites until they are stiff, then
fold in 275 ml/10 fl oz of thick fruit purée. Pile into
serving glasses and set aside, without chilling, for
no more than 1 hour. For a fruit fool, fold fruit
purée or lightly crushed dessert fruits into an equal
amount of thickened yoghurt, and for sorbets
blend the purée with heavy syrup and fold in

Summer Pudding

900 g/2 lb raspberries, hulled (or
    use a mixture of soft fruits)
100 g/4 oz soft brown sugar
125 ml/4 fl oz milk
8 slices stale wholewheat bread
natural yoghurt, beaten with a
    pinch of cinnamon

Place the raspberries in a bowl, sprinkle with the sugar and set aside.

Cut the crusts from the bread and, with a teaspoon, sprinkle a little of the milk over each slice to moisten it.

Well grease a deep pie dish or pudding basin and line it with two-thirds of the bread slices, overlapping the edges slightly and taking care to leave no gaps. Pour the raspberries into the dish and arrange the remaining bread slices on top to cover the fruit completely.

Cover the dish with a sheet of grease-proof or waxed paper and put a plate on top, slightly smaller than the rim. Stand a heavy weight on the plate and put the dish in the refrigerator to chill for at least 8 hours, or overnight.

Run a long-bladed knife round the edge between the walls of the pudding and the dish to loosen it. Invert a large serving plate over the top of the dish and, holding the two firmly together, reverse them, giving them a sharp shake. The pudding should slide out easily. Serve with flavoured yoghurt, but remember the extra calories.

Serves 4-6
Calories 1415 (6010 kJ)
Protein 42 grams

Compôte of Cherries

Pit the cherries and put them in a saucepan with the sugar, cinnamon and a piece of the orange zest. Cover and set over low heat until the juices begin to run and the mixture is almost at boiling point. Pour into a bowl and discard the orange zest.

Cut the remaining orange zest into very thin julienne strips, blanch them in boiling water for 5 minutes, then drain.

Put the piece of cinnamon in the rinsed pan with the red wine. Bring to the boil and cook until the wine is reduced by about one quarter. Remove the pan from the heat and stir in the redcurrant jelly. When it has melted stir in the

orange juice. Drain the syrup from the cherries and stir it into the mixture in the pan with the blended arrowroot. Bring to the boil, stirring. Simmer, still stirring, for 1 minute.

Take the pan from the heat and stir in the cherries, the cherry brandy or kirsch, if using, and the orange strips.

This pudding can be served either hot or cold. To serve it cold, leave it to cool completely then chill it in the refrigerator, until serving time.

Serves 4-6
Calories 800 (3395 kJ)
Protein 6 grams

900 g/2 lb fresh cherries
25 g/1 oz brown sugar
5 cm/2 in cinnamon stick
thinly-pared zest of 1 medium-sized orange
juice of ½ orange
150 ml/5 fl oz dry red wine
30 ml/2 tbls redcurrant jelly
10 ml/2 tsp arrowroot, blended with 30 ml/2 tbls water
60 ml/4 tbls cherry brandy or kirsch (optional)

Making your own yoghurt

Healthy desserts don't know when to stop when it comes to using natural yoghurt, and you'll soon find it will break the bank if you don't make your own. They've been doing it in the Middle East for centuries with no special equipment at all, so you don't have to buy an electric yoghurt maker.
If you have one already, follow the maker's instructions in detail.
You can make yoghurt from any type of milk – though skimmed milk needs the addition of extra dried skimmed milk powder. Without it, the yoghurt is too watery. Obviously, the kind of milk you use affects not only the flavour but the fat content of the yoghurt. Choose the caramel flavour of evaporated milk and watch the calories mount up, go for low-fat milk and you are rewarded with low-fat yoghurt.

575 ml/1 pt pasteurized or homogenized or UHT milk or
575 ml/1 pt boiling water and 100 g/ 4 oz dried skimmed milk powder or
275 ml/10 fl oz evaporated milk and 275 ml/10 fl oz boiling water
30 ml/2 tbls fresh natural yoghurt (this can be either home-made or a commercial brand)

Bring the milk just to the boil in a small pan. Cover the pan and cool until the temperature drops to 46C/115F on a thermometer. Without a thermometer, dip in a scrupulously clean finger and hold it for a count of 10. Your finger should start feeling hot!

Or stir the boiling water into the skimmed milk powder. Or mix together the evaporated milk and boiling water.

Put the yoghurt 'starter' into a sterilized bowl or jug. When the milk is the right temperature, pour a little on to the yoghurt and stir well. Pour it back into the milk and whisk well.

Transfer the mixture to a heated bowl or, preferably, a vacuum jug. Cover the bowl with a cloth and an improvised incubator device such as a warmed rug or a couple of cushions. Or set it in an airing cupboard. Cover the vacuum flask. Leave undisturbed for 6-8 hours, until the yoghurt has set. Tip yoghurt from a flask into a jug or bowl. Cover and chill, if you like, before using.

Thickened Yoghurt
To make absolutely sure that your yoghurt doesn't separate when you add it to hot liquids or use it in cooked dishes – sometimes it would, sometimes it wouldn't – you can stabilize it after the incubation process.

To do this, mix 7.5 ml/1½ tsp cornflour to a paste with a little milk. Tip 575 ml/1 pt yoghurt into a small pan, stir in the cornflour paste and bring very slowly to the boil, stirring constantly in one direction, over low heat. Simmer and stir for 10 minutes, then allow to cool. Now you can use it with even more confidence in cooking.

To thicken (but not stabilize) yoghurt stir 45 ml/32 tbls dried skimmed milk powder into the yoghurt starter. Then pour on a little tepid milk and mix to a smooth paste. Follow the rest of the instructions, leaving the yoghurt for 8 hours. It should set to a rich, creamy consistency that's irresistibly good with fresh and cooked fruits.

Apple and Ginger Sorbet

Turn the refrigerator or freezer to the lowest setting.

Thinly pare the zest from the lemons and squeeze the juice. Put the sugar into a pan with the lemon zest and 275 ml/10 fl oz water. Bring to the boil, stirring, then simmer for 5 minutes. Leave on one side to cool.

Strain the syrup into a jug and add 75 ml/5 tbls lemon juice. Chill for 10 minutes, without freezing.

Peel, quarter and core the apples, put them in a pan with 15 ml/1 tbls lemon juice and cook until soft. Cool, then purée and stir into the chilled syrup. Fold in the ginger. Pour into an empty ice-cube tray and freeze for about 1½ hours, until mushy.

Whisk the egg whites until they will stand in soft peaks. Stir the apple mixture then gradually beat it into the egg whites. When the mixture forms a firm snow, cover the tray and return it to the freezer for about 2 hours, or until it is almost solid.

Beat it again for 3-4 minutes, cover and re-freeze for at least 1 hour.

Remove the tray from the freezer 10 minutes before serving. Serve in scoops in individual glasses decorated with mint sprigs.

Serves 4-6
Calories 920 (3930 kJ)
Protein 13 grams

3 lemons
175 g/6 oz soft brown sugar
40 g/1½ oz stem ginger, finely chopped
2 large ripe dessert apples
2 large-sized egg whites
mint sprigs

Mixed Fruit Suedoise

Begin by making the jelly. Dissolve the sugar in 700 ml/1½ pt boiling water. Dissolve the gelatine in 60 ml/4 tbls hot water. Stir the gelatine and liqueur into the syrup, cool, then chill in the refrigerator until the jelly has thickened and is on the point of setting.

Meanwhile, miss the lemon juice with 30 ml/2 tbls water, toss in the apple slices to cover them completely and set aside.

Rinse a straight-sided 1.4-L/2½-pt mould with cold water. Pour in enough jelly to make a 6-mm/¼-in layer on the bottom. Arrange the cherries, almonds and angelica leaves in a pattern over it – remember that the pattern will be the other way up when the mould is turned out. Spoon a little jelly over the decoration and place the mould in the refrigerator for 15 minutes, or until the jelly has set.

Arrange half the apricots over the jelly and spoon enough jelly to cover them completely. Chill the mould for 30 minutes, or until the jelly has set.

Continue making layers in this way, using the remaining apricots, the apples and plums in sequence, until all the fruit is used up.

Chill the mould for 2 hours, or until the jelly has completely set.

Dip the bottom of the mould quickly into hot water, then wipe the outside to dry it. Place a chilled serving dish over the mould, and, holding the two firmly together, invert, giving a sharp shake. The jelly should slide out easily. Serve at once, or it may start to collapse.

Serves 4-6
Calories 965 (4095 kJ)
Protein 42 grams

10 ml/2 tsp lemon juice
1 large dessert apple, peeled, cored and thinly sliced
6 maraschino cherries
6 blanched almonds
12 angelica leaves
450 g/1 lb fresh apricots, halved, stoned and poached
450 g/1 lb fresh plums, halved, stoned and poached

For the jelly
175 g/6 oz brown sugar
25 g/1 oz gelatine
125 ml/4 fl oz orange-flavoured liqueur

Melon and Lime Mousse

½ medium-sized, very ripe melon, about 700 g/1½ lb
a large pinch ground ginger
30 ml/2 tbls natural yoghurt
grated zest and juice of 1 lime
2 large eggs, separated
50 g/2 oz soft light brown sugar
15 g/½ oz gelatine
slices of kiwi fruit and/or lime

Scoop out and discard the melon seeds. Scoop out the flesh, drain and put in a blender with the ground ginger, yoghurt, grated lime zest and all but 5-10 ml/1-2 tsp of the lime juice. Reduce to a purée and set aside.

Whisk the egg yolks and sugar together. Set the bowl over a pan of hot but not boiling water and whisk until the mixture is pale and thick enough for the whisk to leave trails. Remove the bowl from the heat.

Gradually pour the melon purée into the egg mixture, stirring constantly with a wooden spoon. Dissolve the gelatine in 30 ml/2 tbls hot water. Blend a little of the melon mixture with the dissolved gelatine, then pour the mixture back into the bowl, stirring constantly to mix.

Cover the bowl and chill in the refrigerator for 45 minutes-1 hour, or until the mixture has thickened to a syrupy consistency, but not set.

Whisk the egg whites until stiff and fold them into the melon mixture.

Pour the mousse into a serving bowl, cover and leave in the refrigerator for about 2 hours until set. Just before serving, decorate the mousse with slices of kiwi fruit and/or lime and sprinkle them with the remaining lime juice.

Serves 4-6
Calories 457 (2420 kJ)
Protein 34 grams

Old-fashioned Rice Pudding

Heat the oven to 150C/300F/gas 2.

Put the rice, milk and sugar into a lightly-greased, shallow ovenproof dish. Grate a little nutmeg over the top.

Place the uncovered dish in the oven. Stir the pudding two or three times during the first hour of cooking – this stirs in the skin and helps to make the pudding creamy. Bake for 3-3¼ hours, until the rice is tender and the pudding is thick.

You can turn cooked rice into a delicious and instant peach condé. Chill the rice, divide it between 4-6 serving glasses and top each one with 2 peach halves. Pour over a sauce of redcurrant jelly melted with lemon juice. Fold whisked egg white into a little whipped cream and pipe rosettes to decorate.

*If it is more convenient, you can cook the rice pudding on top of the cooker. Put all the ingredients into a heavy-based saucepan, cover and simmer over a very gentle heat for 2-2½ hours, until creamy. Remove the lid for the last 40 minutes, and stir mixture occasionally.

Serves 4
Calories 615 (2585 kJ)
Protein 23 grams

50 g/2 oz brown short-grain rice
575 ml/1 pt hot milk
15 ml/1 tbls soft light brown sugar
a pinch of freshly-grated nutmeg

Paradise Islands

1 medium-sized pineapple
40 g/1½ oz grated
   coconut, or 20 g/¾ oz
   desiccated coconut
150 ml/5 fl oz thick cream, chilled
150 ml/5 fl oz natural yoghurt,
   chilled
30 ml/2 tbls clear honey
zest and juice of 1 lime or small
   lemon

Cut the leafy foliage from the pineapple and cut into 6 slices. Cut away the skin and remove the woody eyes with the point of a sharp knife. Using an apple corer, carefully stamp out the cores. Trim round the holes with the sharp knife if there is any tough central core remaining. Arrange the pineapple slices on a serving plate.

Whisk the cream and gradually beat in the yoghurt. Fold in the coconut, honey and lime or lemon zest, and gradually stir in the juice. Spoon the coconut cream mixture into a mound in the centre of each pineapple ring. Serve well chilled.

Serves 6
Calories 1235 (5125 kJ)
Protein 15 grams

Mixed Melon Salad

30 ml/2 tbls clear honey
15 ml/1 tbls lemon juice
5 ml/1 tsp ginger syrup
2 medium-sized oranges
1 small honeydew melon
1 small cantaloupe melon
225 g/8 oz black grapes
2 pieces stem ginger
1 banana, thinly sliced

Begin by making the syrup. Put the honey into a small pan with 150 ml/5 fl oz water, the lemon juice, ginger syrup, grated zest and juice of 1 orange. Bring just to the boil, then remove the pan from the heat.

Segment the remaining orange, cut away the membranes and put the sections into a bowl. Cut the melons in half and discard the seeds. Use a melon cutter to cut the flesh into small balls. Seed the grapes by cutting half way into them with a sharp knife and removing the seeds with the knife point. Add all the fruit to the bowl, thinly slice the ginger, stir into the fruit and pour on the syrup. Leave to cool, then chill in the refrigerator for 1-2 hours. Stir in the banana slices just before serving.

Serves 6-8
Calories 700 (2940 kJ)
Protein 12 grams

Orange and Lemon Whip

8 medium-sized oranges
juice of ½ lemon
60 ml/4 tbls clear honey
575 ml/1 pt natural yoghurt
60 ml/4 tbls chopped walnuts,
   hazelnuts or almonds

Thinly pare 3 strips of the rind of one orange and finely chop and reserve it. Cut all the peel and white fibre or pith from this and the remaining oranges.

Finely chop the flesh, removing all the seeds. Put it into a blender with the lemon juice, honey and yoghurt. Blend to make a thick, smooth purée.

Pour the mixture into 4 individual serving glasses and sprinkle each one with the chopped nuts and the reserved orange rind.

Serve chilled.

Serves 4
Calories 965 (4095 kJ)
Protein 42 grams

Brown Sugar Meringues

Heat the oven to 110C/225F/gas ¼.

Beat the egg whites until they are stiff enough to stand in peaks. Add the sugar gradually, beating until the mixture holds its shape.

Using a dessert spoon, shape mounds of the meringue mixture on to a well-greased baking sheet or one lined with non-stick vegetable parchment. Bake in the cool oven for about 2 hours. To test when the meringues are dry and cooked, remove one from the oven and tap the underside. It should sound slightly hollow but will feel moist until it is cold.

Carefully lift the meringues on to a wire rack and allow them to cool.

Grate the zest and squeeze the juice from the orange. Beat the cottage cheese until smooth. Gradually beat in the orange juice and zest, then the liqueur. Beat the mixture well to keep it smooth.

Just before serving sandwich the meringues together in pairs with the orange-flavoured cheese filling.

Serves 4
Calories 720 (3055 kJ)
Protein 39 grams

2 egg whites
100 g/4 oz soft light brown sugar
1 orange
225 g/8 oz low-fat cottage cheese, sieved
15 ml/1 tbls orange-flavoured liqueur

Cinnamon Plum Crumble

Heat the oven to 170C/325F/gas 3

Wash, halve and stone the plums, and place them in a shallow, ovenproof dish. Mix together the brown sugar and cinnamon and sprinkle it over the fruit.

To make the topping, place the flour, oats and cinnamon in a bowl and rub in the fat until the mixture feels like coarse breadcrumbs. Stir in the sugar.

Spoon the crumble mixture lightly over the plums and smooth the top.

Bake for about 40 minutes, or until the topping is crisp and golden and the plums feel tender when pierced with a fine skewer or sharp-pointed knife.

This spiced crumble is delicious served with beaten natural yoghurt.

Serves 4
Calories 1905 (8005 kJ)
Protein 28 grams

450 g/1 lb cooking plums
40 g/ 1½ oz soft light brown sugar
2.5 ml/½ tsp ground cinnamon

For the crumble topping
100 g/4 oz wholewheat flour
100 g/4 oz rolled or porridge oats
5 ml/1 tsp ground cinnamon
100 g/4 oz polyunsaturated margarine
50 g/2 oz soft light brown sugar

Fruit Surprise

Hull the soft fruit and reduce it to a purée in the blender. Rub raspberries or loganberries through a sieve to remove the pips. Stir the sugar into the fruit.

Sieve the cheese into a separate bowl. Using a wooden spoon, gradually stir in the fruit, a little at a time. When all the fruit is incorporated, beat the mixture well until it is smooth.

Divide the fruit mixture between 4 individual serving glasses and chill in the refrigerator for about 1 hour.

Scatter the toasted almonds on top to decorate.

Serves 4
Calories 750 (3140 kJ)
Protein 34 grams

225 g/8 oz raspberries, strawberries, loganberries, or a mixture
30 ml/2 tbls soft light brown sugar
225 g/8 oz yoghurt cheese (see page 88) or low-fat cream cheese
50 g/2 oz blanched almonds, halved and toasted

Health in the Raw

Eating food raw must be the most natural way of all, because it was the first way. And so it appeals to all of us who have mad moments of wanting to scrap progress and start all over again. For primitive people hunted animals, caught fish and gathered wild leaves, seeds and berries long before they had learned how to build a fire or make cooking vessels. That's how health in the raw was really born!

For us, eating food raw enormously extends the flavour range – thinly sliced raw fillets of sole taste very different from grilled fish on the bone, and julienne strips of crisp vegetables suspended in a light, chilled stock bear little resemblance to a hearty country-style soup. Added to that, capturing many foods in the natural state increases their benefit, for some nutrients are inevitably lost in cooking. It does actually save the task of cooking, too, but time won on this count is usually spent in preparation and presentation of the foods. Not being Primitive Man any more, we tend to like our raw fish evenly and daintily sliced (so that the maximum area is exposed to the marinade or sauce), our raw steak twice or thrice minced (so that we can eat it in a reasonably civilised way) and our salads coolly dressed in a tossing of natural fruit juice, vegetable oil or yoghurt.

Meat
Only the tenderest and leanest cuts are suitable. A classic favourite, Steak Tartare (see recipe on page 83) illustrates the general method. If you don't find the sight of a neat pile of raw meat appetizing, you can serve it in trimmed green peppers or hollowed-out tomato shells. In this case stir some of the seasoning vegetables into the meat and bind the mixture with one egg yolk for each 225 g/8 oz of meat. Season well.

Lean leg of lamb can be served raw, too. It takes well to a seasoning of garlic- or curry-flavoured mayonnaise or to being tossed in a little spiced vinaigrette dressing. Mini salads of chopped celery leaves, finely sliced radishes or slivers of fennel make a good balance of colour and texture.

As raw meat isn't famous for its visual appeal – though it wins friends once they actually taste it – put extra effort into the presentation. Attractively-cut tomato 'lilies', spring onion frills or celery curls as garnishes give a pleasing overall impression.

Dried, salted and smoked meats come in a category somewhere between raw and cooked foods. Some products are lightly salted and then cold-smoked to give them a characteristic flavour – which varies according to the region – and are still, to all intents and purposes, raw. Continental hams such as the Italian Parma ham and the German Westphalian are (expensive) examples. Other meats, heavily salted to dry them and hot-smoked to preserve them, have more intensified flavour and more concentrated nutrients. But beware of the enticing array of smoked sausage products on the delicatessen counter. If you have ever watched a piece of salami swim away in fat melted by the summer holiday sun, you will know that they are a calorie-laden trap for the unwary!

Fish
People who would gladly swallow a plateful of oysters might look askance at a dish of raw white fish – but why? Anyone nervous of taking the plunge has only to go to a Japanese restaurant, where the fish will be presented as beautifully as in a still-life painting, to be a convert for life.

Any white fish can be served raw, the only proviso being that it must be absolutely fresh. If you cannot be sure of your supply, don't give up. Frozen fish was absolutely fresh when it was frozen, if not actually on the fishing boat, then on a freezer vessel close by, so thaw it just before you need it and treat it as fresh. Any slight loss of flavour can be overlooked, for raw fish is always marinated or served with a strong 'dipping' sauce or spiced vegetable or salad accompaniments.

Follow the directions for Sashimi (page 85) and arrange the fish in a geometric pattern on individual plates or a single dish with a red or white chrysanthemum flower, a few radish fans or a ring of celery leaves. This is not the occasion for parsley or mint!

Marinating raw fish before serving not only impregnates it with the flavours of your choice – usually a lightly sweetened and delicately spiced mixture – but tenderizes it at the same time. Adapt the recipe for Marinated Salmon to sole, cod, haddock, plaice, any white fish, trout, herring or mackerel and you have an exciting repertoire of first courses.

Pickling is a form of extended marinating, the food being steeped in spiced brine for several days. This is a good way to treat any oily fish – mackerel, herring, sprats, trout or salmon.

Like meat, fish can be smoked just until it has all the evocative flavour of a camp-fire on the beach, when it is still raw, or hot-smoked for a longer period until it is cooked. A mixture of hot-smoked fish, trout, eel, buckling and mackerel, filleted and cut into thin strips, makes an easy-on-the-cook first course or light supper dish, and yoghurt-based horseradish or caper sauce minimizes the richness. Smoked roes (ignoring the painfully expensive caviar) make good opening courses, too. The coral-red cod's roe pounded to a paste with breadcrumbs and vegetable oil evokes the nostalgic flavour of Greece, and lumpfish roe, bright, bright red or black as night and sea-salty tasting, makes a glamorous garnish for such simple dishes as stuffed eggs, scrambled eggs, savoury mousses and soft cheeses.

Soft cheeses

Another back-to-the-beginning food, soft cheese and the yoghurt to make it was discovered accidentally by travelling tribesmen. Bouncing up and down in a non-sterilized saddle bag in the heat all day was enough to make any milk turn to yoghurt!

As the recipes show, you can make a variety of soft cheeses from yoghurt, buttermilk or milk soured with lemon juice, simply by draining it in a scalded cloth. Follow the step-by-step directions on page 89 the first time, then make it an instinctive part of your kitchen routine ever after.

Just as it is, lightly salted or flavoured with herbs, spices, chopped nuts, grated hard cheese or finely chopped vegetables (celery or red or green peppers, for example) soft cheese has a ready appeal as a ready snack. Use it to fill fruit for appetizers or sweetmeats at the end of a meal. Halved and stoned dessert plums, halved and seeded dessert grapes, halved and cored pears, stoned fresh or dried dates, prunes, dried apricots – the marriage is marvellous. Spread it on mini wholewheat or granary crackers or biscuit-cut pumpernickel shapes for parties. Pack the cheese firmly into trimmed pepper cases, cover and chill them and serve them thinly sliced on a salad garnish. Nut-speckled cheese looks good this way, in a fleshy red or green ring. Or serve it as a dip with crudités (see below). For a first course, light lunch or supper dish or even a savoury finale, use a home-made soft cheese in a new role, in a herb-flavoured vegetable-topped cheesecake.

On the sweet side, you can embellish soft cheeses with orange, lime and lemon juice and zest, cinnamon, nutmeg, chopped nuts, toasted coconut, sesame seed, chopped or whole dried fruits (dates especially) crushed soft fruits or banana, a dash of sweet wine or liqueur. Piled into a snowy mountain on a slice of fresh pineapple, in an opened-out whole orange or a cold baked apple, they make a luscious pudding.

Crudités

Soft cheeses and yoghurt are the natural staples of dips and sauces to serve with crisply cut sticks of crunchy-fresh vegetables as crudités, the French way. Arguably, these are vegetables at their best, cut into pencil-slim sticks or broken into bite-sized flowerets and arranged artistically around the sauce. For this is another dish, simplicity itself, where presentation counts.

Dressings

The components of a good dressing should be virtually indistinguishable when mixed with salad ingredients. Most dressings are composed of fat, acid and flavourings, which all have a purpose to serve. The fats, eggs and oils act as carriers for the fat soluble vitamins which are present a-plenty in raw salad vegetables and fruit. The acid – vinegar, wine or fruit juice – protects the ascorbic acid (vitamin C), and the flavouring ensures the variety of taste.

There is a variety of oil to choose from and it will be a matter of personal preference whether, or when, you choose the strong-flavoured olive, the slightly nutty tasting sunflower, the rather sweet sesame seed or almost tasteless corn, groundnut or arachides oils. For lower-calorie dressings, you can substitute low-fat yoghurt or buttermilk for all or some of the oil.

Vinegar is the most usual acid component and you can use those made from cider or red or white wine, or the distilled (white) variety. Lemon juice is an alternative, or when fruit is one of the salad ingredients, use an unsweetened fruit juice, perhaps with some grated citrus fruit zest.

For vinaigrette dressing the proportions are generally one part acid to three parts oil, but vary this to suit your taste. Measure the vinegar into a jug, add salt and lots of freshly ground pepper and stir with a fork to dissolve the salt.

Every season brings a harvest of vegetables to serve in this way – sticks of flame-coloured carrots and milky-white Chinese leaves, celery, turnips and parsnips, (tossed in lemon juice first) flowerets of cauliflower and slivers of cabbage stalk in winter, boat-shaped scoops of cucumber – sticks, too – blanched whole young French beans, spring onions, chicory leaves, thin strips of red, green and yellow peppers and long slices of large radishes in summer. There is scarcely a vegetable that cannot be used in a dish of crudites. Look for colourful contrasts.

To prepare vegetables for crudités, ruthlessly discard any blemished outer leaves or damaged parts – many of them can be used in soup – and taste a sample of any doubtful starters. All but the heart of celery, for example, might be too stringy to be enjoyable.

When you are offering a thin dressing, one based on a simple vinaigrette with added flavouring, or one that is essentially yoghurt, the vegetables can be cut into little more than matchstick proportions, and you can add thin mushroom or leek slices. But for a thicker dressing or dip, one that is more cheese than yoghurt, the sticks need to be of slightly stouter girth.

Preparing Salads

As a meal in its own right, an accompaniment to a hot or cold main dish, a small between-course refresher, and as a thing of beauty – thank Heaven for salad! With such a wealth of leaf and root vegetables, fruits and garnishes to choose from, the problem is not what to put in, but what to leave out.

Whether you go for all the greens – from ice green to evergreen – or a palette of colour in your salads, it is hard to go wrong. Try, however, to ensure balance of texture, colour and shape.

Wash all salads thoroughly. Wash leaves under cold, running water and dry them equally thoroughly. Ideally, put them in a polythene bag, seal and chill in the refrigerator to crisp for 1 hour before serving. Trim and scrub root vegetables and avoid peeling if possible. Chill the salad bowl and – a counsel of perfection – the individual plates.

Pour on the oil gradually, whisking vigorously to mix and thicken the dressing. To give a herby taste, stir in 10 ml/2 tsp chopped parsley, chervil, dill, tarragon, mint or basil or 5 ml/1 tsp dried herbs.

Mayonnaise cannot be advanced, as a low-calorie dressing, delicious though it is with many salad combinations. For a more virtuous version, mix it half-and-half with thickened yoghurt, or settle for a taste-alike alternative using yoghurt cheese. For this Curd Mayonnaise blend together 100g/4 oz soft cheese, 45 ml/3 tbls yoghurt, 5 ml/1 tsp oil, 5 ml/1 tsp cider vinegar and season it well with salt and ground black pepper. It makes a good crudité sauce, too.

Steak Tartare

Trim any excess fat from the meat and cut it roughly into cubes. Using the finest blade of the mincer, mince the meat twice.

Finely chop the onion. Halve the peppers, discard the seeds and white membrane and finely chop the flesh.

Season the meat well with salt and pepper and divide it between 4 serving plates. Arrange the onion, peppers, capers and parsley in mounds around the meat. Using the back of a spoon, push an indent into each meat portion and slide an egg yolk into each one.

To make the sauce, beat the soured cream until smooth, then stir in the chopped capers, gherkins, parsley and onion. Season the sauce with salt, pepper and the lemon juice and serve it separately.

*Connoisseurs of Steak Tartare would claim the meat should be very finely chopped rather than minced. To do this, you need a very sharp knife. Cut the meat off the main chunk in tiny slivers, then chop it again in the way you would a bunch of parsley.

Serves 4
Calories 1155 (4815 kJ)
Protein 99 grams

450 g/1 lb fillet or rump steak
1 medium-sized onion
1 small green pepper
1 small red pepper
salt and ground black pepper
60 ml/4 tbls chopped capers
30 ml/2 tbls chopped parsley
4 large egg yolks

For the sauce
150 ml/5 fl oz soured cream, chilled
15 ml/1 tbls chopd capers
15 ml/1 tbls chopped gherkins
15 ml/1 tbls chopped parsley
1 small onion, finely chopped
2.5 ml/½ tsp lemon juice

Peel onion, de-seed peppers; chop all vegetables finely. Keep them separate. Chop capers and parsley.

Trim meat of all fat. Mince the lean meat finely, then put through mincer again. Season well.

Divide meat between 4 plates. Shape into neat rounds; indent the middle of each one, using a teaspoon.

Separate 4 eggs and slide the yolks into the central indentations. Pile the vegetables, capers and parsley round.

Rollmops

10 salt herring fillets (see method)
350 ml/12 fl oz white wine vinegar
350 ml/12 fl oz water
6 black peppercorns
3 juniper berries
15 ml/1 tbls mustard seed
3 whole allspice berries
1 bay leaf
30 ml/2 tbls German mustard
15 ml/1 tbls capers
10 pickled cucumbers
2 large Spanish onions, thinly
  sliced into rings
6 parsley sprigs

Ask the fishmonger to fillet the herrings for you, or prepare them yourself, following the directions on page 32.

Place the herring fillets in a large bowl and pour over enough water to cover them. Cover the bowl and chill in the refrigerator for 12 hours.

Drain the fillets and wash them under cold, running water. Pat dry with absorbent kitchen paper.

Place the fillets on a wooden board and, using a sharp knife, carefully remove and discard any bones, making sure you keep the fillets intact. Set them aside.

Place the vinegar, water, peppercorns, juniper berries, mustard seed, allspice berries and bay leaf in a large pan and bring to the boil over high heat. Reduce the heat and simmer, uncovered, for 10 minutes. Remove the pan from the heat and set aside to cool.

Lay the fillets flat on the board, skin side down. Spread a little of the mustard over each one and sprinkle with some of the capers. Place a cucumber at the wide end of each fillet and roll up Swiss-roll style. Secure the fillets with a wooden cocktail stick.

Lay one-third of the onion rings in the bottom of a large, deep glass dish. Arrange half of the rollmops over them and continue making layers, ending with onion rings.

Pour the vinegar mixture through a fine strainer over the rollmops and discard the contents of the strainer. Cover the dish with foil and refrigerate, turning the fillets occasionally, for 1 week.

Serves 4-6
Calories 935 (3880 kJ)
Protein 67 grams

Olive "Pretend Caviar"

225 g/8 oz black olives
4 small spring onions, thinly sliced
45 ml/3 tbls chopped parsley
2.5 ml/½ tsp anchovy essence or
  anchovy paste
10 ml/2 tsp white wine vinegar
45 ml/3 tbls olive oil
salt and ground black pepper
about 5 ml/1 tsp sugar
spinach or lettuce leaves, to serve
2 hard-boiled eggs, sliced
2 small celery stalks, very thinly
  sliced
4 thin slices of lemon

Wash the olives thoroughly to rinse off the brine. Stone and chop them very finely. Mix them with the sliced onion and two-thirds of the parsley.

Blend together the anchovy essence or paste and the vinegar and olive oil. Season with salt, pepper and sugar to taste. Toss the chopped olives in this dressing, cover and set aside. Do not chill.

Just before serving, arrange the spinach or lettuce leaves on four individual plates. Arrange slices of hard-boiled egg round the outside. Stir the celery into the olive mixture and spoon on to the plates. Garnish each one with a twisted slice of lemon and the reserved parsley.

Serve the dish, which looks like glistening caviar, with hot buttered toast, and remember the extra calories.

Serves 4
Calories 785 (3240 kJ)
Protein 16 grams

Lumpfish Mousse

If the consommé has solidified, turn it into a small pan and melt it. Measure 60 ml/4 tbls into a cup and reserve to glaze the top.

Stir the curry powder into the consommé in the pan and set aside to cool but not set. Put the consommé and cheese into a liquidizer or beat well with a fork to blend thoroughly. Pour into 4 cocotte dishes and chill until set.

Overlap the cucumber slices to cover the top. Melt the reserved consommé, and spoon it over the cucumber. Put in the refrigerator to set.

Spoon the roe in a ring round each dish, cover and chill.

This mousse is best served with thin slices of brown bread and butter.

Serves 4
Calories 310 (1300 kJ)
Protein 35 grams

125 ml/4 fl oz concentrated consommé
5 ml/1 tsp curry powder
100 g/4 oz low-fat soft cheese
½ small cucumber, thinly sliced
50 g/2 oz red lumpfish roe

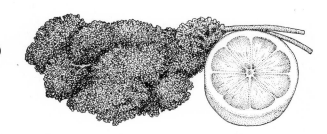

Sliced Raw Fish (Sashimi)

Buy the fish from a very reliable fishmonger, making sure that it is absolutely fresh. To be certain of the quality, it is best to buy whole fish and ask the retailer to fillet it for you. Or do it yourself, following the directions on pages 32 and 33.

Put the fish in a colander, hold it over the sink and pour boiling water through. Then refresh under cold, running water.

Lay the fillets on a carving board and using a very sharp knife, cut them into very thin strips. Cover and chill in the refrigerator while you prepare the garnish.

Cut the red pepper in half, remove the seeds and white membrane and chop the flesh finely. Mix the pepper with the grated radish or turnip. Mix together the soy sauce and lemon juice, pour over the vegetables and toss thoroughly.

To make the serving sauce, mix together the soy sauce, sake or sherry and grated horseradish.

To serve the dish, arrange the fish strips neatly and decoratively in a pattern on 2 or 4 flat serving plates, depending on whether you are serving the dish as a main course or a first course. Arrange the marinated vegetables in a neat mound beside the fish and garnish with the fennel sprigs.

Divide the sauce between 2 or 4 small ramekin dishes. The fish strips are first dipped in the horseradish sauce and eaten with a little raw vegetable.

Serves 2-4
Calories for white fish 460 (1940 kJ)
Protein 76 grams
Calories for fatty fish 1025 (4270 kJ)
Protein 83 grams

450 g/1 lb fillets of very fresh, firm fish such as dover sole, lemon sole or mackerel (see method)
1 red pepper
100 g/4 oz white radish or white turnip, trimmed and grated
30 ml/2 tbls soy sauce
10 ml/2 tsp lemon juice
2 or 4 fresh fennel sprigs

For the serving sauce
45 ml/3 tbls soy sauce
30 ml/2 tbls sake or dry sherry
15 ml/1 tbls grated fresh horseradish

Sweet Pickled Mackerel

2 mackerel, about 350 g/12 oz each

For the pickle
30 ml/2 tbls sea salt
30 ml/2 tbls sugar
5 ml/1 tsp peppercorns, crushed
15 ml/1 tbls brandy (optional)
30 ml/2 tbls fresh dill or 15 ml/
  1 tbls dried dill weed

For the sauce
60 ml/4 tbls French mustard
15 ml/1 tbl sugar
2 large egg yolks
225 ml/8 fl oz olive oil
60 ml/4 tbls red wine vinegar
20 ml/4 tsp fresh dill or 10 ml/2 tsp
  dried dill weed
salt and white pepper

Remove the heads, tails and backbones from the mackerel (see diagrams on pages 32 and 33), but do not skin them.

Mix together all the pickling ingredients and spread a quarter in the bottom of a large, shallow dish.

Lay one of the mackerel, skin side down, on the pickling mixture and spread half the remaining mixture on top. Place the other mackerel on top, skin side up, facing the opposite way to the first fish. (This way the top will be level for putting on a weight).

Cover with the remaining pickle, then with foil and a board weighted down with one or two cans. Leave in the refrigerator for at least 12 hours, or up to 4 days.

For the sauce, beat the mustard with the sugar and egg yolks until smooth. Add the oil and vinegar a little at a time, mixing constantly. Season to taste with dill, salt and pepper.

To serve, drain the fish and thoroughly scrape away the herb and spices. Cut the fish in thin, slanting slices. Serve the sauce separately.
*You can pickle trout in just the same way.

Serves 4
Calories 3195 (13,180 kJ)
Protein 91 grams

Marinated Salmon

Place the slices of salmon in a large, shallow dish.

Mix together all the other ingredients, beating well until the sugar has dissolved. Pour the mixture over the salmon, cover and chill in the refrigerator for 1 hour, turning the fish occasionally in the marinade.

Transfer the fish to a serving dish and strain over the marinade, discarding the contents of the strainer.

Serve well chilled as an hors d'oeuvre, with thinly sliced bread and butter.

Serves 4-6
Calories 745 (3100 kJ)
Protein 62 grams

450 g/1 lb fresh salmon, very
    thinly sliced
2 cm/1 in fresh root ginger, peeled
    and finely chopped
1 garlic clove, crushed
2 spring onions, finely chopped
5 ml/1 tsp sugar
5 ml/1 tsp salt
45 ml/3 tbls soy sauce
125 ml/4 fl oz dry sherry

Buttermilk Cheese

575 ml/1 pt cultured buttermilk
salt to taste

Place the buttermilk in a double boiler or a bowl over a pan of simmering water and heat gently to 71°C/160°F, stirring from time to time. The buttermilk will separate as it heats.

Remove from the heat, cover and leave for 2 hours.

Line a colander with a double thickness of scalded butter muslin or cheese cloth and stand in a large bowl. Tip the buttermilk into the colander, gather up the cloth and tie at the top. Hang over the bowl to drain for 2 hours.

Scrape the cheese from the bag and beat in salt to taste. You can flavour the cheese in any of the ways suggested for Yoghurt Cheese.

Makes about 100-150 g/4-5 oz
Calories 155 (645 kJ)
Protein 15 grams

Yoghurt Cheese

575 ml/1 pt yoghurt
salt and other flavourings (see notes opposite)

Line a colander with a double thickness of scalded buttermuslin or cheesecloth. Stand the colander in a large bowl and tip in the yoghurt. Fold the cloth over the top and leave to drain for at least 2 hours. Gather up the top of the cloth, tie securely with string and hang over a bowl for about another 2 hours to catch the remaining drips of whey.

Pour off the whey and store it in the refrigerator. You can use it as a light stock for soups, sauces and casseroles, in scones, teabreads and some breads, or mix it with milk or fruit juice.

*If the yoghurt was made with skimmed milk and skimmed milk powder, the resulting cheese will be very similar in flavour and texture to cottage cheese.

Makes about 200-225 g/7-8 oz
Calories 255 (1045 kJ)
Protein 23 grams

Soft Soured Milk Cheese

575 ml/1 pt cow's or goat's milk
juice of 1 lemon

Heat the milk to 38°C/100°F, checking the temperature with a thermometer. Pour the milk into a large bowl.

Squeeze the juice of the lemon and strain into a bowl. Stir well, cover and leave in a warm place for 15 minutes – beside the cooker, or in an airing cupboard, for example. You will notice that the milk has begun to set.

Line a colander with a double thickness of scalded buttermuslin or cheesecloth. Ladle the curd into it a little at a time, allowing most of the whey to drip through before adding more.

Gather up the cloth and tie the top. Hang over a bowl and leave for 1 hour to drain.

Scrape the cheese in to a bowl, flavour with salt or in any of the other ways suggested for Yoghurt Cheese. Cover and store in the refrigerator.

Makes about 100-150 g/4-5 oz
Calories 378 (1588 kJ)
Protein 19 grams

To make yoghurt cheese: line colander with double thickness of scalded cheesecloth. Tip in yoghurt.

Gather up top of cloth and tie securely with string. Suspend (by tying to upturned chair for eg) over a bowl to catch dripping whey.

Turn cheese in cloth into bowl; add chopped herbs or other flavourings (see below). Beat well, cover and store in refrigerator.

Yoghurt cheese can be used in many ways. For an appetizer, roll into small balls and coat in finely chopped nuts.

Flavouring the Cheese

Many people consider the addition of about 5 ml/1 tsp sea salt (or to taste) brings out the flavour of the cheese.

You can make a variety of delicious savoury cheeses by adding chopped fresh herbs such as chives, parsley, basil or marjoram – about 15 ml/1 tbls gives a subtle flavour to 225 g/8 oz cheese, but add more if you wish. And as a good combination with the herbs, or alone, you can add 2 crushed garlic cloves.

Chopped mixed nuts such as walnuts and cashews beaten into the cheese give it a delightful texture. Or you can roll the cheese into small balls and then roll them in chopped nuts to serve, on cocktail sticks, as appetizers.

Ground spices make interesting flavourings. Try curry powder, paprika pepper, coriander or cayenne, beating in a little at a time and testing until you have just the right degree of spiciness.

For fish lovers, beat finely-chopped anchovies, shrimps or prawns into the cheese. Add a dash of anchovy paste or cayenne pepper to give extra 'bite'.

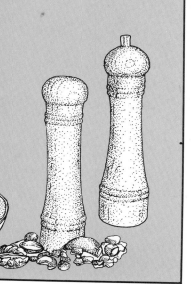

Plum Salad

175 g/6 oz dessert plums
1 medium-sized round lettuce
¼ cucumber
6 spring onions
4 sage leaves, chopped
15 ml/1 tbls chopped tarragon
15 ml/1 tbls chopped parsley
60 ml/4 tbls sunflower oil
30 ml/2 tbls white wine vinegar
salt and ground black pepper

Halve and stone the plums and cut them lengthways into thin slices. Shred the lettuce. Cut the cucumber lengthways into 4 long sticks, then across into thin slices. Finely chop the spring onions.

Put the plum and cucumber slices, lettuce and spring onion in a salad bowl and mix in the herbs.

Beat the oil, vinegar and seasonings together and fold into the salad just before serving. Toss well.

*This salad, with its mixture of sweet and sharp flavours, is particularly good with lamb, pork or grilled mackerel.

Serves 4
Calories 590 (2430 kJ)
Protein 3 grams

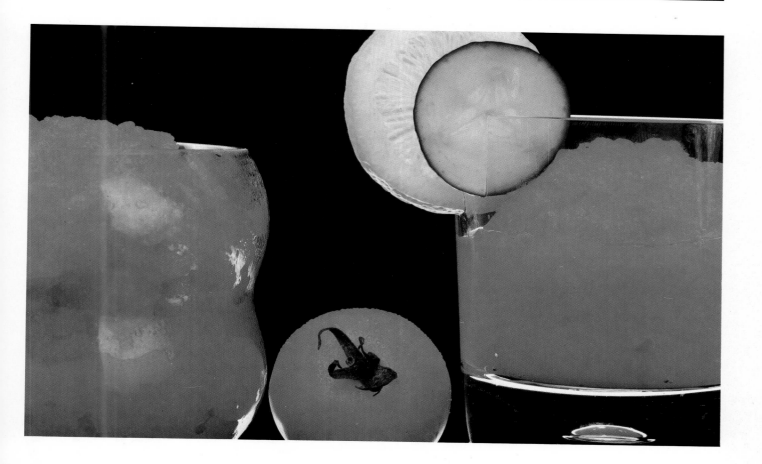

Russian Tomato Ice

Turn the refrigerator or freezer to the lowest setting.

Put the tomato juice, vodka, lemon juice, Worcestershire sauce and crushed ice into a liquidizer and blend until the ice has been completely crushed. Pour the mixture into a plastic container, stir in the celery leaves and chopped mint and season well with salt, pepper and red pepper sauce. Cover and freeze for 2 hours, or until the mixture has frozen around the edges. Beat it well, turning the frozen sides into the middle. Cover and freeze again for 2-3 hours, or until the mixture is completely frozen.

Take the container from the freezer 30 minutes before serving and leave it in the main part of the refrigerator to soften. Spoon into 6 goblets. Slice lemon and cucumber thinly and use to decorate the glasses. Serve as a tinglingly refreshing first course.

Serves 6
Calories 215 (900 kJ)
Protein 3 grams

275 ml/10 fl oz tomato juice
75 ml/5 tbls vodka
juice of 2 lemons
6 drops Worcestershire sauce
6 ice cubes, crushed
4 celery leaves, finely chopped
90 ml/6 tbls chopped mint
salt and ground black pepper
a few drops of red pepper sauce
1 lemon
small piece of cucumber

Mixed Salad Soup

6 large tomatoes
6 spring onions, thinly sliced
1/2 cucumber, peeled and thinly
    diced
1 red pepper, de-seeded and very
    thinly sliced
6 radishes, very thinly sliced
60 ml/4 tbls fresh wholewheat
    breadcrumbs
2 garlic cloves, finely chopped
salt and ground black pepper
a large pinch of cayenne
90 ml/6 tbls sunflower oil
45 ml/3 tbls lemon juice
450 ml/15 fl oz strong chicken stock
2 large carrots, grated
15 ml/1 tbls chopped parsley

Dip the tomatoes into boiling water, skin them and remove the seeds and juice. Chop the flesh and put it into a large bowl. Stir in the sliced spring onions, the cucumber, red pepper, radishes, breadcrumbs and garlic. Season the vegetables well with salt, pepper and cayenne pepper and stir in the oil and lemon juice. Stir in the chicken stock, cover the bowl and refrigerate overnight. Taste the soup and adjust the seasoning if necessary.

Turn into a chilled serving bowl or soup tureen and, just before serving, scatter with the grated carrot and the chopped parsley.

Serves 4
Calories 965 (4005 kJ)
Protein 11 grams

Pear and Brie Salad

4 small firm pears, chilled
juice of 1/2 a lemon
100 g/4 oz ripe Brie
45 ml/3 tbls dry white wine
50 g/2 oz walnut halves
bunch of watercress

Cut the pears in half lengthways, scoop out the cores and peel thinly. Brush the pears all over with the lemon juice to preserve their colour and arrange them on a serving dish.

Mash the Brie with a fork and blend in the wine until the mixture is smooth and creamy. Roughly chop all but 8 of the walnut halves and stir them into the cheese mixture.

Pile the mixture on to the pears, and top each with a walnut half. Serve surrounded with sprigs of watercress.

Serves 4
Calories 740 (3085 kJ)
Protein 29 grams

Cucumber and Yoghurt Salad

250 ml/8 fl oz natural yoghurt,
    chilled
1 large cucumber, peeled and
    thinly diced
1 garlic clove, crushed
30 ml/2 tbls chopped mint or 10
    ml/2 tsp dried mint
salt and ground black pepper

Beat the yoghurt until it is smooth, stir in the remaining ingredients, cover and chill until ready to serve.

This salad is served as a side dish with highly-spiced dishes such as curry or with barbecued dishes like grilled lamb or spring chicken.

Serves 4-6
Calories 150 (625 kJ)
Protein 14 grams

Uncooked Fruit Soup

Stone and chop the peaches, plums and cherries. Peel and slice the banana.

Put all the fruit into a liquidizer with the honey and blend until it forms a thick purée.

Transfer purée to a large bowl and pour in the milk. Beat with a wire whisk or rotary beater until it is thoroughly blended. Stir in the lemon juice and beat in the yoghurt or cream.

Pour the soup into a large soup tureen.

or serving bowl, cover and chill in the refrigerator for 1 hour. The soup must be served well chilled.

Serves 4-6
Calories with yoghurt
   1095 (4640 kJ)
Protein 35 grams
Calories with thin cream
   1335 (5630 kJ)
Protein 31 grams

4 large fresh peaches
225 g/8 oz Victoria plums
225 g/8 oz cherries
1 large banana
60 ml/4 tbls clear honey
575 ml/1 pt milk
juice of 1 lemon
150 ml/5 fl oz natural yoghurt or
   thin cream

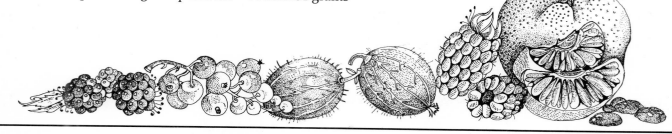

Herb Cheesecake

To make the base, melt the margarine in a small pan and stir in the biscuit crumbs, lemon rind and juice. Season lightly with salt and pepper. Press the mixture into a greased loose-bottomed 20-cm/8-in cake tin. Leave in the refrigerator to chill.

To make the filling, put the grated cucumber into a colander, sprinkle with salt and leave over a bowl for 30 minutes, to draw off some of the moisture. Rinse well under cold, running water and dry thoroughly. Pat off excess moisture with a wad of absorbent kitchen towel.

Beat the cheese in a bowl, then beat in the egg yolks one at a time, followed by the lemon rind and yoghurt. Stir in the garlic, mint and basil. Soften the gelatine in 30 ml/2 tbls water in a small bowl standing in a pan of hot water. Stir until

dissolved, then beat into the cheese mixture, making sure it is well mixed.

Whisk the egg whites until they are stiff. When the cheese mixture is almost set, carefully fold in the egg whites. Pour the mixture on to the biscuit base and level the top. Chill in the refrigerator for about 2 hours, or until set.

Transfer the cheesecake to a flat serving plate. Whip the yoghurt until it is smooth and thick and spread it evenly over the cheesecake. Thinly slice the cucumber and arrange the slices to overlap in a ring around the outside.

Serves 6-8
Calories 1700 (7075 kJ)
Protein 78 grams

50 g/2 oz polyunsaturated
   margarine
150 g/5 oz digestive biscuits,
   crushed
grated rind and juice of 1/2 lemon
salt and ground black pepper

For the filling
1/2 large cucumber, peeled and
   grated
225 g/8 oz yoghurt cheese
   (see page 89)
2 medium-sized eggs, separated
grated rind 1/2 lemon
150 ml/5 fl oz natural yoghurt
1 garlic clove, crushed
30 ml/2 tbls chopped mint
15 ml/1 tbls chopped basil
15 g/1/2 oz powdered gelatine

For the topping
100 ml/31/2 fl oz natural yoghurt
1/4 large cucumber

Healthy Beverages

'Tea! Tea!' a much-loved comedian once exclaimed. 'A cup of tea! Is that your only answer to the world's ills – a cup of *tea*?!' Well, often it is. We rush to put the kettle on whenever we are called upon to comfort a friend in need. We vow we're all but dying for a cup of coffee as our workaday energy flags, and from childhood days onward we warm our hands gratefully around a steaming mug of cocoa or malted milk at night-time. At other times, of course, it's an ice-cold drink that is worth its weight in gold – lemon barley water, or a glass of fruit-floaty Sangria on a hot summer's evening.

Whatever the occasion, the time or the temperature, it seems that what we have to drink plays a vital part in our health and happiness, not always directly affecting our physical health, maybe, but crucial to our feeling of well-being. If we are convinced that a sip of what we fancy does us good, then surely it will. From the sweetly scented herbal teas that cured our grandmothers of fits of the vapours to the vitality yoghurt drinks of today; from the log-fire-inspiring bowls of mulled wine punch to the fresh-as-the-mountain-air bottles of mineral waters – whatever our needs or our moods, there's a drink to cater for them.

Tisanes

Long before China and Indian teas were imported in the West people knew the value of a cup of tea, made from the infused leaves, flowers and seeds of wild or cultivated plants. These tisanes took the place of medicines for centuries, but then fell by the wayside, swept out of mind by modern drugs. Although no claims are made for the healing properties of the tisanes listed here, recent research has to a large extent backed up old beliefs – many herbs have indeed been found to have the properties that earlier devotees relied upon.

Camomile tea, for example, has long been taken in the hope of dispelling mild infections and as a relaxant. Now scientific tests show that the flowers contain, in the bright blue volatile oil, two valuable

antiseptics, bisabolol and chamazulene. And in a hospital experiment cups of camomile tea induced sleep in ten out of twelve heart patients.

A brief list of some of the tisanes you can make from herbal plants is given on page 102, but this is only the tip of the iceberg of possibilities. Experiment, if you like the idea, with other herbs (if you can borrow an old herbal, it will give literally hundreds of examples) and with the proportions of plant-to-water.

Milk in drinks

Ever since the fifties, dairy-producers' advertising campaigns have encouraged us to 'Drinka pinta milka day' or to 'Go to work on an egg' and promised that we would be all the healthier for doing so. And indeed a glass of milk whizzed up with an egg, full of vital proteins, vitamins, calcium and other minerals is one of the most complete foods we could have – even if it is not, for some non-devotees, the most enjoyable. But milk comes in many forms – yoghurt is an increasingly popular one – and is the easiest of foods to disguise with other more powerful flavours. Children who clamour for a strawberry or chocolate milk shake on a hot day might well refuse to drink the yoghurt or milk ingredients straight 'because it is good for them'.

Most milk on sale now has been treated in some way (in the U.K. untreated milk, when available, is sold in bottles with green caps). In the various processes used – pasteurization, homogenization, ultra-heat treatment and sterilization – the milk is heated, to destroy any harmful bacteria and to improve its keeping properties, and then rapidly cooled. The flavour, fat content and calorific values of the different types of milk vary considerably. If you enjoy a creamy taste but are anxious to restrict your fat intake, a compromise is the only answer.

The milk with the highest cream content (sold with gold tops in the U.K.) comes from Jersey, Guernsey or South Devon cattle breeds and has a minimum 4 per cent butterfat content. The other pasteurized type (with silver caps in the U.K.) has a slightly reduced vitamin content. Homogenized milk lacks a thick 'cream line' on top because the fat globules, though still present, are distributed evenly. Some homogenized milk is ultra-heat treated (UHT), a process which affects neither the flavour nor nutritional value, and some is sterilized – heat treated and vacuum sealed. Sterilized milk has a rich, creamy look and a slight caramel flavour, but has been robbed of many of its vitamins. Skimmed milk, much in demand now by weight-watchers and others who want to follow a low-fat programme, is homogenized milk with the fat extracted. Both whole and skimmed homogenized milk is available dried, and it is in this powdered form that many people find it most convenient.

Vitality drinks

Yoghurt made from skimmed milk and dried skimmed milk powder has the lowest fat content of all. Buttermilk, which was originally made from the residue from the butter churn, is now made with milk and an added culture.

A delightfully cooling summer drink with the fragrance of the herb garden, offered in Turkey in little brass bowls by street sellers, is made with equal parts of yoghurt and water beaten together with clear honey, salt and roughly chopped mint leaves. Served in chilled glasses with tinkling ice cubes, it is as good as a cool shower.

Fruit and yoghurt go perfectly together in so many different vitality drinks and can be served just as 'coolers' or as a light and easy first course for a summer meal. Blend together equal quantities of grapefruit juice and yoghurt, stir in chopped mint and sprinkle the tops with toasted coconut, or season a 50-50 mix of yoghurt and tomato juice with Worcestershire sauce, stir in chopped basil and garnish with sprigs of herb.

Citrus fruits, like milk, have one of the strongest claims for consideration as 'health' drinks and they, too, can make a nutritionally substantial meal in a glass. For breakfast, blend together the juice of 2 oranges, a small banana, 10 ml/2 tsp of wheatgerm and 5 ml/1 tsp of clear honey.

Punches, toddies, nogs, mulls and possets

All these highly evocative names describe drinks that warmed, cheered or revived our male ancestors for centuries. Some mixtures of wine and spirit can, of course be very powerful, but others can actually be less potent than a 'straight' drink, because the wine is diluted with fruit juice or even water. Spice was the variety of life in all these drinks, disguising the somewhat 'off' flavours of the wine and beer.

Many of these popular eighteenth- and nineteenth-century drinks are well worth reviving for winter parties and celebrations, or just a cosy family evening at home. The spirit in the glass is infectious – even if there isn't actually any spirit content at all!

To make mulled drinks, put all the ingredients, the liquid, fruit and spices, into an enamel or other lined saucepan (not an aluminium one) and bring them slowly to just under boiling point. It is

wasteful to allow the mixture to boil – unless you actually want to evaporate the alcohol. Strain the mull into a heatproof or warmed glass jug or bowl. Float the whole or sliced fruit on top and ladle the drink into warmed or heatproof glasses. A spoon transferred from one glass to the next as you pour helps to eliminate the danger of glasses cracking.

Mulled drinks can be based on fortified wines, table wines, beer or cider, sometimes mixed and sometimes with added spirit. It is never necessary, or even advisable, to buy a good quality wine for a mull. The spices disguise good flavours as well as bad. Choose full-bodied wines that are hearty rather than delicate. For Negus, a drink immortalized by Dickens, you need 1 bottle of 'cheap' sweet sherry, 1 lemon, 6 cloves, 2 cinnamon sticks and 5 ml/1 tsp grated nutmeg. Stick the cloves into the lemon, put all the ingredients in a pan and heat slowly. Taste and add 15-30 ml/1-2 tbls brown sugar if you like. Pour on 575 ml/1 pt boiling water and add (optionally) 60 ml/4 tbls brandy. This will make 12 glasses.

It is, perhaps, a mistake in any recipe for these drinks to say 'you need', for the essence of them is their versatility. You can use red wine instead of sherry, oranges instead of a lemon, other spices to replace the cloves and cinnamon, and honey when any extra sweetening is needed.

A Victorian recipe for Wassail Bowl, a term originating from the 15th century, calls for 3 cored dessert apples filled with 100 g/4 oz brown sugar, 150 ml/5 fl oz water, 2.5 ml/½ tsp grated nutmeg, 1 clove, 2.5 ml/½ tsp ground ginger, 1 stick of cinnamon, 1 bottle cheap dry white wine, 90 ml/6 tbls clear honey and 3 eggs. Bake the sugar-filled apples in a moderate oven until they are tender. While they are cooking, put the water and spices in a large pan and bring slowly to the boil. Pour in the wine, stir in the honey and heat gently. In a warmed bowl, beat the eggs with a little of the warmed wine mixture, pour on the remainder and beat briskly until the mull is frothy. Add the baked apples and stir in 60 ml/4 tbls brandy if you like. This makes 8 drinks.

Assuming that it's not a toe-tinglingly cold evening, but a warm and sultry one, here's how to make Sangria, an appropriately exotic cooler. Chill 1 bottle of red wine and 700 ml/1¼ pt low-calorie lemonade. Mix them together in a chilled bowl, stir in 60 ml/4 tbls of brandy and add sugar if you like; stir until it dissolves. Float on top 1 thinly-sliced apple, lemon and orange, a few strawberries and a couple of sliced peaches tossed in lemon juice – and drink at sundown.

Favourite 'night-caps'

Hot milk drinks, traditionally comforting 'night-caps', can seem even more reassuring with a little alcohol added. To make Mocha Toddy for 3-4 people, mix 15 ml/1 tbls carob powder (or cocoa) to a paste with a little cold milk taken from 575 ml/ 1 pt. Stir in the rest of the milk and heat in a small pan. Add 15 ml/1 tbls brown sugar and 60 ml/4 tbls coffee-flavoured liqueur. Stir and bring to just below boiling point (boiling would ruin the flavour) and pour into beakers. Top each one with 15 ml/1 tbls thickened yoghurt, (see page 72).

Dieter's Pinkers

125 ml/4 fl oz low-calorie bitter
  lemon
10 drops of Angostura bitters
1 thin slice of lemon

Chill the glass in the refrigerator or by swirling ice cubes round in it.
  Pour in the bitter lemon, add the Angostura bitters and stir. Float the lemon slice on top.
*For an even pinker Pinkers, try making this drink with similar proportions of low-calorie tonic water and bitters.

Serves 1
Calories } negligible
Protein

Apple Cocktail

about 275 ml/10 fl oz crushed ice
275 ml/10 fl oz unsweetened apple
  juice
150 ml/5 fl oz unsweetened orange
  juice
150 ml/5 fl oz unsweetened
  pineapple juice
275 ml/ 10 fl oz soda water
1 dessert apple, cored and thinly
  sliced
15 ml/1 tbls lemon juice
sprigs of mint

Put the ice into a chilled jug and pour over the three fruit juices and the soda water. Toss the apple slices in the lemon juice and float on top. Decorate with the mint sprigs and serve in chilled glasses.

Serves 4-6
Calories 300 (1270 kJ)
Protein 3 grams

Ginger Vine

575 ml/1 pt low-calorie ginger ale
275 ml/10 fl oz white grape juice
8-12 sugar cubes
1 lemon, washed
a few sprigs of applemint or
  peppermint

Mix together the ginger ale and grape juice in a chilled jug. Rub the sugar cubes over the lemon to extract the zest and add them to the drink. Float mint leaves on top to decorate.

Serves 4
Calories 390 (1660 kJ)
Protein 3 grams

Grape Juice Bitters

about 150 ml/5 fl oz crushed ice
2-3 drops of Angostura bitters
60 ml/4 tbls black grape juice
125 ml/4 fl oz soda water
1 small bunch black grapes
  (optional)

Put the crushed ice into a chilled tumbler and shake on the bitters. Add the grape juice, then the soda water and stir well. Decorate the rim of the glass, if liked, with a bunch of 2 or 3 black grapes.

Serves 1
Calories 45 (180 kJ)
Protein negligible

Spanish Orange

juice of 3 large oranges
juice of 1 large grapefruit
90 ml/6 tbls sweet sherry
575 ml/1 pt soda water, or to taste
twists of grapefruit zest, to
*   decorate*
4-6 cocktail cherries

Squeeze the juice of the oranges and the grapefruit and mix with the sherry. Dilute with soda water to taste.

Pour into 4-6 glasses and decorate each one with a cocktail cherry and a twist of thinly-pared grapefruit zest on a cocktail stick.

Serves 4-6
Calories 340 (1440 kJ)
Protein 6 grams

Lemon Barley Water

100 g/4 oz pearl barley
50 g/2 oz cube sugar
2 large lemons, washed

Put the barley in a saucepan and add enough cold water to cover. Bring to the boil and boil for 4 minutes. Strain into a large jug.

Rub the sugar cubes over the lemon rind to extract the zest and add to the barley. Squeeze the lemons and strain the juice into the jug. Pour on 1 L/1¾ pt of boiling water and stir well. Cover and leave to cool. Strain, then chill before serving in long glasses.

Serves 6-8
Calories 600 (2570 kJ)
Protein 10 grams

Fresh Tomato Refresher

450g/1 lb tomatoes
1 lemon
10 ml/2 tsp caster sugar
15 ml/1 tbls tomato purée
275 ml/10 fl oz chicken or vegetable
*   stock, chilled (see method)*
salt and ground black pepper
crushed ice, to serve
thin slices of cucumber

Skin the tomatoes and discard the seeds. Grate the zest of the lemon and squeeze the juice. Put the tomato, lemon zest and juice, sugar, tomato purée and stock in a liquidizer, season with salt and pepper and blend until the mixture is smooth. Taste and adjust the seasoning if necessary.

Put some crushed ice into tall, chilled glasses, pour over the tomato juice and decorate with cucumber slices.

*For a delightful combination of flavours, try Orange and Tomato Refresher. Make it in the same way, but substitute the juice of 3 oranges for the chicken or vegetable stock, and add the grated zest of 1 orange. Decorate the drink with thin slices of orange or with finely-snipped chives. (Calories 235 (1010 kJ). Protein 8 grams).

*As the drink is to be served chilled, make very sure that there is no fat in the chicken stock. If the stock has solidified and there is a fat content, it might be necessary to warm the stock and skim off the fat as it rises to the surface. Mop up the last traces with two or three layers of absorbent kitchen towel.

Serves 4-6
Calories 130 (550 kJ)
Protein 7 grams

Prairie Oyster

1.5 ml/¼ tsp malt vinegar
yolk of 1 large egg
5 ml/1 tsp Worcestershire sauce
5 ml/1 tsp tomato ketchup
ground black pepper

To make this tried and, by some, trusted 'morning after' reviver, shake all the ingredients together without breaking the egg yolk. The trick is to swallow it in one gulp!

Serves 1
Calories 80 (330 kJ)
Protein 4 grams

Tomato and Tequila Cocktail

575 ml/1 pt canned tomato juice, chilled
juice of 2 large oranges
100 ml/3½ fl oz tequila
2.5 ml/½ tsp hot red pepper sauce
crushed ice, to serve
orange slices

Pour the tomato juice into a large jug and stir in the orange juice, tequila and pepper sauce. Stir well to blend thoroughly.

One-quarter fill 4 tall glasses with crushed ice. Pour on the cocktail, garnish with the orange slices and serve at once as a fiery 'pick-you-up'!

Serves 4
Calories 395 (1665 kJ)
Protein 9 grams

Spring Cocktail

225 g/8 oz tomatoes
575 ml/1 pt chicken or vegetable stock (see note with Tomato Refresher recipe)
1 large carrot, grated
2 stalks celery, roughly chopped
1 bunch watercress
salt and ground black pepper

Skin the tomatoes and discard the seeds. Put flesh in a liquidizer with the stock, carrot, celery and most of the watercress leaves. Season and blend until smooth.

Put some crushed ice into chilled glasses and pour on the cocktail. Decorate with the reserved watercress.

Serves 4-6
Calories 70 (305 kJ)
Protein 7 grams

Fruit Juice Fling

2 apples
1 lemon
275 ml/10 fl oz fresh orange juice
2 slices fresh pineapple, peeled
30 ml/2 tbls clear honey
twists of orange zest

Peel and core the apples and roughly chop the flesh. Grate the zest and squeeze the juice of the lemon. Put all the ingredients, except the orange zest, into a liquidizer, add 150 ml/5 fl oz iced water and blend until smooth. Chill.

Pour into chilled glasses and decorate with twists of thinly-pared orange zest.

Serves 4-6
Calories 390 (1660 kJ)
Protein 4 grams

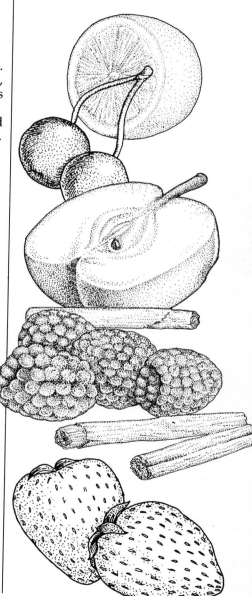

Tisanes

Over the centuries, herb teas have been credited with many medicinal and digestive properties, and have been drunk as much for these as for their undoubtedly refreshing and invigorating qualities.
You can make tisanes with fresh herb leaves, some herb flowers, and spice seeds from the garden, or with dried herbs and seeds – you can buy the more specialized ones in health food shops.
Follow the sample recipes below, and experiment with the herbs suggested in the following list. The quantities are always the same. Note that calorie and protein values are not included as the amounts are negligible.

Herb Tea

Makes 2-3 cups

45 ml/3 tbls chopped fresh herb leaves or flowers or
15 ml/1 tbls dried herb leaves, or
20 ml/4 tsp dried herb flowers (or more to taste)

Warm the pot with boiling water. Discard this and put in the herb leaves or flowers. Add 575 ml/1 pt boiling water, stir well, cover the pot and allow to steep for 5-10 minutes. Drain.

Herb teas, if they are sweetened at all, are usually served with a spoonful of honey (5 ml spoon = 14 calories/60 kJ). A slice of lemon in each cup adds fragrance to the tisane, and is decorative, too.

Try these herbs

Angelica Use the young leaves. This tea is considered good for nervous headaches.

Basil Serve hot or cold. It is soothing for colds and gastric upsets.

Bergamot Said to be sleep-inducing, this tisane can be served alone, or the herb leaves added to China tea.

Borage Use the leaves or flowers to make this refreshing tonic-tea and try it 'on the rocks', poured over crushed ice.

Camomile Make the tea from the dried flowers, using double the usual quantity. This one is popular in France.

Coltsfoot Fresh or dried, the flowers make a tea which has been used in the treatment of catarrh and chest troubles.

Dandelion The fresh or dried leaves make a tea favoured for rheumatic conditions and digestive disorders.

Elder The delightfully fragrant elder flowers make a tisane recommended by some for cold and throat infections.

Horehound This tea was used for coughs and colds.

Lemon Balm Add a slice of lemon to the pot while the tea is steeping.

Lemon Verbena Mix the leaves with a few mint leaves for a subtle fragrance.

Lovage This tea, almost a savoury drink, is usually seasoned with salt.

Meadowsweet The flowers are used for a tisane given to treat diarrhoea.

Mint A favourite in North African countries, Mint Tea is refreshing served hot or ice cold.

Nettle Said to be good for purifying the blood, but very pleasant anyway!

Parsley Use the young, fresh leaves for the most delicate flavour.

Rosemary This tisane is said to help alleviate headaches.

Sage Used as a tonic and to ward off winter ills and headaches.

Thyme Thought to be good for coughs and sinus troubles.

Violet The leaves make a refreshing and stimulating tonic-tea.

Yarrow Slightly bitter to many tastes, and definitely a candidate for a spoonful of honey. It is taken for colds and chest complaints.

Tea Punch

½ 75-cl/1¼-pt bottle dark rum
½ 75-cl/1¼-pt bottle brandy
250 g/9 oz soft brown sugar
juice of 1 large lemon
1.5 L/1½ pt strong tea, boiling

Pour the rum and brandy into a warmed bowl. Add the sugar and lemon, stir to dissolve the sugar, then set alight. Pour on the tea to put out the flames.

Ladle the tea into warmed heatproof glasses. If you use ordinary glasses, put a silver spoon in each before pouring, to avoid cracking.
*The calorie count will vary depending on how much alcohol is burnt off before the tea quenches the flames. The count given assumes that none has been burnt and is therefore the highest.

Serves 16-18
Calories 2675 (11195 kJ)
Protein 2.5 grams

Spiced Lemon Tea

575 ml/1 pt tea, hot
1 lemon, quartered
4 cloves
2 small pieces of cinnamon
slices of lemon

Stud the lemon quarters with cloves, pushing them well into the skin. Place them in 2 tall, heatproof glasses and put a piece of cinnamon in each. Strain on the hot tea and leave to infuse for about 4 minutes. Decorate with the lemon slices.

Serves 2
Calories 20 (80 kJ)
Protein 1 gram

Ceylon Punch

juice of 2 oranges
juice of 3 lemons
60 ml/4 tbls clear honey
275 ml/10 fl oz tea, hot
a few ice cubes
575 ml/1 pt soda water
575 ml/1 pt low-calorie ginger ale
slices of orange and lemon and
    sprigs of borage and mint

Mix together the orange and lemon juice, the honey and tea and stir to dissolve the honey. Set aside to cool.

Put the ice cubes into a large jug, strain over the tea mixture and pour on the soda water and ginger ale. Stir to mix well and float the fruit and herbs on top. Serve well chilled.

Makes about 1.7 L/3 pt
Calories 280 (1205 kJ)
Protein 4 grams

Iced Mint Tea

crushed ice
4 thin slices of orange
4 thin slices of lemon
12-16 crushed mint leaves
575 ml/1 pt strained tea, cold
sugar or honey to taste
sprigs of mint

Place crushed ice in the base of two tall, chilled glasses. Add the fruit and crushed mint and pour over the tea. Sweeten to taste. Decorate with sprigs of mint and serve chilled.

Serves 2
Calories 55 (235 kJ)
Protein 1 gram

Cucumber Cooler

1 medium-sized cucumber,
  roughly chopped
275 ml/10 fl oz buttermilk, chilled
6-9 fresh basil or mint leaves
salt and ground black pepper
borage or mint sprigs

Put the cucumber and buttermilk into a liquidizer with the basil or mint leaves and salt and pepper. Blend until the mixture is smooth and creamy. Taste and adjust seasoning. Serve in chilled glasses, garnished with herb sprigs.
*For a Pineapple Cooler, add 3 slices of peeled, cored and roughly chopped fresh pineapple to the goblet and omit the seasoning. A little honey blended with this drink is delicious.

Serves 2
Calories 110 (475 kJ)
Protein 11 Grams

Banana Nog

275 ml/10 fl oz natural yoghurt
15 ml/1 tbls clear honey
2 small bananas, peeled and sliced
1 large egg
a large pinch of cinnamon
extra cinnamon to decorate

Put the ingredients into a liquidizer goblet and blend until the mixture is smooth. Serve in pottery beakers and decorate, if you like, with an extra pinch of cinnamon.

Serves 2
Calories 370 (1550 kJ)
Protein 23 grams

Watercress Express

2 bunches of watercress
4 medium-sized oranges
1/2 a lemon
6 crushed ice cubes
150 ml/5 fl oz yoghurt
salt and ground black pepper

Discard the rough stalks of the watercress. Reserve a few of the best sprigs for decoration and put the remainder into a liquidizer goblet. Squeeze the oranges and lemon and strain the juice into the goblet. Add crushed ice cubes, yoghurt and seasoning. Blend until smooth.
   Serve in chilled glasses, decorated with the reserved watercress sprigs.

Serves 4-6
Calories 255 (1100 kJ)
Protein 14 grams

Ale Posset

1 slice wholewheat bread, toasted
1 L/1¾ pt boiling milk
2 medium-sized egg yolks, beaten
25 g/1 oz butter, melted
30 ml/2 tbls clear honey
1 L/1¾ pt draught brown ale

Place the toast in a large bowl and pour on the boiling milk. Whisk the egg yolks with the butter and honey. Strain milk on to the egg mixture and whisk to blend.
   Pour the milk mixture into a saucepan, add the ale and warm gently. Pour into a warmed, heatproof serving jug and serve in warmed glasses.
*Calorie count will vary – see note at end of Tea Punch.

Serves 8-10
Calories 1415 (5920 kJ)
Protein 46 grams

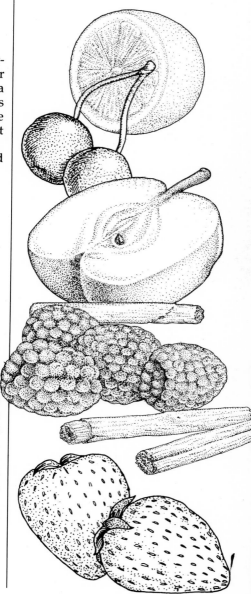

Bran and Fibre Cooking

Quite unwittingly over the last one hundred years or so we have been frittering away the fibre and nutrients in our natural foods – and jeopardizing our good health at the same time. For every time we choose highly refined white flour, a product made possible by the new mechanization techniques of the Industrial Revolution; every time we cook polished white rice instead of natural brown rice; indeed every time we unnecessarily peel a potato or an apple, we are depriving ourselves of valuable dietary fibre.

Recent medical research has shown that this dietary fibre, which is present in all grains, fruit and vegetables, can help to protect us from many of the diseases now so prevalent in the Western world – diseases virtually unknown before the development of 'refined' flours, polished rice and so-called convenience foods, and still little known in the underdeveloped countries of the world.

This is not to say that all processed foods are bad for us – in fact the problem has arisen more because of what we do not eat than because of what we do.

And what we do not eat in sufficient quantity for our health's sake is the fibre or 'roughage' which allows our bodies to function properly, for in refined white flours and polished white rice which, in various forms, make up so much of our diet, the main fibre element, the bran, has been processed away. True, for a couple of generations or so anxious mothers have prescribed a bowl of bran cereal as a cure for constipation. Yet not until recently have experts become convinced that adequate amounts of these most natural of foods would go a very long way to preventing digestive disorders and intestinal diseases.

Dietary fibre is the supportive structure of all cereals, fruit and vegetables, the woody tissues and the cellulose and gums which bind them together. Because it contains no nutrients and we cannot digest it, fibre has been largely overlooked as an important element in our daily needs. If all it does is to pass through our digestive systems, then what good is it?

The explanation is not perhaps quite the kind of thing you would discuss at the meal table – but important to understand, nonetheless. As fibre travels through the digestive tract it absorbs liquid, like a sponge, and therefore increases considerably in bulk. Digestive juices have to penetrate the fibre to extract the nutrients combined with it. This takes time, and so the nutrients are passed into the bloodstream in a steady flow. When nutrients are released too quickly, large amounts of insulin have to be released to digest them; and now there is growing reason to believe that this 'emergency

service' can lead to diabetic disorders.

Food matter which has a high fibre content – and is therefore bulky – is quickly and readily transported through the digestive system, as muscles can easily get a grip on it. Without this bulk, or roughage, food materials linger too long in the intestine, and there are fears that poisons could be reabsorbed into the body.

Finally, without the liquid that is absorbed by the fibre, these waste materials are less bulky and very hard, and are reluctant to be evacuated at all – back to the remedial bowl of bran!

It is important not to be confused by the terms 'dietary fibre' and 'fibrous' which are not at all the same thing. Soft fruits such as bananas and strawberries and even vegetables with a very high moisture content, such as spinach, have valuable dietary fibre; meat and fish have none at all.

A high-fibre diet is not a crash course, but a perfectly balanced and sensible long-term plan for healthy cooking and eating. Once you have become used to making a few fundamental changes in the basic ingredients you use, and to a slight change of emphasis in your menus, you can adapt all your own favourite recipes, as well as trying new ones from this book.

When you have to eat away from home regularly, at lunchtime at your job for instance, and cannot easily keep to the whole-grain foods, you can compensate by adding a little natural bran to the meals you prepare for yourself. If you sprinkle bran on your breakfast cereal, or into a soup, sauce or casserole either when you are making it or when you serve it, if you add bran to your bread and other baking, it will redress the balance. But this is not to say that you can eat whatever you like as long as you mix it with bran!

Approximate cooking times for Pulses

Beans	Average cooking times
Aduki	30 minutes
Black-eyed beans	25-30 minutes
British field beans	30 minutes
Butter beans	2-2½ hours
Chick peas	1-2 hours
European lentils	30-60 minutes
Gunga peas	1¼-1½ hours
Haricot beans	1-1½ hours
Kidney beans	1-1¼ hours
Mung beans	30 minutes
Peas	45 minutes
Pinto beans	1-1¼ hours
Red lentils unsoaked	20-30 minutes
soaked	15-20 minutes
Soya beans	3-4 hours
Split peas	30-40 minutes

Cereals

If you follow the advice of a Swiss physician, Dr. Bircher Benner, there is no better way to start the day than with a bowl of muesli. At the beginning of the century he introduced his recipe for the perfect food, a mixture of rolled oats, hazelnuts, chopped apple and lemon juice that would provide us with the dietary fibre, minerals, vitamins, protein, iron and fat we need to spring energetically into action. But how long it has taken us to believe him!

Rolled oats are crushed and partly cooked but, like oatmeal, still contain the oat kernel. Apart from muesli porridge they can be used to make flan cake, crumble toppings or added to scones, bread and biscuits.

Barley, a less familiar grain but probably the world's oldest cereal crop, is just as versatile. Buy the whole grain (sometimes sold as 'pot barley') and cook it in boiling, salted water, like rice for about 45 minutes, or simmer it in stock for a pilaff with a difference.

Burghul, or bulghar, is another of the 'good grains' which can be added to casserole dishes or simply soaked in water, thoroughly drained and served without further cooking as a crunchy salad.

Buckwheat, although not strictly a grain, is sold in 'groat' form. The crushed and hulled seeds can be added for extra fibre and crunch to baked goodies, or cooked like rice.

Rye flakes are a popular ingredient in muesli mixtures, and rye groats, the whole grains of the cereal plant, can be cooked like rice. Pre-soaking for 1 hour shortens the cooking time to around 20 minutes. Again, the flour, too, is becoming more widespread. The dark version is the equivalent to wholewheat flour and contains the whole bran.

Rice

Switch from white rice to natural brown rice, and you increase your fibre intake seven-fold with every bite! There are three main types of brown rice. Short-grain rice is very absorbent and slightly glutinous, almost always used for puddings, and for some savoury dishes when separation of the grains is not essential. Medium-grain rice, also rather absorbent, is served with meat or vegetable sauces, or in puddings. Long-grain rice is most often chosen for savoury dishes because it looks well, each grain separate, dry and fluffy.

Brown rice can be cooked in a large pan of salted water and then drained, as for boiled white rice,

but most people find the 'one cup, two cups' method most reliable. Measure the rice into a pan, add twice its volume of water and add salt. Bring the water to the boil, stir the rice and boil for 3 minutes. Reduce the heat to very low, cover the pan and simmer without stirring, for 40-45 minutes, or until the rice is barely tender and has absorbed all the water.

Wholewheat flour

Flour is sometimes described in vague terms, such as 'wheatmeal' or just 'brown', leaving the bewildered shopper – bewildered. What counts from the fibre standpoint is the extraction rate. Wholewheat flour, containing the whole grain is expressed as 100 per cent – nothing has been taken away except the inedible husk. Lighter flour, sometimes with a leavening agent added, is expressed as 85 per cent or 81 per cent, indicating that 15 or 19 per cent of the bran, respectively, has been removed. Refined white flour, way down the scale, has an extraction rate of 72 per cent.

The absorbency rate of wholewheat flour varies with individual brands, so you have to experiment to find just how much water is needed (usually slightly more than for refined flours) to give the texture you enjoy.

Whether you buy pasta or take the time to make your own, this is another chance to 'go with fibre' and choose wholewheat. Always follow the directions on the packet for exact cooking times.

Vegetables, fruit and pulses

It takes an expert to assess which vegetables and fruits are highest in fibre, for similarity in appearance is nothing to go by. Cooked spinach, for example, has 6.3 per cent of fibre, whilst raw lettuce has 1.5, with all the root vegetables in between, at 2.5-3.0 per cent. Soft fruits can have a higher fibre content than hard orchard types – blackberries at 7.3 per cent and strawberries at 2.2 per cent both beat apples, which have 2.0 per cent.

Statistics apart, all vegetables and fruit have a significant fibre content with legumes and dried pulses most of all (frozen peas have 12.0 per cent).

Most pulses, with the exception of red lentils and split soya beans (soya splits) benefit from being soaked before cooking – a step that also makes them more digestible. Depending on the time you have available, soak them for between 4 and 8 hours in a large bowl of cold water. They absorb three times their volume during this partial re-hydration process. (See page 107 for approximate cooking times).

Red Bean and Lamb Casserole

1 kg/2 lb boned leg of lamb
2 medium-sized onions, finely
    chopped
2 garlic cloves, crushed
5 ml/1 tsp turmeric
5 ml/1 tsp salt
2.5 ml/½ tsp ground black
    pepper
6 medium-sized tomatoes,
    peeled, de-seeded and
    coarsely chopped
275 g/10 oz dried red kidney
    beans, soaked, rinsed and
    drained
15 ml/1 tbls lemon juice
15 ml/1 tbls chopped coriander
    leaves
15 ml/1 tbls chopped mint
175 ml/6 fl oz chicken stock, hot
150 ml/5 fl oz natural yoghurt
15 ml/1 tbls chopped parsley

Heat the oven to 180C/350F/gas 4.

Trim any excess fat from the lamb and cut it into 2.5-cm/1-in cubes. Gently heat a non-stick pan and fry the meat, turning and stirring it all the time, until the 'hidden' fat begins to run. Fry until the meat is evenly brown, then remove it with a draining spoon and keep it warm.

Add the onion and garlic to the fat in the pan and fry, stirring occasionally, for about 5 minutes, until the onion is soft and translucent but not brown. Pour off any excess fat.

Stir in the turmeric, salt and pepper, then the tomatoes, kidney beans, lemon juice, coriander and mint and stir well to mix. Pour over the hot stock and bring slowly to the boil.

Transfer to a heatproof casserole and cook in the centre of the oven for 1¼-1½ hours, or until the lamb and beans are tender. Taste and adjust the seasoning if necessary.

Stir in the yoghurt, sprinkle over the parsley and serve at once.

Serves 4-6
Calories 2155 (9085 kJ)
Protein 232 grams

Red Lentil Soup

Melt the margarine in a large pan and fry the onion and celery over moderate heat for about 5 minutes until soft but not brown. Stir in the cloves, allspice, salt and pepper, then add the washed lentils. Pour on the stock, bring to the boil and cover the pan. Lower the heat and simmer gently for 30-35 minutes, or until the lentils are soft.

Put the soup into a liquidizer goblet in 2 batches and blend until it is smooth. Reheat it gently in the rinsed pan, taste and adjust the seasoning if necessary.

Pour into a warmed serving dish and sprinkle on the parsley to garnish.
*You can substitute dried split peas for the lentils to make a delicious corn-coloured soup with just as much healthy goodness. Soak the split peas in boiling water for 1 hour, then rinse and drain them. Proceed as in recipe.

Serves 4
Calories 680 (2875 kJ)
Protein 38 grams

25 g/1 oz polyunsaturated margarine
1 large onion, chopped
2 stalks celery, chopped
1.5 ml/¼ tsp ground cloves
1.5 ml/¼ tsp ground allspice
salt and ground black pepper
150 g/5 oz split red lentils
1 L/1¾ pt vegetable stock
15 ml/1 tbls chopped parsley

Bean and Barley Casserole

225 g/8 oz smoked streaky bacon
225 g/8 oz pork spare rib
15 ml/1 tbls flour
2.5 ml/½ tsp paprika
25 g/1 oz polyunsaturated
  margarine
1 large onion, chopped
450 g/1 lb dried haricot beans,
  soaked, rinsed and drained
100 g/4 oz pearl barley
salt and ground black pepper
15 ml/1 tbls chopped coriander or
  parsley

Cut the rind from the bacon and cut the bacon and pork into chunks. Mix together the flour and paprika and toss the meats to coat them them thoroughly.

Melt the margarine in a flameproof casserole and fry the meats and the onion, turning and stirring them frequently, for about 5-7 minutes, or until the meat is evenly brown.

Stir in the beans and the barley, add just enough water to cover and bring slowly to the boil. Cover the casserole and simmer over very low heat for 1½-2 hours, or until the beans and the meat are tender and nearly all the liquid has evaporated. Sprinkle with the coriander or parsley to garnish.

Serves 6
Calories 3525 (14760 kJ)
Protein 170 grams

Burghul Lamb Pilau

700 g/1½ lb lean shoulder of lamb
  cut into 2.5-cm/1-in cubes and
  trimmed of excess fat
3 medium-sized onions, chopped
salt and ground black pepper
15 ml/1 tbls chopped oregano or
  5 ml/1 tsp dried herbs
6 large tomatoes, skinned,
  de-seeded and chopped
45 ml/3 tbls tomato purée
50 g/2 oz polyunsaturated
  margarine
225 g/8 oz burghul wheat
15 ml/1 tbls chopped parsley

Gently fry the lamb cubes in a non-stick pan until the fat begins to run. Turn them until they are evenly brown, remove with a slotted spoon and keep warm. Add the onions to the pan and fry in the remaining fat until they are soft and translucent, but not brown. Pour off any excess fat.

Return the meat to the pan, season with salt and pepper and add the herbs, tomatoes and tomato purée. Stir well, add just enough water to cover the meat, bring slowly to the boil, then cover the pan and simmer for 1 hour, or until the meat is tender. Check from time to time that the meat is not drying out. Add a little more water if necessary.

Meanwhile, melt the margarine in another pan and fry the burghul over low heat for 10 minutes, stirring all the time. Add the meat mixture to the wheat and simmer uncovered until the burghul has almost absorbed the liquid.

Cover the pan with a cloth (taking care that it does not overlap the pan, particularly on a gas cooker). Place over the lowest possible heat or on a heat-dispensing mat and steam for 30 minutes, or until the burghul is tender. Serve very hot, garnished with the chopped parsley.

Serves 4-6
Calories 1900 (7985 kJ)
Protein 124 grams

Cassoulet

Put the beans in a large saucepan and add the onions, garlic, bouquet garni and bay leaf. Cover them completely with some of the stock, bring to the boil and cover the pan. Simmer for 1 hour, adding more boiling water if necessary.

Meanwhile, prepare the meat. Cut the rind from the belly of pork and cut it into 2.5-cm/1-in slices. Trim any excess fat from the lamb and cut it into 2.5-cm/1-in slices. Cut the chicken flesh from the bones and cut it into bite-sized pieces.

Heat the oven to 150C/300F/gas 2.

Drain the beans, onions and garlic into a colander. Discard the bouquet garni and bay leaf and reserve the stock. Season the beans well with salt and pepper.

Put a layer of beans into the bottom of a very large casserole, arrange the pork strips over them and cover with another layer of beans. Arrange half the lamb, then more beans, half the chicken, beans, the remaining lamb, more beans, and chicken in layers. Finish with a layer of beans.

Mix the canned tomatoes and tomato purée with the reserved hot stock and pour on the remaining stock. Season well with salt and pepper. Pour this into the casserole until it reaches the level of the beans. (This will depend on the size of the dish – add more if necessary.)

Mix the breadcrumbs with the herbs and sprinkle half over the beans, reserving the remainder.

Cook the Cassoulet, uncovered, for 3 hours, checking from time to time and adding more stock if necessary to keep up the level.

Using the back of a large spoon, push down the crumb crust until it is covered by beans and top up the level of the stock again. Sprinkle on the remaining crumbs and return to the oven for a further 30 minutes or until a new crust has formed.
*Long, slow-cooking dishes like this are marvellous for a supper party. They also reheat particularly well. To heat the cooked Cassoulet from cold, put it in the oven for a minimum of 1 hour and up to 2 hours.

Serves 8-10
Calories 4075 (17160 kJ)
Protein 352 grams

575 g/1¼ lb dried haricot beans,
  soaked, rinsed and drained
225 g/8 oz onions, chopped
6 large garlic cloves, halved
1 bouquet garni
1 bay leaf
about 2.8 L/5 pt unsalted chicken
  stock
225 g/8 oz belly of pork
900 g/2 lb shoulder of lamb, boned
2 wing joints chicken, weighing
  275 g/10 oz each
salt and ground black pepper
400 g/14 oz canned tomatoes
30 ml/2 tbls tomato purée
175 g/6 oz fresh wholewheat
  breadcrumbs
15 ml/1 tbls chopped oregano or
  5 ml/1 tsp dried herb
15 ml/1 tbls chopped thyme or
  5 ml/1 tsp dried herb

Butter Bean and Tomato Soup

Melt the margarine in a large pan and fry the onion and garlic over moderate heat for about 5 minutes, until soft but not brown. Add the tomatoes, stir well and cook for 3 minutes. Add the butter beans, stock, and basil and season with salt and pepper. Bring to the boil, cover the pan and simmer for 2 hours, or until the butter beans are soft. Discard the bay leaf.

Blend the soup in a liquidizer in 2 batches until it is smooth and creamy. Return it to the rinsed pan and reheat gently. Taste and adjust seasoning if necessary. Pour the soup into a warmed serving bowl and garnish with the sunflower seeds.
*Calorie count does not include sunflower seed garnish. The amount stated in the recipe adds an extra 105 calories (439 kJ) and 5.4 grams protein.

Serves 6
Calories 540 (2285 kJ)
Protein 25 grams

25 g/1 oz polyunsaturated
  margarine
1 large onion
1 garlic clove, crushed
450 g/1 lb tomatoes, peeled,
  de-seeded and roughly chopped
100 g/4 oz butter beans, soaked,
  rinsed and drained
1 L/1¾ pt chicken stock, hot
15 ml/1 tbls chopped basil or
  5 ml/1 tsp dried herb
salt and ground black pepper
30 ml/2 tbls sunflower seeds

Barley Bake

25 g/1 oz polyunsaturated
  margarine
2 medium-sized onions, sliced
1 garlic clove, crushed
225 g/8 oz mushrooms, thinly
  sliced
225 g/8 oz barley, washed
5 ml/1 tsp paprika
1.5 ml/¼ tsp cayenne pepper
350 ml/12 fl oz chicken or
  vegetable stock
30 ml/2 tbls chopped parsley

Heat the oven to 170C/325F/gas 3.

Melt the butter in a flameproof casserole and fry the onion and garlic over moderate heat for about 5 minutes, until they are soft. Stir in the mushrooms and cook for a further 2 minutes, then stir in the barley, paprika and cayenne and season with salt. Pour on the stock and bring slowly to the boil. Remove from the heat and cover the pan.

Cook in the oven for 40 minutes, or until the grains are tender. Garnish the dish with the chopped parsley.

Serves 4
Calories 1070 (4540 kJ)
Protein 25 grams

Sambar

225 g/8 oz toovar dhal, or other
  lentils
1.5 ml/¼ tsp ground fenugreek
50 g/2 oz fresh coconut, finely
  chopped
10 ml/2 tsp cumin seeds
15 ml/1 tbls coriander seeds
2.5 ml/½ tsp ground cinnamon
50 g/2 oz tamarind
10 ml/2 tsp soft brown sugar
5 ml/1 tsp hot chilli powder
30 ml/2 tbls chopped coriander
  leaves
5 ml/1 tsp salt
30 ml/2 tbls vegetable oil
5 ml/1 tsp mustard seeds
5 ml/1 tsp ground turmeric
⅛ tsp asafoetida (optional)
2 garlic cloves, crushed
1 green chilli, finely chopped

Wash the dhal, soak it in cold water for 1 hour, then drain. Put it in a saucepan with the fenugreek and 1.1 L/2 pt water. Bring to the boil, reduce the heat and simmer, uncovered, for 1 hour, or until the dhal is soft.

Meanwhile, cook the coconut, cumin, coriander seeds and cinnamon for 3 minutes over moderate heat, stirring constantly. Allow to cool, then purée in a blender with 60 ml/4 tbls cold water. Spoon the spice purée into a small bowl and set aside.

Pour 225 g/8 fl oz boiling water over the tamarind, stir and leave to cool. Strain into a small pan, pressing as much of the tamarind as possible through the mesh. Discard the pulp remaining in the strainer. Stir in the sugar, chilli powder, coriander leaves and salt and simmer for 5 minutes.

Heat the oil in a small pan and add the mustard seeds. When they begin to pop stir in the turmeric, asafoetida, if used, the garlic and chilli. Reduce the heat to low and fry, stirring constantly for 2 minutes. Spoon into the dhal with the tamarind mixture and the coconut and spice purée. Stir well to mix.

Return the pan to a low heat and cook for 10 minutes, stirring frequently. Pour into a warmed serving bowl and serve hot.

Serves 4
Calories 1295 (5445 kJ)
Protein 56 grams

Butter Beans in Yoghurt Sauce

225 g/8 oz dried butter beans,
   soaked
850 ml/1½ pt stock
1 large onion
1 large carrot
25 g/1 oz polyunsaturated
   margarine
15 ml/1 tbls wholewheat flour
60 ml/4 tbls natural yoghurt
60 ml/4 tbls chopped parsley
juice of ½ lemon
salt and ground black pepper

Drain and rinse the beans and put them in a pan with the stock. Bring to the boil, cover the pan and simmer for 1 hour. Chop the onion, dice the carrot and add them to the beans. Bring back to the boil and continue cooking for 1 hour, or until the beans are tender.

Strain the vegetables and keep them hot. Reserve the stock. Melt the margarine in a pan, stir in the flour and cook for 1 minute. Gradually pour on the stock and bring to the boil, stirring. Simmer for about 3 minutes, until the sauce has thickened. Take the pan from the heat and stir in the yoghurt, parsley and lemon juice. Season well and stir in the beans.

Reheat gently, but do not allow the sauce to boil.

Serves 4
Calories 955 (4030 kJ)
Protein 55 grams

French Bean Sambal

450 g/1 lb French beans
2 fresh red chillies
1 medium-sized onion, chopped
2 garlic cloves, crushed
small piece of tamarind
30 ml/2 tbls peanut oil
30 ml/2 tbls brown sugar
salt
1 large bay leaf
275 ml/10 fl oz thin coconut milk,
   made with 100 g/4 oz creamed or
   desiccated coconut (see right)

Top and tail the beans and cut them into 5-cm/2-in lengths. De-seed the chillies and put them in a blender with the onion, garlic and tamarind. Blend to a smooth paste.

Heat the oil in a heavy-based frying-pan and fry the paste for about 5 minutes over moderate heat. Stir in the beans, add the sugar, salt and bay leaf and stir well. Gradually add the coconut milk, stirring until it is well blended. Simmer uncovered for a further 10-12 minutes, or until the beans are tender.

Transfer to a warmed serving dish and serve hot.

Serves 4-6
Calories 1070 (4440 kJ)
Protein 11 grams

*To make 275 ml/10 fl oz thin coconut milk break 100 g/4 oz creamed coconut into a liquidizer. Pour on 275 ml/10 fl oz boiling water, leave to soak for 10 minutes, then blend until smooth. Strain through buttermuslin, pressing out as much liquid as possible.

Or place the desiccated coconut in a bowl, pour on 275 ml/10 fl oz boiling water and leave to soak for 10 minutes. Strain through muslin, pressing the liquid through with a spoon.

You can make thick coconut milk in a similar way. For 275 ml/10 fl oz, break 100 g/4 oz creamed coconut into a bowl, add 150 ml/5 fl oz of boiling water, a little at a time, and stir to a smooth paste.

Hummus with Sesame Seeds

Drain and rinse the chick peas and cook them in unsalted water for at least 2 hours, or until they are soft. Drain them and reserve 150 ml/5 fl oz of the cooking liquor.

Put most of the cooked peas and liquor into a liquidizer and blend until smooth, or pass the peas through a vegetable mill and beat in the liquor to make a smooth purée. Reserve about 10 of the chick peas. Gradually beat in the lemon juice, tahini, oil, garlic, pepper and sesame seeds.

Put the hummus into a serving bowl, sprinkle the parsley thickly on top and garnish with the reserved chick peas. Alternatively, stir the whole peas into the purée to give a variation in texture, and scatter the parsley on top.

225 g/8 oz chick peas, soaked
juice of 2 lemons
90 ml/6 tbls tahini (sesame paste)
30 ml/2 tbls vegetable oil
2 garlic cloves, crushed
ground black pepper
15 ml/1 tbls toasted sesame seeds
15 ml/1 tbls chopped parsley

Serves 4
Calories 1560 (6565 kJ)
Protein 66 grams

Three-bean Salad

Soak the dried beans and peas overnight, then rinse and drain them. Put the red kidney beans in one pan, the chick peas in another and divide the onion, garlic, parsley and celery between them. Well cover them with water, cover the pans and cook the kidney beans for 1-1¼ hours. Cook the chick peas for 1 hour before adding the haricot beans. Cook for a further 1½ hours, or until they are tender. Drain the pulses and discard the flavouring vegetables.

To make the dressing, put the mustard and sugar into a bowl, blend to a smooth paste with a little of the vinegar, then gradually stir in the oil. Stir in the remaining vinegar and the orange juice and season the dressing with salt and pepper. Taste and adjust seasoning.

Pour the dressing over the pulses while they are still warm and toss to coat them thoroughly, taking care not to break them.

Allow to cool, then stir in the herbs. Cover, and chill if you wish.

75 g/3 oz dried red kidney beans
75 g/3 oz dried chick peas
75 g/3 oz dried haricot beans
1 small onion, quartered
1 garlic clove, halved
a few stalks of parsley
1 stalk celery, quartered

For the dressing
2.5 ml/½ tsp mustard powder
2.5 ml/½ tsp brown sugar
30 ml/2 tbls red wine vinegar
15 ml/1 tbls vegetable oil
60 ml/4 tbls unsweetened orange juice
salt and ground black pepper
30 ml/2 tbls chopped chives
15 ml/1 tbls chopped coriander leaves

Serves 4-6
Calories 815 (3445 kJ)
Protein 49 grams

Applejacks

75 g/3 oz polyunsaturated
  margarine
50 g/2 oz demerara sugar
90 ml/6 tbls clear honey
225 g/8 oz rolled oats
a large pinch of salt
45 ml/3 tbls apricot jam
10 ml/2 tsp orange juice
2 dessert apples, peeled, cored and
  thinly sliced
15 g/½ oz polyunsaturated
  margarine
2.5 ml/½ tsp ground cinnamon

Heat the oven to 180C/350F/gas 4. Grease a swiss roll tin 28 x 18 cm/11 x 7 in.

Melt the margarine, sugar and honey over low heat and stir until the sugar has dissolved. Remove the pan from the heat and stir in the rolled oats, a little at a time, and the salt. Turn the mixture into the prepared tin, spread it evenly and press it down with the back of a spoon.

Sieve the jam into a small pan and add the orange juice, stirring until the mixture is well blended and runny. Spread some of the jam mixture over the flapjack and arrange the apple slices in 3 long rows, leaving a slight gap between each row to facilitate cutting.

Add the margarine and cinnamon to the remaining jam mixture and brush it over the fruit.

Bake for 30-35 minutes, until the apples are tender and the flapjack has turned gold brown at the edges. Cut into finger-sized pieces while the flapjack is still warm, then leave to cool completely in the tin.

Store in an airtight tin.

Makes 18
Calories 2220 (9350 kJ)
Protein 29 grams

Chicken Pilaff

Remove skin from chicken joints and cut each into two pieces and season with salt and pepper. Heat the oil and margarine in a large pan and fry the chicken, turning it frequently, until it is evenly brown. Remove the chicken and keep it warm. Fry the onion in the same pan for 10 minutes over gentle heat, then add the garlic, ground cumin, cinnamon, cardamoms and cloves, and fry for a further 3 minutes. Return the chicken pieces to the pan and cook over gentle heat for 5 minutes, stirring occasionally.

Add the rice, stock, saffron powder or turmeric and bay leaves, bring to the boil, cover the pan and simmer gently for 20 minutes or so.

Stir in the raisins and cook for a further 20 minutes, or until the rice is just tender. Discard the bay leaves and any pieces of cinnamon. Turn on to a warmed serving dish and fork up the rice so that it looks fluffy. Scatter with the toasted almonds and serve hot.

Serves 4
Calories 2180 (9160 kJ)
Protein 124 grams

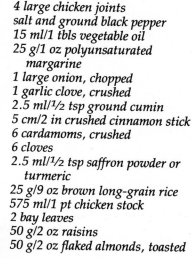

4 large chicken joints
salt and ground black pepper
15 ml/1 tbls vegetable oil
25 g/1 oz polyunsaturated
   margarine
1 large onion, chopped
1 garlic clove, crushed
2.5 ml/½ tsp ground cumin
5 cm/2 in crushed cinnamon stick
6 cardamoms, crushed
6 cloves
2.5 ml/½ tsp saffron powder or
   turmeric
25 g/9 oz brown long-grain rice
575 ml/1 pt chicken stock
2 bay leaves
50 g/2 oz raisins
50 g/2 oz flaked almonds, toasted

Traditional Porridge

150 g/5 oz medium or porridge
   oatmeal (not quick oats)
a pinch of salt

Bring 575 ml/1 pt of water to the boil in a small, heavy-based pan. Sprinkle on the oatmeal, stirring all the time. Bring slowly to the boil, stirring. Reduce the heat, cover the pan and simmer gently for 10 minutes. Add the salt. Simmer for a further 10 minutes.

Serve the porridge in cereal bowls with natural yoghurt, milk or buttermilk and, if you like, heather honey to sweeten.

Serves 4
Calories 600 (2550 kJ)
Protein 19 grams

Wholewheat Pizza

150 g/5 oz 81% wheatmeal self-
   raising flour
1.5 ml/¼ tsp salt
5 ml/1 tsp dried oregano
5 ml/1 tsp soft brown sugar
40 g/1½ oz polyunsaturated
   margarine
15 ml/1 tbls natural yoghurt

For the filling
50 g/2 oz polyunsaturated
   margarine
1 medium-sized onion, chopped
2 garlic cloves, crushed
800-g/1 lb 12-oz can tomatoes,
   drained
15 ml/1 tbls chopped basil or
   5 ml/1 tsp dried herb
15 ml/1 tbls chopped thyme or
   5 ml/1 tsp dried herb
5 ml/1 tsp soft brown sugar
salt and ground black pepper
100 g/4 oz button mushrooms,
   sliced
1 green pepper, de-seeded and
   thinly sliced into rings
100 g/4 oz Mozzarella cheese,
   thinly sliced
12 black olives, pitted

Heat the oven to 200C/400F/gas 6.

Begin by making the filling. Melt half the margarine in a pan and fry the onion and garlic over moderate heat for about 5 minutes. Add the drained tomatoes, the basil, thyme and sugar, stir well and bring to the boil. Simmer, stirring occasionally, for about 40 minutes, or until the mixture is reduced to a paste. Season with salt and pepper.

In a separate pan, melt the remaining margarine and fry the mushrooms for about 3 minutes. Remove them with a slotted spoon and fry the green pepper rings for 5 minutes or until they are just softened. Set them aside.

To make the pizza base, sift together the flour and salt and stir in the herb and sugar. Rub in the margarine and mix to a soft dough with the yoghurt. Roll the pastry on a lightly-floured board and line a 25-cm/10-in flan case. Cover the pastry with foil and baking beans and bake 'blind' for 15 minutes.

To assemble the pizza, remove the baking beans and foil and spread the tomato sauce over the pastry. Arrange the mushrooms in a pattern over the tomatoes and cover them with the cheese slices. Arrange the green pepper rings in an overlapping circle around the outside and scatter the olives between them. Return the pizza to the oven and bake for a further 15 minutes, or until the cheese topping is bubbling and brown. Serve hot.

Serves 4
Calories 1695 (7080 kJ)
Protein 59 grams

Cauliflower and Nut Quiche

Heat the oven to 190C/375F/gas 5.

Sift together the flour and salt and rub in the fat. Add just enough cold water to form a dough. Wrap closely in foil and chill the dough for 1 hour. Roll out the pastry to line a 25-cm/10-in flan case. Prick the base all over and cover with foil and baking beans. Bake 'blind' for 15-20 minutes until pastry is pale brown.

To make the filling, break the cauliflower into flowerets and put them in a pan with the onion, bouquet garni and stock. Bring to the boil and simmer for 10 minutes, until the vegetables are tender and most of the stock has evaporated. Discard the bouquet garni and rub the vegetables through a food mill or liquidize them in a blender.

Grind the nuts and mix them with the grated cheese and beaten eggs. Stir in the vegetable purée and season well with salt and pepper.

Remove the foil and baking beans from the pastry case. Pour in the vegetable mixture and level the top. Bake for 40 minutes, or until the filling is well risen and golden brown. Serve warm or cold. This is ideal picnic fare.

Serves 6
Calories 2615 (10905 kJ)
Protein 93 grams

225 g/8 oz wholewheat flour
salt
100 g/4 oz white vegetable fat

For the filling
1 small cauliflower
1 small onion, thinly sliced
1 bouquet garni
150 ml/5 fl oz vegetable stock
50 g/2 oz walnuts
50 g/2 oz hazelnuts
75 g/3 oz Cheddar cheese, grated
4 eggs, beaten
ground black pepper

Brown Rice with Cheese Sauce

Put the rice and salt in a large, heavy-based saucepan, pour on 575 ml/1 pt water and bring to the boil. Stir once to separate the grains, cover the pan and cook over a low heat for 40-50 minutes, or until the rice is tender and all the water has been absorbed.

Meanwhile, make the sauce. Melt two-thirds of the margarine in a pan and stir in the flour. Cook for 1 minute, then gradually pour on the milk, stirring. Stir until the sauce thickens, then simmer gently for 5-10 minutes. Stir in the mustard and cheese and season with salt and pepper. Dot the remaining margarine over the top and leave the sauce in a warm place.

Fry the onion and celery in the oil for 10 minutes, without letting them brown. Add the spring onion and cook for a further 2 minutes.

Mix the vegetables into the cooked rice and stir in the apple, raisins, almonds and peanuts. Pile the mixture on to a warmed serving dish. Stir the sauce – gently reheat if necessary – and serve it separately in a sauce boat.

Serves 4
Calories 2950 (12340 kJ)
Protein 85 grams

250 g/9 oz brown long-grain rice
5 ml/1 tsp salt
1 large onion, chopped
2 stalks celery, finely chopped
30 ml/2 tbls vegetable oil
12 spring onions, chopped
1 red-skinned dessert apple,
  cored and chopped
50 g/2 oz raisins
50 g/2 oz flaked almonds
50 g/2 oz roasted peanuts

For the sauce
40 g/1½ oz polyunsaturated
  margarine
25 g/1 oz wholewheat flour
300 ml/11 fl oz milk
15 ml/1 tbls mild, wholegrain
  mustard
100 g/4 oz grated cheese

Gnocchi Romana

575 ml/1 pt milk
½ small onion, thinly sliced
1 garlic clove, finely chopped
1 bay leaf
25 g/1 oz polyunsaturated
    margarine
salt
40 g/1½ oz polenta or corn meal
15 ml/1 tbls melted butter
100 g/4 oz grated Parmesan cheese
ground black pepper

Heat the oven to 200C/400F/gas 6.

Put the milk, onion, garlic, bay leaf, margarine and salt in a pan and bring slowly to the boil. Strain into a clean pan, bring back to the boil, then tip in the polenta or corn meal. Stir until thick, then simmer for 5 minutes, stirring constantly to prevent the mixture from sticking.

Pour the paste on to a well-oiled surface, then spread it to a thickness of 12 mm/½ in. Leave it to become cold, then cut it into rounds, using a 7.5-cm/2½-in biscuit cutter.

Arrange the rounds in overlapping rows in a well-greased baking dish, brush them with the melted butter and sprinkle with a little of the Parmesan cheese and plenty of ground black pepper. Bake for 15-20 minutes, until they are golden brown.

Serve the Gnocchi piping hot with Tomato Sauce (see page 125). Hand the remaining Parmesan cheese separately.

Serves 4
Calories 1220 (5070 kJ)
Protein 58 grams

Spaghetti with Aubergine Sauce

450 g/1 lb aubergines, cut into
    thin strips
1 medium-sized onion, thinly
    sliced
salt
450 g/1 lb wholewheat spaghetti
75 ml/6 tbls sunflower oil
2 large garlic cloves, very finely
    chopped
ground black pepper
150 ml/5 fl oz soured cream or
    natural yoghurt
75 g/3 oz grated Parmesan cheese

Mix together the aubergine and onion in a colander, sprinkle with salt and leave to drain for 30 minutes. Rinse under cold running water, drain thoroughly and pat dry with kitchen towels.

Cook the spaghetti in a large pan of boiling, salted water with 15 ml/1 tbls of the oil for 12-13 minutes, or until it is just tender.

Heat 30 ml/2 tbls of the oil in a pan, add half of the aubergine and onion mixture and fry over gentle heat, turning occasionally, until the vegetables are golden brown and crisp. Remove with a slotted spoon and keep warm. Heat the remaining oil and fry the second batch, adding the chopped garlic for the last 2 minutes.

When the spaghetti is cooked, tip it into a colander and refresh it by pouring boiling water through it. Drain it thoroughly and pile it into a warmed serving dish.

Add the vegetables, season with salt and pepper and gently toss them into the spaghetti. Stir in the soured cream or yoghurt and serve at once. Hand the grated Parmesan cheese separately.

Serves 4
Calories using natural yoghurt
    2720 (11330 kJ)
Protein 104 grams
Calories using soured cream
    2960 (12320 kJ)
Protein 100 grams

Spaghetti with Aubergine Sauce, Gnocchi Romana, Ravioli with Tomato Sauce (see overleaf)

Ravioli

For the basic pasta dough
450 g/1 lb wholewheat bread flour,
   or unbleached strong white flour
2-3 eggs (see recipe)
5 ml/1 tsp salt
15-30 ml/1-2 tbls water
1 egg, well beaten
15-30 ml/1-2 tbls oil

For the filling
15 g/½ oz butter
15 ml/1 tbls finely-chopped onion
225 g/8 oz cottage cheese
100 g/4 oz grated Parmesan cheese
60-75 ml/4-5 tbls chopped parsley
a little lemon juice
1 egg, well beaten
salt and ground black pepper
about 350-450 ml/12-15 fl oz
   Tomato Sauce (see page 125)
30-45 ml/2-3 tbls grated Parmesan
   cheese

To make the basic pasta dough, put the flour in a large bowl or a mound on a working surface and make a well in the centre. Break in 2 eggs, add the salt and work these lightly into the flour until they are evenly distributed. The mixture should resemble fine breadcrumbs. If necessary, add a little of the remaining egg to achieve the correct consistency.

Work the mixture to a firm dough, adding a little water to bind together.

Knead the dough for 5-10 minutes until it feels elastic, keeping your hands, the dough and the working surface well sprinkled with flour. The dough is now ready to shape. Use half for this recipe. (You can freeze the other half).

Roll out the dough and stretch it on a lightly-floured surface until it is about 50 cm/20 in square. Keep both sides of the dough well floured, then cut it in half. Mark one half into squares measuring about 4.5 cm/scant 2 in.

To make the filling, melt the butter and fry the onion until transparent. Mix it with the rest of the filling ingredients and beat well. Place a small spoonful of the filling in the centre of each square of dough. Brush the edges of each square with the beaten egg, then place the other sheet of dough on top. Seal the filling into the squares (see instructions below).

Cut the squares apart with a serrated-edged pastry wheel. Place the ravioli in a single layer on floured plates, then cover with a dampened and floured cloth. Leave to rest for at least 30 minutes.

Cook the ravioli in a large pan of boiling, salted water with 15-30 ml/1-2 tbls of oil for 5-7 minutes, or until just tender.

Meanwhile, gently heat the Tomato Sauce (see opposite).

Remove the ravioli with a slotted spoon, drain it thoroughly and pile it into a warmed serving dish. Pour the hot tomato sauce over, and serve with grated Parmesan cheese separately.
*Calorie count is based on using half the dough, as recipe states.

Serves 4
Calories 2035 (8525 kJ)
Protein 128 grams

Roll dough into 2 sheets. Mark one into squares without cutting through. Spoon filling into centre of each square.

Wrap second sheet of dough round floured rolling pin. Carefully unroll it directly on top of first sheet and mounds of filling.

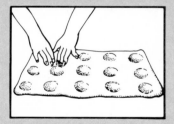

Using fingertips, press gently round each mound of filling to push out trapped air and to press together the sheets of dough.

Cut dough into squares using a pastry wheel with a serrated edge. Separate these and proceed as instructed above.

Tagliatelle

You can use the other half of the basic pasta dough to make Tagliatelle.

Roll the dough into a long sausage shape, keeping the work surface, the dough, rolling pin and your hands well sprinkled with flour.

Starting at one end of the sausage, roll a small section of the dough out lengthways, using fairly gentle pressure. Roll from the centre to the left, and from the centre to the right, stretching the dough gently and trying to keep an even thickness.

Continue rolling out the dough in this way, a section at a time, until you reach the end of the sausage, then work back the other way.

Roll and stretch the dough until it is about 45.5 cm/18 in long and almost thin enough to see through. Use more flour if necessary. Keep the ends of the dough square and the sides straight by pushing inwards with the rolling pin from time to time as you work.

Roll up the sheet of dough loosely, then cut across the roll at about 6-mm/¼-in intervals. Use a sharp knife with a thin blade, and a sawing action, Do not press too hard or the layers will stick together.

Unroll the dough ribbons and spread them out on a clean cloth until required.

Cook the tagliatelle in boiling, salted water for 5-7 minutes, until it is just tender. Drain it into a colander and refresh it by running boiling water through it. Drain it well and serve it with a vegetable sauce such as Tomato Sauce (see below) or the Aubergine Sauce (see page 122).

Serves 4
Calories 805 (3420 kJ)
Protein 37 grams

½ recipe basic pasta dough

Tomato Sauce

Heat the oil in a pan and fry the onion until it is soft and transparent but not brown. Stir in the flour, then gradually pour on the stock or water. Stir until the sauce is thick, then add the tomatoes, bay leaf and garlic. Season with salt and pepper, bring to the boil and simmer for 30 minutes.

Rub the sauce through a sieve or purée in a liquidizer. Taste and adjust seasoning and add a pinch of sugar.
*For a sauce with a deeper flavour, you can add 15 ml/1 tbls chopped basil or oregano or 5 ml/1 tsp dried herb. And for a more piquant flavour, add 15 ml/1 tbls cider vinegar after puréeing.

Serves 4
Calories 230 (970 kJ)
Protein 7 grams

15 ml/1 tbls vegetable oil
1 medium-sized onion, finely chopped
15 ml/1 tbls wholewheat flour
150 ml/5 fl oz stock or water
450 g/1 lb tomatoes, skinned and coarsely chopped (or canned ones)
1 bay leaf
1 garlic clove, crushed
salt and ground black pepper
a pinch of sugar

Rosemary Bread

2.5 g/½ oz fresh yeast
2.5 g/½ oz sugar
350 g/12 oz strong unbleached
   flour
5 ml/1 tsp salt
100 g/4 oz wholewheat flour
30 ml/2 tbls dried rosemary,
   crumbled

Crumble the yeast into a small bowl and mash in the sugar. Add 15 ml/1 tbls lukewarm water and mix well. Leave in a warm place for 15-20 minutes.

Sift the flour and salt into a large, warmed bowl. Stir in the wholewheat flour and 20 ml/1½ tbls of the rosemary. Make a well in the centre and pour in the frothy yeast mixture and 275 ml/10 fl oz lukewarm water. Gradually draw the flour into the liquid and mix until the dough leaves the side of the bowl.

Turn on to a lightly-floured board and knead until dough is smooth and elastic. Shape into a ball and put in a lightly-greased bowl. Cover with a damp cloth and return to a warm place for 1-1½ hours.

Turn the dough on to a floured surface and knead for about 3 minutes. Shape it into a greased 450-g/1-lb loaf tin and return it to a warm place for 30-45 minutes, or until it has risen to the top of the tin.

Meanwhile, heat the oven to 240C/475F/gas 9. Sprinkle the loaf with the remaining rosemary. Bake for 15 minutes, lower the temperature to 190C/375F/gas 5 and bake for a further 25 minutes.

Remove the loaf from the tin and rap the underside. If it does not sound hollow reduce the oven heat to 170C/325F/gas 3, and bake for a further 5-10 minutes. Cool on a wire rack.

Makes 1 450 g/1-lb loaf
Calories 1510 (6415 kJ)
Protein 53 grams

Nutty Treacle Tart

Sift the flours and salt into a mixing bowl and tip in the bran remaining in the sieve. Rub in the margarine until the mixture resembles fine breadcrumbs. Gradually stir in just enough iced water to bind the mixture together and knead until it is smooth. Wrap in cling film and chill for about 15 minutes.

Roll out the dough to a circle about 22 cm/9 in in diameter. Line an 18-cm/7-in diameter flan case, reserving the trimmings. Chill the pastry case and trimmings for 15 minutes.

Heat the oven to 200C/400F/gas 6.

Measure the honey and black treacle or molasses into a heavy-based saucepan. Stir in the breadcrumbs and lemon zest. Rub the skins from the hazelnuts, chop them coarsely and stir them in. Allow the melted honey-syrup to cool a little, then spread it over the pastry case. Roll out the pastry trimmings thinly and cut into long, narrow, strips. Arrange in a lattice pattern over the filling. Lightly brush the lattice and the rim with the beaten egg or milk.

Bake the tart for 30-35 minutes, until the pastry is cooked.

Serves 4-6
Calories 1725 (7245 kJ)
Protein 30 grams

100 g/4 oz wholewheat flour
50 g/2 oz self-raising flour
a pinch of salt
75 g/3 oz polyunsaturated
 margarine
beaten egg or milk to glaze

For the filling
60 ml/4 tbls clear honey
60 ml/4 tbls black treacle or
 molasses
75 g/3 oz fresh brown breadcrumbs
grated zest of ½ lemon
50 g/2 oz hazelnuts, toasted

Bran Loaf

275 g/10 oz strong plain flour
5 ml/1 tsp salt
5 ml/1 tsp bicarbonate of soda
275 g/10 oz bran
75 g/3 oz polyunsaturated
    margarine
15 ml/1 tbls honey
575 ml/1 pt milk

Heat the oven to 180C/350F/gas 4.

Sift the flour, salt and soda into a bowl and stir in the bran. Rub in the margarine, make a well in the centre of the mixture and stir in the honey and milk. Mix well to make a stiffish dough.

Shape the dough into a greased 700-g/1½-lb loaf tin and bake on the bottom shelf of the oven for 1½ hours. Tap the underside of the loaf to see if it sounds hollow. If it does not, return it to the oven, out of the tin, to bake for about another 5 minutes.

Makes 1 700-g/1½-lb loaf
Calories 2465 (10365 kJ)
Protein 89 grams

Buckwheat Biscuits

100 g/4 oz buckwheat flour
100 g/4 oz wholewheat flour
salt and ground black pepper
175 g/6 oz polyunsaturated
    margarine
25 g/1 oz cashew nuts, chopped
175 g/6 oz Cheddar cheese, grated

Heat the oven to 230C/450F/gas 8.

Mix together the flours, salt and pepper and stir in the margarine. Add the chopped nuts and grated cheese and knead until the mixture forms a dough.

Carefully roll out the dough on a floured board until it is 6 mm/¼ in thick. Cut it into rounds with a 5-cm/2-in biscuit cutter. Transfer the biscuits to a floured baking tray and prick them with a fork to stop them rising. Bake for about 15 minutes, or until they are golden brown all over.

Leave the biscuits to cool on the tray, then transfer them to a wire rack to become completely cold. Store in an airtight tin.

Makes about 30 biscuits
Calories 2765 (11480 kJ)
Protein 76 grams

Honey Scones

225 g/8 oz wholewheat flour
20 ml/4 tsp baking powder
50 g/2 oz polyunsaturated
    margarine
30 ml/2 tbls clear honey
about 125 ml/4 fl oz milk
10 ml/2 tsp sesame seeds

Heat the oven to 220C/425F/gas 7.

Sift together the flour and baking powder and tip in the bran remaining in the sieve. Mix in the margarine and honey, then add just enough milk to make a soft dough. On a floured board, carefully roll out the dough to a thickness of about 12 mm/½ in. Cut it into rounds with a 5-cm/2-in pastry cutter and lift them on to a floured baking sheet. Brush the tops with a little milk and scatter on the sesame seeds.

Bake near the top of the oven for about 10 minutes, or until the scones are well-risen. Transfer them to a wire rack to cool. If possible, serve warm. The scones are delicious with sieved cottage cheese stirred with a little yoghurt and honey.

Makes 12 scones
Calories 1290 (5420 kJ)
Protein 35 grams

Wheat Germ Bread

Line 2 450-g/1-lb loaf tins with grease-proof paper and grease the paper. Heat the oven to 180C/350F/gas 4.

Put the milk and margarine into a small pan and melt the fat over low heat. Remove the pan from the heat and beat in the egg, wheat germ, cracked wheat and sugar. Set aside to cool.

Sift together the flours, soda, salt and baking powder and tip in the bran remaining in the sieve. Stir the dry ingredients into the cooled milk mixture and turn into the prepared tins. Level the top, sprinkle with a little extra wholewheat flour or cracked wheat and bake for 45-50 minutes.

Remove the loaves from the tins and tap the underside with your knuckles. The loaves should sound hollow. If they do not, return them to the oven for about 5 minutes. Cool on a wire tray.

Makes 2 450-g/1-lb loaves
Calories 1585 (6690 kJ)
Protein 63 grams

275 ml/10 fl oz milk
25 g/1 oz margarine
1 egg
50 g/2 oz wheat germ
30 ml/2 tbls cracked wheat
40 g/1½ oz soft brown sugar
175 g/6 oz wholewheat flour
50 g/2 oz 81% wheatmeal self-raising flour
2.5 ml/½ tsp bicarbonate of soda
5 ml/1 tsp salt
15 ml/1 tbls baking powder

Apple Crumble Tart

Heat the oven to 200C/400F/gas 6.

Mix together the flour and salt, rub in the margarine and mix to a dough with about 60 ml/4 tbls iced water. Wrap the dough in cling film and chill in the bottom of the refrigerator for about 15 minutes.

To make the filling, peel, core and thinly slice the apples. Mix with the honey, sultanas and cinnamon.

Roll out the chilled dough and line a 20-cm/8-in flan ring. Fill the pastry case with the apple mixture.

For the topping, mix together the flour and sugar and rub in the margarine until the mixture resembles fine bread-crumbs. Sprinkle the mixture evenly over the apples.

Bake the tart for 30 minutes, or until the top is golden brown and crunchy. Serve hot, with natural yoghurt.

Serves 6-8
Calories 2770 (11610 kJ)
Protein 39 grams

200 g/7 oz wholewheat flour
a pinch of sea salt
100 g/4 oz polyunsaturated margarine

For the filling
700 g/1½ lb cooking apples
30 ml/2 tbls clear honey
50 g/2 oz sultanas
2.5-5 ml/½-1 tsp ground cinnamon

For the topping
75 g/3 oz wholewheat flour
50 g/2 oz Barbados sugar
75 g/3 oz vegetable margarine

Natural Foods

The wholefood revolution has brought new sensations of taste and healthy eating to us all. It has caused us to consider what we eat, where our food comes from, what happens to it before it reaches us, and what it actually consists of. A glance at many an attractively-designed packet on a supermarket shelf might soon reveal a list of ingredients we have probably never heard of, and certainly do not want to pay good money for. Read the contents table for a packet of some instant puddings and it can sound more like the requirements for a chemical experiment. Make it yourself at home, from milk, wholewheat flour, raw sugar and fruit purée and you know exactly what you and the rest of the family are eating.

That is what 'wholefoods' are all about – knowing and choosing exactly what you eat – and yet until recently they have been surrounded in mystery and doubt.

Throughout this book so far there have been many healthy recipes that are wholefood recipes. But to complete the delicious natural food revolution, there are a number of other important ingredients which, used with discrimination – and, in the case of the sweeteners, restraint – help to provide the right balance between what is good for you and what you enjoy eating. Eggs and cheese, basic foods that are infinitely versatile, full of nutrients (but also high in fat) and all the natural sweeteners – raw sugar, molasses and honey; dried fruits that are so rich in natural sugars they can even replace other sweeteners; seeds and nuts that put protein and texture into both sweet and savoury dishes; and herbs and spices that have flavoured the national and cultural cuisines of the world for thousands of years – these complete the taste of wholefoods.

Eggs
Eggs are one of the most nutritious foods we know, containing protein, fat, iron, Vitamins A, D and B12, Riboflavin. The white comprises 86 per cent water, whilst the yolk contains essential amino acids – and is also high in cholesterol. An egg weighing 55-60 g/approx. 2¼ oz will contain about 250 mg, and so anyone trying to limit their cholesterol intake will use eggs judiciously.

Cheese
The calorific values of cheeses vary considerably according to the type of milk the cheeses are made from. For the lowest fat content of all, choose the low-fat soft cheeses, cottage cheese (26 calories per 25 g/1 oz) or yoghurt cheese made from low-fat or skimmed milk. Lowest among the semi-hard cheeses is Camembert (85 calories per 25 g/1 oz) and among the hard cheeses, Edam or Gouda.

For tasty sauces that will not go 'over the top' in a calorie count, try blending sieved cottage cheese with a grated hard cheese; using sieved yoghurt cheese very lightly spiced with nutmeg, or halving the cheese content and compensating the flavour by adding 15-30 ml/1-2 tbls chopped herbs.

Natural sweeteners

Perhaps in an ideal world we would not sweeten our foods at all and should make every effort to return to the enjoyment of the natural and original flavours of each ingredient. However, many 'sweet' foods have been family favourites for generations, and are now part of our heritage, so that somehow life would seem duller without them.

One positive achievement of the wholefood revolution has been to make us aware that there is a better alternative to refined white sugars and the brown sugars that are chemically tampered with. Recipes in this book use unrefined raw sugars in almost every case. Because they are sweeter you need less of them and because they are 'natural', you are at least getting the benefit of the nutrients they – naturally – contain.

How can you tell the difference between natural and refined sugars? By reading the packet! Natural sugars will always have the country of origin – Barbados, Guyana or wherever – and perhaps the name of the packer – but not a processor. Neither

will they have a list of ingredients because, apart from the sugar itself, there aren't any.

There are several types of raw sugar, from almost black to very pale. The darkest of the natural sugars is molasses sugar, which is almost black. Use it for heavy fruit cakes and puddings and for barbecue sauces. Dark Muscovado sugar, also from Guyana, is very dark brown. Use it when cooking rhubarb, apples, quinces, plums and for a new taste in jams and marmalades, as well as in cakes and biscuits. Light-coloured Muscovado sugar can be used in sponge cakes, biscuits and light fruit cakes. True demerara sugar comes from Mauritius. The light golden crystals are slow to melt and are used to sweeten coffee, sprinkle on cereal, as a crunchy topping for cakes and pies, and in biscuits and rock cakes. Golden Granulated is natural pale brown unrefined sugar in crystal form, which can be used in place of refined granulated sugar. And like all natural sugars, it contains all the original nutrients and has not been artificially coloured.

Molasses is the residue taken from crude sugar after all the crystallization has taken place, and can still contain about 50 per cent sugar. The dominant flavour makes a very rich 'treacle' tart when spooned over an oatmeal base, and gives Boston baked beans the deep, characteristic flavour.

Treacle, less sweet than molasses, is extracted at an early stage of the sugar refining process.

Honey, the natural syrup manufactured by bees from the nectar of flowers and plants, is a rich source of vitamins, enzymes and acids and, like sugar, of energy. Clear honey, which has been heat treated, is most often used in cooking, to flavour yoghurt, fruit, biscuits, cakes, sauces, milk drinks, and so on. Like raw sugars, honey is by no means blameless in terms of its calorie count – but wholefooders point out that it is at least natural.

Dried fruit
Left on the plants to dry naturally in the sun (and then finished off under controlled conditions or on racks in the sun) dried fruits have a high concentration of natural sugar – fructose – and dietary fibre. Because of this natural sweetness, dried fruits can be added raw to muesli and other breakfast cereals, to fruit cakes and puddings and actually take the place of any further sweetness. You can add the raw fruits whole or chopped to casseroles and stews and to rice or breadcrumbs in the stuffings for fish, meat and poultry.

To bring dried orchard fruits back to their original plumpness, you can give them a short, hot soak or a long, cold one, or cook and soak them in one operation. For the short-time method, put the fruits in a pan with twice their volume of cold water or other liquid. Bring to the boil, cover the pan and simmer for 10 minutes. Remove the pan from the heat and leave the fruit to soak for 40 minutes. Alternatively, put them to soak for 8 hours or overnight in cold liquid. You can use water, cider, red or white wine, unsweetened orange or apple juice or even strained tea (for

prunes) and black coffee (for figs). A slice of orange, a twist of orange or lemon peel, a stick of cinnamon, a few gratings of nutmeg or a few cloves added to the soaking or cooking liquor can enhance the flavour of the fruit.

All of these dried fruits can bring the taste of sunshine to your winter menus, but don't forget them for the rest of the year. Try adding chopped dried dates to apple pie and crumble, dried apricots with even the sourest quinces, and dried pears with cooking pears or apples, and you can cut out extra sweeteners completely.

Nuts and seeds
Nuts and seeds feature so prominantly in vegetarian cooking that you might almost think vegetarians have exclusive rights to them. It is

because of their very high protein content that these natural foods are particularly valuable in a programme that excludes meat and fish.

Whether served whole or ground or in any of the stages in between – halved, flaked, shredded, nibbed or chopped – and toasted or not, nuts have a multitude of uses. They can thicken sauces, coat fish or poultry before it is cooked, add flavour to bland foods, texture to smooth ones, and interest to everyday ingredients. They are, however, high in fat and so should be used sparingly in a meal containing other high-fat foods.

Seeds can have an even higher protein content than nuts – with sunflower seeds highest of all. Get used to scattering sunflower, sesame or melon

seeds into salads, over milk puddings or into soups, to using seeds as toppings, for bread, cakes and biscuits or stirring them into anything from crumble mixtures to muesli.

Coconuts, too, are worthy of more experiment, although, too, they are high in fat. If you cannot find a whole one at the greengrocer's, you can buy desiccated coconut as strands, chips or shreds. Toast it in the oven or under the grill and it takes on a new, dark-brown personality. Either way it is good as a garnish for cakes, fools and creams, stirred into muesli or other cereals, or sprinkled on to cream soups.

Herbs and spices
Hundreds of years ago when meat and fish were unobtainable or prohibitively expensive to many communities, herbs and spices were used to flavour the 'staple' ingredients like rice, pulses and cereals to ring the changes and make them more palatable. If we adopt this practice today, we can cut down on fats, salt, calories and expense.

Fresh herbs give the true, natural flavour and are so valuable in the kitchen that it is worth growing them even in pots on the windowsill, so that they are always readily available. When you have to substitute dried herbs, use between one half and one-third of the stated quantity.

Use herbs liberally in the liquor when cooking rice and other grains and pulses so that the foods will absorb the flavour as they absorb the moisture. Use them generously in sauces to serve with rice, wheat, barley, pasta or whatever, and you will find that you can cut down – or cut out – high-fat ingredients.

A hint of spice in a fruit dish, and it can disguise the lack of extra sweetening, a heavier hand with a blend of spices in a curry – and, strange but true, it actually makes the meat or fish go further. Never slavishly follow spice or herb charts and stick rigidly to set ideas of what goes with what. Some people like pepper on strawberries, allspice on oranges, cumin seeds as a topping on wholewheat bread – and others, perhaps, have so far missed out on the experience!

Dried Fruit Salad (Khoshaf)

450 g/1 lb dried whole apricots
225 g/8 oz prunes
100 g /4 oz seedless raisins
100 g/4 oz blanched almonds, split
25 g/1 oz pine nuts
50 g/2 oz stoned dates
30 ml/2 tbls rose-water

Put all the ingredients together into a large bowl and pour on enough water to cover. Cover the bowl and leave at room temperature for at least 48 hours, stirring occasionally.

By then, the flavours will have blended and the liquid should be well sweetened by the fruit. If you wish to sweeten it further, melt 30-45 ml/2-3 tbls of clear honey in a small pan, add about the same volume of the fruit syrup and heat until the honey has melted. Stir the syrup into the fruit salad.

This dried fruit salad is delicious served with chilled natural yoghurt or thin or thick cream. It also makes a good start to the day – serve it with a generous sprinkling of muesli, or add a spoonful of the fruit to a bowl of muesli. The combination of dried fruits and whole grains is quite delicious.

Serves 6-8
Calories 2345 (9915 kJ)
Protein 56 grams

Stuffed Vine Leaves

Drain the vine leaves, cut off the stem ends and blanch them in boiling water for 1 minute. Drain.

Fry the lamb in a dry non-stick frying pan over moderate heat, stirring frequently, until it is evenly browned. Remove the meat and discard the fat.

Add the oil and fry the onion until it begins to brown. Add the rice and stir for 1 minute, then stir in the tomato purée, paprika, salt and 50 ml/2 fl oz water. Return the meat to the pan, bring to the boil, and remove from the heat. Stir in the herbs and pepper.

Dip the vine leaves in water and pat them dry. Spoon a rounded tablespoon of the filling at the stalk end, then roll up.

Brush the base of a large pan with oil, arrange a few torn vine leaves to cover and arrange the rolls, seam sides down, closely packed in a single layer if possible. Place an inverted plate over the rolls to keep them steady. Pour on water barely to cover the plate, cover the pan and simmer for 1½ hours.

To make the sauce, put the cornflour into a small pan and mix with 45 ml/3 tbls water. Beat in the egg yolks and yoghurt. Strain off the cooking juices and make them up to 150 ml/5 fl oz with water if necessary. Stir into the egg mixture.

Put the pan over very low heat and, stirring constantly, bring to simmering point. Do not allow to boil, or the egg yolks will scramble. Simmer, stirring, until the sauce thickens enough to coat the back of a spoon. Remove from the heat and season with salt, pepper and lemon juice.

Arrange the lamb rolls on a serving dish and serve the sauce separately.

Serves 4
Calories 1520 (6350 kJ)
Protein 114 grams

225 g/8 oz jar of vine leaves
450 g/1 lb lean lamb, minced
30 ml/2 tbls olive oil
1 large onion, finely chopped
50 g/2 oz brown short-grain rice
15 ml/1 tbls tomato purée
5 ml/1 tsp paprika
7.5 ml/1½ tsp salt
30 ml/2 tbls chopped parsley
10 ml/2 tsp chopped mint
30 ml/2 tbls chopped dill
2.5 ml/½ tsp ground black pepper

For the sauce
45 ml/3 tbls cornflour
3 medium-sized egg yolks
275 ml/10 fl oz natural yoghurt
15-30 ml/1-2 tbls lemon juice,
   to taste

Dried Fruit Syllabub

100 g/4 oz dried apricots
50 g/2 oz prunes
275 ml/10 fl oz unsweetened
    orange juice
275 ml/10 fl oz thickened yoghurt
    (see page 72)
45 ml/3 tbls sweet sherry or
    Marsala
30 ml/2 tbls toasted hazelnuts,
    chopped

Soak the apricots and prunes in the orange juice for at least 8 hours. Stone the prunes. Put the fruit and juice into a liquidizer and blend until the mixture forms a smooth purée.

Beat the yoghurt, then gradually beat in the fruit purée a little at a time. Stir in the wine if you use it.

Spoon the syllabub into individual serving glasses and scatter the hazelnuts on top. Serve chilled.

Serves 4
Calories 635 (2665 kJ)
Protein 23 grams

Peach and Fig Muesli

50 g/2 oz dried peaches
25 g/1 oz dried figs
4 dessert apples
60 ml/4 tbls orange juice
150 ml/5 fl oz natural yoghurt
15-30 ml/1-2 tbls clear honey
100 g/4 oz rolled oats
50 g/2 oz toasted hazelnuts,
    coarsely chopped
30 ml/2 tbls desiccated coconut,
    toasted

Soak the peaches and figs in lukewarm water for at least 8 hours, drain well and chop them coarsely.

Core the apples and grate them into the orange juice. Mix together the yoghurt and honey and stir it into the apple mixture. Stir in the chopped dried fruit and the oats and stir to mix thoroughly and evenly.

Turn the muesli into a bowl and sprinkle on the toasted nuts and coconut. This muesli, delicious at breakfast-time, also makes a lovely dessert for an informal or family supper.

Serves 4-6
Calories 1180 (4985 kJ)
Protein 29 grams

Crab and Ginger Foo Yung

6 eggs
45 ml/3 tbls sesame seed oil
100 g/4 oz crabmeat, flaked
1 piece ginger root, peeled and
    finely chopped
2 spring onions, finely chopped
15 ml/1 tbls soy sauce
15 ml/1 tbls dry sherry

Break the eggs into a bowl and beat until they are frothy.

Heat 10 ml/2 tsp of the oil in a small, heavy-based pan over high heat. Add the crabmeat, ginger, onion, soy sauce and sherry and stir-fry for 1 minute. Heat half the remaining oil in a frying pan and tip in half the egg mixture. Scatter half the crabmeat mixture on top and cook for 1 minute drawing the egg mixture into the middle from the sides of the pan. Invert a plate over the pan and tip the omelette onto it. Slide it back into the pan the other side up and cook for a further 1 minute. Tip the cooked omelette onto a plate and keep warm. Cook the second omelette using the remainder of the oil, egg mixture and crabmeat. Divide each omelette into two.

Serves 4
Calories 1015 (4200 kJ)
Protein 63 grams

Ricotta Cheesecake

Heat the oven to 190C/375F/gas 5.

Mix together the cheese, salt, flour, sugar, egg yolks, saffron if you use it, and orange zest. Stir in the raisins, orange peel and almonds.

Whisk the egg whites until they are stiff but not dry and fold them into the cheese mixture with a metal spoon.

Turn the mixture into a greased 20-cm/8-in loose-bottomed cake tin and bake in the centre of the oven for 40 minutes, or until the cake is firm.

Remove the cake from the oven and allow to cool slightly before turning it out on to a plate. Sprinkle with the cinnamon or, if you wish, first mix the spice with the icing sugar. Serve warm as a pudding or cold as a cheesecake.

Serves 6
Calories 1590 (6700 kJ)
Protein 93 grams

450 g/1 lb Ricotta cheese
a pinch of salt
15 ml/1 tbls wholewheat flour
100 g/4 oz soft brown sugar
2 medium-sized eggs, separated
2.5 ml/½ tsp saffron (optional)
5 ml/1 tsp grated orange zest
25 g/1 oz seedless raisins
25 g/1 oz candied orange peel,
  chopped
50 g/2 oz blanched almonds,
  chopped
2.5 ml/½ tsp powdered cinnamon
30 ml/2 tbls icing sugar (optional)

Zabaione

Whisk the egg yolks in the top of a double boiler off the heat until they are pale yellow. Gradually add the sugar and beat until the mixture becomes foamy and paler still.

Place the pan over simmering water and gradually beat in the wine. Continue whisking until the mixture is very thick and has tripled in size. To serve in the traditional Italian way, pour into tall glasses and serve warm.

If you prefer to serve the dessert cold – an advantage being that it can be made in advance – pour the warm mixture into a serving bowl, stand it in a larger bowl of ice and continue whisking until it is cold. Decorate the top of the cold pudding with toasted almonds or a few ratafia biscuits, or serve with langue de chat biscuits.

Serves 6
Calories 605 (2525 kJ)
Protein 19 grams

6 egg yolks
45 ml/3 tbls soft brown sugar
175 ml/6 fl oz dry white wine
toasted almonds or ratafia biscuits,
  (see method)

Lebanese Milk Pudding

Mix the ground rice and cornflour to a smooth paste with a little of the milk. Gradually bring the rest of the milk to the boil in a heavy-based saucepan. Stir a little into the rice paste, then tip the paste into the milk. Stir constantly over low heat until the mixture thickens.

Add the honey, orange-flower water and ground almonds and stir for a further 2 minutes. Remove the pan from the heat, allow the pudding to cool slightly and pour it into a glass serving bowl. Cool completely and just before serving sprinkle sesame seeds over the top.

Serves 6
Calories 2035 (8530 kJ)
Protein 65 grams

1.1 L/2 pt milk
65 g/2½ oz ground rice
50 ml/2 tbls cornflour
75 ml/5 tbls clear honey
45 ml/3 tbls orange-flower water
100 g/4 oz ground almonds
30 ml/2 tbls sesame seeds

Gougère

50 g/2 oz butter
75 g/3 oz unbleached white flour
3 eggs
75 g/3 oz Cheddar cheese, cut into
* 6-mm/¼-in cubes*
about 275 ml/10 fl oz Tomato
* Sauce (see page 125)*

Heat the oven to 150C/300F/gas 2.

Put the butter and 150 ml/5 fl oz of water into a medium-sized pan and bring it just to the boil. Remove the pan from the heat and tip in all the flour at once. Beat vigorously with a wooden spoon until all the flour has been absorbed and the mixture comes away from the side of the pan and forms a smooth ball. Cool the mixture slightly and beat in the eggs one at a time, beating thoroughly between each one so that the mixture is always smooth and glossy. The mixture must be stiff enough to hold its shape, so it may be necessary to add only part of the third egg. Fold in two-thirds of the cheese.

Pipe or spoon the mixture into a 25-cm/10-in circle on a well-oiled baking sheet. Dot the top with the remaining cheese cubes and pin a double band of non-stick vegetable parchment round the outside to hold the Gougère in shape so that it rises neatly.

Place in the centre of the oven and immediately increase the heat to 200C/400F/gas 6. Bake the Gougère for 40 minutes, then turn off the heat, prop open the oven door slightly and leave it in the oven for 5-10 minutes to cool. Transfer to a warmed serving dish and serve the heated sauce separately.

Serves 4
Calories 1375 (4730 kJ)
Protein 51 grams

Spinach and Cheese Soufflé

40 g/1½ oz polyunsaturated
* margarine*
25 g/1 oz wholewheat flour
200 ml/7 fl oz milk
100 g/4 oz Cheddar cheese, grated
225 g/8 oz cooked spinach, well
* drained and chopped*
salt and ground black pepper
a pinch of grated nutmeg
4 egg yolks
5 egg whites

Heat about 25 g/1 oz of the margarine in a pan over gentle heat, then sprinkle in the flour. Cook for 1-2 minutes, stirring continuously until it thickens and forms a roux. Remove the pan from the heat, then gradually pour on the milk, stirring well all the time. Return the pan to the heat and bring to the boil, stirring until the sauce thickens.

Remove the pan from the heat again, stir in the cheese and spinach and season with salt, pepper and nutmeg. Leave the mixture to cool slightly.

Heat the oven to 200C/400F/gas 6. Set a 1½-L/3-pt soufflé dish on top of the cooker to warm.

Stir the egg yolks into the cheese mixture. Whisk the whites until they stand in stiff peaks. Pour half of the cheese mixture over the egg whites and fold it in from the bottom to the top until it is well blended. Fold in the remaining mixture in the same way.

Heat the remaining margarine and brush it over the inside of the soufflé dish. Pour in the soufflé mixture and draw a circle in the top of the mixture, using an oiled knife – this will produce the 'top hat' effect that characterizes a well-risen soufflé.

Bake in the middle of the oven for about 20 minutes if you like the centre to be semi-liquid, or for 25 minutes if you prefer a drier soufflé. Serve at once, while the soufflé is at its peak.

Serves 4
Calories 1315 (5470 kJ)
Protein 78 grams

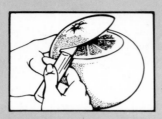
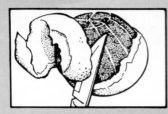

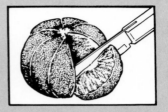

To segment oranges or grapefruits, cut off a small slice from the stalk end of the fruit.

Cut away the peel in a spiral, removing all the pith and a sliver of flesh. Cut in a gentle sawing motion.

Put fruit on a plate to catch juice. Cut into centre of fruit close to membrane of one segment.

Cut again close to membrane on other side of segment. Lift out flesh. Repeat all round fruit.

Rhubarb and Orange Chutney

2 oranges
700 g/1½ lb rhubarb, trimmed and cut into 2.5-cm/1-in lengths
2 medium-sized onions, chopped
225 g/8 oz seedless raisins
425 ml/15 fl oz malt vinegar
450 g/1 lb demerara sugar
8-12 black mustard seeds
4-8 white peppercorns
about 12 coriander seeds
1.5 ml/¼ tsp ground allspice

Wash and dry the oranges. Thinly peel the zest and shred it finely. Squeeze the juice. Put the rhubarb into a heavy-based pan with the orange zest and juice, chopped onions, raisins, vinegar and sugar. Tie the whole spices into a piece of muslin and add to ingredients in the pan with the ground allspice.

Bring the mixture slowly to the boil, stirring frequently. Reduce the heat and simmer, stirring occasionally, for about 1½ hours, or until the chutney is thick and pulpy. Remove the pan from the heat and discard the bag of spices.

Ladle the chutney into clean warmed jars to within 15 mm/½ in of the tops. Cover with waxed discs, wax side down, then with vinegar-proof covers – coffee jars with plastic-lined lids are ideal for chutney. Label the jars and store in a cool, dry place for 3 months to mellow before using.

Makes about 1.4 kg/3 lb
Calories 2495 (10650 kJ)
Protein 13 grams

Arabian Oranges

6 large oranges
100 g/4 oz fresh dates
225 ml/8 fl oz dry white wine
100 g/4 oz blanched almonds, flaked

Cut 4 of the oranges into segments, removing all peel, pith, membrane and pips, and place them in a bowl. Cut the dates in half, stone them and cut them into slivers. Add them to the oranges.

Squeeze the juice from the 2 remaining oranges, stir in the wine and pour over the fruit. Cover and chill for at least 4 hours, turning the fruit occasionally. Scatter with almonds just before serving.

Serves 4
Calories 1030 (4325 kJ)
Protein 24 grams

Grapefruit and Sesame Seed Salad

Wash, drain and trim the lettuce and cut it into shreds. Put it in a polythene bag and chill in the refrigerator for 30 minutes to crisp.

Cut the rind and pith from the grapefruit, cut away the membrane, discard the pips and separate the fruit into segments (see left).

Divide the shredded lettuce between 4 individual plates and arrange the grapefruit segments in a wheel pattern over it. Spoon the tahini over the grapefruit and scatter the sesame seeds on top. Cut off the mustard tops and arrange neatly in a ring to garnish each plate.

If you like to serve an extra dressing, an orange-flavoured vinaigrette is very good with this simple salad.

1 small, firm head of lettuce
2 large grapefruits
60 ml/4 tbls tahini (sesame seed paste)
40 ml/8 tsp sesame seeds
1 box mustard and cress

Serves 4
Calories 670 (2790 kJ)
Protein 23 grams

Garlic and Orange Soup

Heat the oil in a saucepan over medium-low heat and sauté the garlic gently until it is just beginning to brown. Cut the crusts from the bread, cut it into 2.5-cm/1-in pieces and add them to the pan gradually, turning them in the oil.

Remove the pan from the heat and add 1 L/1¾ pt water. Season with salt and add the tomatoes, orange zest and rind and the cumin seed. Simmer the soup for about 15 minutes, stir well and allow to stand for at least 1 hour for the flavours to blend. Reheat the soup, pour into a warmed tureen or serving dish and scatter with the parsley.

45 ml/3 tbls sunflower oil
4 large garlic cloves, finely chopped
225 g/8 oz 1-day old wholewheat bread
salt
4 large, ripe tomatoes, skinned and de-seeded
grated zest and juice of 2 oranges
5 ml/1 tsp cumin seed, crushed
15 ml/1 tbls chopped parsley

Serves 4
Calories 965 (4055 kJ)
Protein 24 grams

Carrot Cake

Heat the oven to 170C/325F/gas 3.

Beat the egg yolks until they begin to thicken, then gradually add the sugar and continue beating until the mixture is thick and creamy. Add the remaining ingredients and stir to mix thoroughly.

Whisk the egg whites until they form stiff peaks, then fold them into the carrot mixture, using a metal spoon.

Pour the mixture into a greased 23-cm/9-in loose-bottomed cake tin and bake in the centre of the oven for about 50 minutes, or until a skewer inserted into the middle of the cake comes out clean.

Remove the cake from the oven and leave it to cool in the tin for 15 minutes. Turn it out on to a wire rack to cool completely. Serve cut in slices.

6 eggs, separated
225 g/8 oz light Muscavado sugar
350 g/12 oz carrots, cooked and puréed
15 ml/1 tbls grated orange zest
15 ml/1 tbls orange juice
225 g/8 oz ground almonds
100 g/4 oz wholewheat semolina
5 ml/1 tsp ground allspice

Serves 8
Calories 3055 (12800 kJ)
Protein 96 grams

Herb Pâté

900 g/2 lb courgettes
15 ml/1 tbls salt
50 g/2 oz butter
4 medium-sized eggs
275 ml/10 fl oz thick cream
30 ml/2 tbls chopped mixed herbs,
*   such as chervil, parsley, mint,*
*   tarragon*
a pinch of cayenne pepper
ground black pepper
45 ml/3 tbls thick cream
extra chopped fresh herbs
sprigs of fresh herbs
lettuce leaves and tomato slices

Coarsely grate the courgettes into a colander. Sprinkle with the salt, stir well and set aside for 1 hour. Rinse under cold, running water, drain well and pat dry with absorbent kitchen paper.

Melt the butter in a saucepan, add the courgettes and cook over a low heat for about 10 minutes, stirring occasionally, until they are soft. Leave to cool. Heat the oven to 180C/350F/gas 4. Line a 1.5-L/3-pt loaf tin with greased greaseproof paper or foil.

Mix together the eggs and cream, add the courgette mixture and the herbs. Stir well and season with cayenne and black pepper to taste. Pour the mixture into the prepared tin, level the top and cover with foil. Stand in a roasting tin and pour in enough cold water to come halfway up the sides of the loaf tin.

Bake in the centre of the oven for 1¼ hours, until the pâté is firm. Leave to cool in the tin, then turn out on to a serving dish.

Whip the cream and spread it over the top of the pâté. Scatter with chopped fresh herbs and decorate with herb sprigs. Arrange lettuce leaves and tomato slices around the edge of the dish.

**Serves 6 as a starter, 4 as a
  main course**
Calories 2390 (9890 kJ)
Protein 38 grams

142

Pears Ambrosia

To make the syrup, place the honey and 275 ml/10 fl oz water in a heavy-based saucepan and stir over low heat until the honey is dissolved. Bring to the boil and boil for 3-4 minutes. Remove pan from the heat and add the vanilla pod.

Peel, core and thickly slice the pears and add them straight away to the syrup. Poach them over a low heat for 10-15 minutes until they are tender but not mushy. Turn the pears and syrup into a bowl, allow to cool completely then cover and chill in the refrigerator for at least 15 minutes and up to 2 hours.

Meanwhile, mix together the fromage blanc or cottage cheese, honey and essences. Cover and chill.

When ready to serve, drain the pears, reserving the syrup. Remove the vanilla pod, wash, dry and store it for future use. Divide the fruit between 4 dessert plates, arranging in a circular pattern. Dip a pastry brush into the reserved syrup and brush lightly over the pears. Spoon the cheese mixture into the centre of each plate and scatter the praline on top.

To make the praline, put the un-blanched almonds and caster sugar into a pan over a low heat and cook until the sugar caramellizes. Turn the mixture on to a piece of oiled foil and leave to set. Crush the praline between greaseproof paper with a rolling pin.

Serves 4
Calories 820 (3470 kJ)
Protein 30 grams

4 small, firm dessert pears

For the syrup
60 ml/4 tbls clear honey
1 vanilla pod

For the topping
175 g/6 oz fromage blanc or cottage
    cheese
10 ml/2 tsp clear honey
3 drops vanilla essence
2 drops almond essence
60 ml/4 tbls finely crushed praline
    (see below)

For the praline
100 g/4 oz unblanched almonds
100 g/4 oz caster sugar

Italian Honey Cake

75 g/3 oz light Muscavado sugar
175 g/6 oz orange blossom honey
50 g/2 oz wholewheat flour
30 ml/2 tbls carob powder
5 ml/1 tsp ground cinnamon
50 g/2 oz candied peel, chopped
50 g/2 oz blanched almonds,
   toasted
150 g/5 oz toasted hazelnuts
15 ml/1 tbls grated orange zest
icing sugar to decorate (optional)

Heat the oven to 140C/275F/gas 1.

Put the sugar and honey in a heavy-based pan over a low heat, stirring occasionally, for 15 minutes. Sift together the flour, carob and cinnamon. Remove the honey from the heat and stir in the flour mixture. Stir in all the other ingredients and turn at once into a greased 25-cm/10-in pie plate.

Bake in the centre of the oven for 30 minutes, or until the cake is firm. Allow the cake to cool in the tin for 15 minutes, then slide it on to waxed paper and leave it on a wire rack to cool completely.

Sift icing sugar over the cake if you wish.

The cake can be served as a dessert – it is very rich – or with coffee.

Makes 12 slices
Calories 2010 (8460 kJ)
Protein 34 grams

Honey Bread

300 g/11 oz clear honey, warmed
150 g/5 oz dark Muscavado sugar
300 g/11 oz light rye flour
a pinch of salt
15 ml/1 tbls bicarbonate of soda
30 ml/2 tbls dark rum
15 ml/1 tbls ground aniseed
2.5 ml/1/2 tsp ground cinnamon
1.5 ml/1/4 tsp ground mace
1.5 ml/1/4 tsp almond essence
50 g/2 oz ground almonds
100 g/4 oz candied peel, chopped

Heat the oven to 180C/350F/gas 4. Grease a 2-L/3-pt loaf tin, line it with greaseproof paper and grease again.

Mix the warmed honey with the sugar and 50 ml/2 fl oz of boiling water and beat until the sugar has dissolved.

Mix together the flour, salt and soda. Add enough of the flour mixture to the honey to make a stiff, heavy dough and beat hard for 5 minutes. Beat in the remaining ingredients and any remaining flour. Turn the mixture into the prepared tin, smooth the top with the back of a spoon dipped into hot water and dome it slightly in the middle.

Bake in the centre of the oven for 1½ hours. Do not open the door during this time, or the bread will sink.

When the bread is cooked it will shrink from the sides of the tin. Allow it to cool in the tin for 15 minutes, then turn it on to a wire rack. Peel off the paper and turn the loaf right side up. Allow it to cool completely for about 2 hours, then wrap it closely in foil and store for 48 hours before cutting.

Makes 10 slices
Calories 2955 (12560 kJ)
Protein 36 grams

Honey and Apricot Crunch

Heat the oven to 160C/325F/gas 3.

Mix together the hazelnuts, sunflower and sesame seeds, coconut and wheat germ. Put the honey and oil into a small pan and heat together gently until the honey melts. Stir into the cereal until all the ingredients are well coated.

Spread the cereal out in a single layer on non-stick baking trays and bake for 25 minutes, turning occasionally with a fish slice or spatula.

Snip the dry apricots into small pieces and mix into the cereal while it is still warm.

Cool and store in airtight jars. You can eat this granola as a deliciously crunchy snack, or serve it for breakfast with natural yoghurt.

Makes about 700 g/1½ lb
Calories 2090 (8775 kJ)
Protein 51 grams

50 g/2 oz hazelnuts, roughly chopped
50 g/2 oz sunflower seeds
50 g/2 oz sesame seeds
50 g/2 oz shredded coconut
50 g/2 oz wheat germ
150 ml/5 fl oz clear honey
30 ml/2 tbls sunflower oil
175 g/6 oz dried apricots

Honeyed Spare Ribs

Separate the ribs, cutting down between the bones. Spread them in a single layer in a large, shallow ovenproof dish.

Mix together all the remaining ingredients and pour the marinade over the meat. Toss the bones so that all the ribs are evenly coated. Cover the dish and leave in a cool place for about 3 hours, turning the ribs occasionally.

Heat the oven to 200C/400F/gas 6.

Roast the ribs in the uncovered dish for 1 hour, turning them and basting them with the sauce from time to time.

Reduce the heat to 180C/350F/gas 4 and cover the dish. Continue cooking for a further 1 hour, basting from time to time.

Serves 4
Calories 2390 (9895 kJ)
Protein 116 grams

900 g/2 lb pork spare ribs
75 ml/5 tbls tomato purée
30 ml/2 tbls clear honey
30 ml/2 tbls soy sauce
45 ml/3 tbls red wine vinegar
275 ml/10 fl oz beef stock
a pinch of salt

Honey Mousse

Mix the egg yolks with the honey in the top of a double boiler or a bowl over a pan of gently simmering water. Stir constantly until the mixture thickens like custard. Remove the pan from the heat, lift off the top pan or bowl and allow the mixture to cool.

Whisk the egg whites until stiff and fold them into the cooled honey mixture, taking care to blend thoroughly.

Pour the mousse into 4 individual serving dishes and chill for at least 3 hours. Decorate the tops with the chopped nuts.

Serves 4
Calories 1760 (7455 kJ)
Protein 35 grams

4 large eggs, separated
450 g/1 lb clear honey
25 g/1 oz toasted hazelnuts, coarsely chopped

Low-Fat Cooking

When you or anyone in your family is first advised to observe a low-fat diet, it is, to say the least, a stimulating challenge to the cook. As in any other diet, do not look down the list of prohibited foods, pile them up on one side of an imagined balance-scale and, visualising this, allow your enjoyment of food to come crashing to the ground.

Think positive! Think instead of all the foods you are encouraged to eat – and the exciting dishes you can create with them. The sparklingly clear meat soups fragrant with herbs, the golden-spiced chicken simmered with sun-dried fruits, the crunchy, fresh fruit and vegetables, the pride of our horticultural harvests, dressed with yoghurt and fruit juices.

Once you know by heart the list of foods to avoid – forget it! As you can see from the guidelines there are many alternatives and so it isn't by any means a diet of deprivation.

The medical factors
Coronary heart disease (C.H.D.) is a condition caused when the arteries supplying the heart (coronary arteries) become narrowed or blocked restricting the blood which supplies the heart with oxygen. This may result in a fatal heart attack, or less severely in a heart attack in which only a part of the heart muscle dies, and the patient survives. The narrowing of the arteries is caused by the deposition of fatty tissue which includes cholesterol.

No one knows exactly what causes C.H.D. but

One-step White Sauce

A quick and easy way to a comparatively low-fat white pouring and coating sauce.
Use them with caution in conjunction with low fat foods.

Makes 275 ml/½ pt

For pouring sauce
15 g/½ oz polyunsaturated margarine
15 g/½ oz wholewheat (or plain white) flour
275 g/½ pt skimmed milk
salt and ground black pepper

Calories 250 (1040 kJ)
Protein 11 grams
Fat 13 grams

For coating sauce
25 g/1 oz polyunsaturated margarine
25 g/1 oz flour
275 ml/½ pt skimmed milk
salt and ground black pepper

Calories 350 (1480 kJ)
Protein 13 grams
Fat 21 grams

Put all the ingredients in a small, heavy-based pan, set it over medium heat and whisk continuously. As the margarine melts the sauce will thicken. When it does, remove the pan from the heat and stir in any flavouring. Return the pan to a gentle heat if you use cheese, just to melt it.

For flavouring, select from:
10 ml/2 tsp anchovy essence
15 ml/1 tbls chopped capers
25 g/1 oz grated Edam cheese and 10 ml/2 tsp mustard
15 ml/1 tbls mustard and 5 ml/1 tsp vinegar
2 onions, boiled and chopped and a pinch of grated nutmeg
15-30 ml/1-2 tbls chopped parsley, oregano, chives, basil or other herbs.

For Sweet White Sauce
Pouring
Calories 345 (1450 kJ)
Protein 13 grams
Fat 13 grams

Coating
Calories 450 (1885 kJ)
Protein 14 grams
Fat 21 grams

*Flavourings (left) will add energy, protein and fat counts to the sauces. Cheese, in particular, is a high source of fat.

Follow the same method as for pouring and coating sauces. Omit the seasoning, add 15 ml/1 tbls brown sugar, up to 150 ml/5 fl oz thick fruit purée and a pinch of nutmeg or cinnamon.

there are many factors involved. Those that put us highest at risk are smoking, high blood pressure and a high concentration of cholesterol in the blood. Other factors include diabetes, family history, obesity, stress, personality, lack of exercise and soft tap water.

The more risk factors present, the greater the likelihood of developing the disease.

Fats and cholesterol
In the U.K. we eat a lot of fat; 38% of our total energy comes from fat. The incidence of C.H.D. is consequently very high. Countries with low fat diets have much lower rates of heart disease.

Types of fat. Fats and oils (fats liquid at normal room temperature) are made up of a mixture of 3 types of fatty acids in different proportions. They are known as saturated fatty acids, polyunsaturated fatty acids (p.u.f.a.) and mono-unsaturated fatty acids. When a fat contains a high proportion of saturated fatty acids we call it a **'saturated fat'**. These are usually hard at room temperature. Animal fats, that is, those from meat, cheese, lard and cream, come in this category. But note that coconut and palm oil, as well as hard and some soft margarines, are also 'saturated fats'.

A **polyunsaturated fat** contains a high proportion of p.u.f.a.'s. They are normally liquid at room temperature (i.e. oil) and come from vegetable sources such as corn and sunflower oil. Other sources are fish oils and margarines marked high in polyunsaturated fatty acids.

Mono-unsaturated fatty acids make up the final proportion of the fat. They predominate in olive oil and some soft margarines. So far they haven't played a significant part in the fats and heart disease debate!

Cholesterol is a fat-like substance vital to our body's functioning and a certain amount must always be available. People with high circulating concentrations in the blood do appear to be at greater risk of a heart attack. Much of the cholesterol present is in fact made by the body. For this reason foods rich in cholesterol such as eggs and shellfish need not be shunned, although they should still be used cautiously. (Cholesterol is not present in vegetables, fruit or cereals.)

Blood cholesterol levels can be lowered by eating less fat, particularly saturated fat. (A blood cholesterol concentration considered to be associated with a small risk of C.H.D. can be achieved with a diet of which 30% of the energy comes from fat.)

Which foods?
The single most important message is to eat less fat – particularly saturated fat. The Guidelines table on page 161 will help you with this.

An average person with a daily intake of 2,400 calories (10,000 kJ) should aim to eat approximately 80 grams of fat per day. (This represents 30% of the total food energy.) The recipes in this chapter have been selected so that for a main course, the amount of fat present does not exceed 25 grams, and for a sweet does not exceed 10 grams of fat per portion.

Change the emphasis of your diet so that you eat less foods rich in saturated fatty acids such as meat, cheese, butter and cream. Avoid those invisible fats in cakes, pastries, biscuits, processed meats and snack foods. Eat more foods high in starch and fibre such as vegetables (including pulses), fruit and cereals. Also eat more fish and shellfish; even the 'fatty' fish are fine.

There will be moments when you need to use some added fat in your cooking, especially for non-meat dishes. For preference use pure vegetable oils such as sunflower seed, safflower seed or corn (maize) oil. Olive oil is a good choice too. Avoid 'blended vegetable oils' as these may contain coconut or palm oil which are high in saturated fatty acids.

When using margarine stick to those specifically labelled 'high in polyunsaturated fatty acids'. Hard margarines and some soft margarines have a high

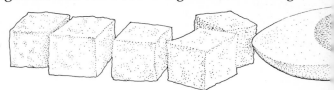

proportion of saturated fatty acids.

You can use the recommended oils or margarine (but with great restraint) for shallow frying. Have the fat hot enough, first, to brown a cube of bread in a few seconds, before you add the food to be fried. This is important; at a lower temperature, the food will absorb far more fat.

You can make 'cream' soups using skimmed milk and low-fat yoghurt, let all the flavours of the vegetables really come through and complement them, if you like, with just a dash of spice. Add texture and flavour to casseroles and stews by ladling out some of the stock and cooked vegetables and whizzing or sieving it to a purée, the most natural thickening agent of all.

You will soon get used to cutting off all the excess fat from every piece of meat before you cook it. Skin whole chickens, joints or portions before cooking – the skin is the birds' fatty overcoat. Always stand meat for roasting on a rack in the roasting pan, so that the fat drops below and the meat is not left swimming in it. Baste the meat if necessary with a polyunsaturated oil or margarine, and not with the pan juices. A 'cook's brush' works like magic on any little pools of risen fat on casseroles. Dip the long white fibres in the fat, wait a few seconds while the fat is drawn up the bristles, and wash it away in hot, soapy water.

Take special note of all the ideas using low-fat yoghurt, thickened yoghurt and cottage or yoghurt cheese in Chapters 4, 5, 6 and 8 – so good that they could not possibly be kept a secret until we reached this special-diet section!

Develop a demand in the family for more fish meals every week by cooking and presenting them deliciously. Wrap fillets or fish steaks in fresh herbs, dribble them with yoghurt and seal them up in foil parcels, or sprinkle them with subtle spices like mace or a pinch of saffron to give them a golden flavour glow.

Enjoy your 'low-fat' cooking' but do watch the calories! Remember that overweight is associated with high blood pressure, diabetes and lack of exercise, and all are black marks towards developing heart disease.

Too much salt has been linked to high blood pressure. Try to use a little less salt in your cooking and at the table – you may be pleasantly surprised by the delicious new flavours. Beware of the high salt content in certain processed foods such as processed meats, meat and yeast extracts, dried and tinned soups, cheese spreads and cheeses such as Camembert, Danish Blue and Stilton. Also some breakfast cereals contain a certain amount of salt.

German Beef and Clove Casserole

1.5 kg/3½ lb lean topside beef in one piece, trimmed of all fat
1 garlic clove, crushed
5 ml/1 tsp dried marjoram
salt and ground black pepper
8 whole cloves
60 ml/4 tbls sunflower oil
225 ml/8 fl oz dry red wine
225 ml/8 fl oz beef stock, skimmed of all fat
1 onion, chopped
3 carrots, scraped and chopped
1 celery stalk, chopped

Beat the meat with a meat mallet to tenderize it. Combine the garlic and marjoram and add salt and pepper to taste. Rub the mixture all over the meat, roll up the meat and tie it with string. Make small incisions in the meat and push in the cloves.

Heat the oil in a flameproof casserole over moderate heat and brown the meat on all sides. Pour in the wine and stock and bring to the boil. Add the onion, carrots, celery and salt and pepper to taste. Cover the casserole and simmer on top of the stove for 1¾ hours, or until the meat is tender.

Transfer the meat to a warmed serving dish. Skim any fat from the surface of the cooking juices, then strain the juices over the meat.

The meat is delicious served cold on the second day.
*For a reduced fat content, brown the meat in a non-stick pan without using any oil. This will reduce the calories to 1485 (6250 kJ) and the fat to 55 grams.

Serves 6-8
Calories 1730 (7250 kJ)
Protein 245 grams
Fat 82 grams

Clear Beetroot Soup

Pour the chicken stock into a large pan. Wash the beetroot and grate it into the stock. Blanch the onion in boiling water for 1 minute, then drain. Scrub and chop the celery stick. Add the onion, celery and all the remaining ingredients to the pan, adding the egg white and crushed shell last of all.

Set the pan over medium heat and whisk until the liquid has almost reached boiling point. A thick scum will rise to the top. Simmer gently for 1 hour.

Line a large sieve with a double layer of scalded muslin and set it over a large jug or bowl. Carefully pour the contents of the pan into the sieve and discard them. Rinse the muslin in hot water and strain the soup again. Blot the top of the hot liquid with several layers of absorbent kitchen paper to remove any fat. Taste the soup and adjust the seasoning.

Pour the soup into heated bowls and float a slice of lemon in each. Or swirl the thickened yoghurt on top.

Serves 4
Calories 102 (430 kJ)
Protein 12 grams
Fat 1 gram

1.15 L/2 pt fat-free chicken stock
1 medium-sized beetroot
1 small onion
1 celery stick
2.5 ml/¹/₂ tsp peppercorns
1 pinch of salt
45 ml/3 tbls dry sherry
white and shell of 1 large egg
1 lemon, thinly sliced
60 ml/4 tbls thickened yoghurt
  (see page 72-optional)

Tomato Nut Ring

30 ml/2 tbls fine, dry breadcrumbs
6 tomatoes, peeled, de-seeded and
    chopped
225 g/8 oz ground brazil nuts
150 g/5 oz wholewheat
    breadcrumbs
30 ml/2 tbls wholewheat flour
60 ml/4 tbls skimmed milk powder
30 ml/2 tbls rolled oats
75 ml/5 tbls tomato juice
10 ml/2 tsp dried basil
5 ml/1 tsp salt
100 g/4 oz broccoli
450 g/1 lb new potatoes, scrubbed
15 ml/1 tbls chopped parsley

Heat the oven to 190C/375F/gas 5.

Grease a ring mould, tip in the dry breadcrumbs and shake the mould to line it with the crumbs.

Mix together the tomatoes, nuts, fresh breadcrumbs, flour, milk powder, oats, tomato juice, basil and salt. Spoon the mixture into the mould and level the top. Bake for 50 minutes, or until a fine skewer inserted through the mould comes out clean.

Meanwhile, cook the broccoli and potatoes in boiling, salted water until they are just tender. Drain them well. Put the potatoes into a bowl and toss with the parsley. Keep the broccoli and potatoes warm.

Turn out the nut ring on to a warmed serving plate. Fill the centre with the broccoli and arrange the potatoes around the edge. Serve hot.
*Brazil nuts are a rich source of fat. If the content is too high for you, reduce the amount of nuts in the recipe. 138 grams of the total 147 grams of fat comes from the brazil nuts.

Serves 4-6
Calories 2635 (11000 kJ)
Protein 83 grams
Fat 147 grams

Mexican Chicken with Fruit

50 g/2 oz wholewheat flour
salt and ground black pepper
2.5 ml/½ tsp chilli powder
1.8 kg/4 lb chicken, skinned
50 g/2 oz polyunsaturated
    margarine
30 ml/2 tbls sunflower oil
1 onion, finely chopped
1 garlic clove, crushed
2.5 ml/½ tsp ground cinnamon
1.5 ml/¼ tsp ground ginger
15 ml/1 tbls tomato purée
275 ml/10 fl oz chicken stock
2 bananas, thinly sliced
2 oranges, peeled and thinly sliced
1 small pineapple, peeled, cored
    and thinly sliced
15 ml/1 tbls soft brown sugar

Mix the flour with salt and pepper and half the chilli powder. Cut the chicken into serving pieces and toss them in the seasoned flour.

Melt the margarine with the oil in a frying-pan and add the chicken pieces. Fry them over moderate heat, turning occasionally, until they are brown on all sides. Transfer the chicken to an oven-proof dish and keep warm.

Heat the oven to 180C/350F/gas 4.

Fry the onion and garlic until the onion is soft but not beginning to brown. Stir in the cinnamon, ginger, remaining chilli powder, tomato purée and salt and pepper to taste. Cook for 2 minutes, stirring constantly. Skim any fat from the top of the chicken stock and pour it into the pan, stirring. Bring to the boil, re-duce the heat and simmer for 5 minutes.

Pour the sauce over the chicken pieces, then cover the chicken with layers of bananas, oranges and pineapple. Sprinkle the sugar over the top.

Bake the dish uncovered for 45-50 minutes, or until the chicken is tender and the top glazed and syrupy. Serve the dish piping hot.

Serves 4-6
Calories 2355 (9875 kJ)
Protein 180 grams
Fat 103 grams

Marinated Roast Chicken

Skin the chicken and discard the skin – which is very high in fat. Prick the chicken all over many times with a fork. Mix together the salt, lemon juice and chillies and rub them into the chicken. Place the chicken in a large bowl, cover and set aside for about 30 minutes.

Mix together the yoghurt, coriander or other herbs, ginger and garlic. Rub this mixture all over the chicken, cover the bowl and set aside for 8 hours.

Heat the oven to 200C/400F/gas 6.

Heat the oil in a roasting pan and add the chicken and the marinade. Roast in the centre of the oven for 20 minutes. Reduce the heat to 180C/350F/gas 4 and continue roasting, basting the chicken frequently, for a further 30 minutes, or until the chicken is tender when pierced with the point of a sharp knife.

Transfer the chicken to a warmed serving dish and keep it warm. Place the pan over moderate heat and, stirring constantly, boil the pan juices for about 3 minutes until they have reduced. Taste this sauce and add more seasoning if necessary. Pour the sauce over the chicken and garnish the dish with the slices of lemon. Serve at once.

Serves 4-6
Calories 1655 (6920 kJ)
Protein 201 grams
Fat 83 grams

1.8 kg/4 lb chicken
5 ml/1 tsp salt
juice of ½ lemon
2 green chillies, de-seeded and very finely chopped
225 ml/8 fl oz natural low-fat yoghurt
90 ml/6 tbls chopped fresh coriander leaves, or parsley and mint combined
5-cm/2-in piece fresh root ginger, peeled and finely chopped
4 garlic cloves, crushed
45 ml/3 tbls vegetable oil
1 lemon, thinly sliced

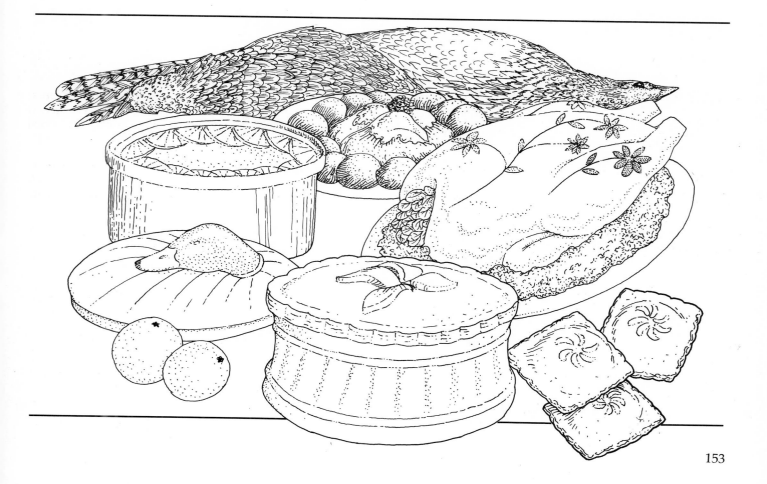

153

Italian Bananas

25 g/1 oz polyunsaturated
   margarine
1 onion, finely chopped
225 g/8 oz tomatoes, skinned and
   chopped
5 bananas, sliced
salt
60 ml/4 tbls dry white wine

Melt the margarine in a frying-pan. Add the onion and fry until it is soft but not brown. Add the tomatoes, bananas, salt to taste and the wine. Stir well and simmer gently for 10-15 minutes or until the bananas are tender.

Turn into a warmed serving dish and serve hot.

Serves 4
Calories 555 (2330 kJ)
Protein 7 grams
Fat 22 grams

Bean Sprout Salad

Wash fresh bean sprouts and drain them thoroughly. Drain canned ones, rinse them under cold, running water and drain them well. Drain and chop the canned pimento. Put the bean sprouts, pimento, cucumber and chives in a salad bowl and toss them together.

Mix together the oil, vinegar, mustard and soy sauce and season the dressing with salt and pepper. Taste and add a little brown sugar if necessary. Pour the dressing over the salad, toss to coat the salad evenly, cover and chill for 1 hour.

*For an even lower calorie and fat count, omit the oil from this recipe. This will bring the fat content down to 1 gram. For those not so concerned with the fat content, sprinkle some roasted peanuts over the salad as shown in the picture.

Serves 4
Calories 190 (785 kJ)
Protein 9 grams
Fat 14 grams

450 g/1 lb bean sprouts
50 g/2 oz canned pimento
1 pickled cucumber, chopped
15 ml/1 tbls chopped chives
15 ml/1 tbls sunflower oil
15 ml/1 tbls wine vinegar
2.5 ml/½ tsp made mustard
10 ml/2 tsp soy sauce
salt and ground black pepper

Lamb and Apricot Pilaff

700 g/1½ lb boned leg of lamb
15 ml/1 tbls vegetable oil
1 medium-sized onion, thinly
 sliced
100 g/4 oz dried apricots, soaked
 and drained
45 ml/3 tbls seedless raisins
2.5 ml/½ tsp ground cinnamon
1 pinch of ground ginger
salt and ground black pepper
225 g/8 oz brown long-grain rice

Trim the lamb of all excess fat and cut it into 2.5-cm/1-in cubes. Heat a non-stick frying-pan and fry the meat over gentle heat until the fat runs. Increase the heat slightly and fry, stirring frequently, for about 5 minutes. Lift out the meat with a slotted spoon. Drain off and discard fat.

Melt the oil in the pan and fry the onion until it is soft but not brown. Halve the apricots and add them to the pan with the raisins, meat cubes, cinnamon and ginger. Season with salt and pepper and pour on 425 ml/16 fl oz water. Stir well and bring slowly to the boil. Stir again, reduce the heat and cover the pan. Simmer for 1-1¼ hours, or until the lamb is tender. Taste and adjust seasoning if necessary.

Meanwhile, put the rice into a large saucepan with 575 ml/1 pt water and 2.5 ml/½ tsp salt. Bring the water to the boil, stir the rice and boil for 3 minutes. Stir again, cover the pan, lower the heat and simmer for 40-45 minutes, or until the rice is just tender. The water should all have been absorbed.

Heat the oven to 180C/350F/gas 4.

Spread one-third of the rice in an ovenproof dish and cover with one-third of the meat and fruit mixture. Continue making layers, ending with a layer of rice. Cover the dish and bake for 10 minutes. Serve hot.

Serves 4
Calories 2095 (8830 kJ)
Protein 140 grams
Fat 67 grams

Lentil Rissoles

225 g/8 oz split red lentils
75 ml/5 tbls sunflower oil
1 medium-sized onion, chopped
15 ml/1 tbls lemon juice
2.5 ml/½ tsp ground cumin
2.5 ml/½ tsp ground coriander
2.5 ml/½ tsp ground turmeric
30 ml/2 tbls chopped parsley
salt and ground black pepper
1 medium-sized egg, lightly beaten
wholewheat flour, to coat

For the sauce
1 garlic clove, crushed
30 ml/2 tbls chopped parsley
275 ml/10 fl oz natural low-fat
 yoghurt

Wash and drain the lentils. Put them into a pan with 275 ml/10 fl oz water and bring to the boil. Half cover the pan with the lid and simmer over low heat until the lentils are cooked and all the water has been absorbed – about 25 minutes. Check that the lentils are not drying out and add a little more water if necessary.

Purée the lentils in a vegetable mill to make a thick, smooth paste. If the purée is runny, return it to the saucepan and dry over a low heat for a few minutes, stirring, until the paste is firm.

Heat 30 ml/2 tbls of the oil in a pan and fry the onion until it is soft and light brown. Remove the pan from the heat and add the lentils, lemon juice, spices and parsley. Season the mixture and stir in the beaten egg.

Turn the mixture on to a plate and divide it into 8 portions. Flour your hands and form each portion into a roll, like a sausage. Chill the rissoles in the refrigerator for 30 minutes.

Heat the remaining oil in a frying-pan and fry the rissoles over moderate heat until they are crisp and evenly browned – about 10-12 minutes. Remove them with a slotted spoon and toss them on absorbent kitchen paper to dry.

Stir the garlic and parsley into the yoghurt and season with salt and pepper. Serve the chilled sauce separately, with the hot rissoles.

Serves 4
Calories 1590 (6645 kJ)
Protein 77 grams
Fat 79 grams

Red Cabbage Casserole

Discard the tough outer leaves of the cabbage, cut it into quarters and cut away the stalk. Shred the cabbage finely and put it into a large bowl. Add the red wine vinegar and sugar and toss to coat the cabbage thoroughly.

Melt the oil in a heavy-based pan. Chop one onion and add it to the pan with the apples. Cook over moderate heat for about 5 minutes, stirring frequently. Skin the remaining onion and press the cloves into it. Add the whole onion to the pan with the cabbage, bay leaf and raisins. Add 575 ml/1 pt boiling water,

stir well and cover the pan. Simmer over low heat for 1¾-2 hours, or until the cabbage is tender. Top up the pan with a little more boiling water if necessary.

Stir in the red wine, discard the bay leaf and whole onion and turn the cabbage into a warmed serving dish. Serve at once, piping hot.

Serves 4
Calories 890 (3745 kJ)
Protein 12 grams
Fat 32 grams

700 g/1½ lb red cabbage
75 ml/5 tbls red wine vinegar
50 g/2 oz soft brown sugar
45 ml/3 tbls vegetable oil
2 medium-sized onions
2 medium-sized cooking apples,
  peeled, cored and chopped
2 cloves
1 bay leaf
50 g/2 oz seedless raisins
30 ml/2 tbls dry red wine

Fish Mousse

Place the haddock fillets in a pan with the bay leaf and pour on just enough boiling water to cover. Cover the pan and set aside for 10 minutes.

Sieve the cheese into a bowl and stir in the lemon juice and parsley.

Skin the fish and remove any small bones, flake it and leave to cool. Fold the fish into the cheese and mix well. Season the mixture with salt, pepper and

cayenne and divide it between 4 small ramekin dishes. Cover and chill.

Garnish the dishes with the lemon wedges and parsley sprigs.

Serves 4
Calories 350 (1465 kJ)
Protein 60 grams
Fat 10 grams

225 g/8 oz smoked haddock fillet
1 bay leaf
225 g/8 oz cottage cheese
juice of ½ lemon
45 ml/3 tbls chopped parsley
salt and ground black pepper
a pinch of cayenne
1 lemon, quartered
parsley sprigs

Baked Cauliflower

Trim off the the green leaves and the hard stalk and divide the cauliflower into large flowerets.

Heat the oven to 180C/350F/gas 4.

Partly cook the cauliflower in boiling, salted water for 10 minutes, then drain.

To make the sauce, stir together the yoghurt, tomato purée and nutmeg and season with salt and pepper. Transfer the cauliflower to an ovenproof dish and

pour over the sauce. Sprinkle a little paprika on top if you like.

Bake the cauliflower on a low shelf in the oven for 20 minutes. Serve hot.

Serves 4
Calories 200 (860 kJ)
Protein 25 grams
Fat 2 grams

1 medium-sized cauliflower
150 ml/5 fl oz natural low-fat
  yoghurt
30 ml/2 tbls tomato purée
salt and ground black pepper
2.5 ml/½ tsp grated nutmeg

German Fruit Bread

25 g/1 oz fresh yeast
100 g/4 oz sugar plus 5 ml/1 tsp
1.3 k/3 lb flour
2.5 ml/½ tsp ground coriander
1.5 ml/¼ tsp ground fennel
1 pinch of ground cloves
5 ml/1 tsp salt
100 g/4 oz polyunsaturated
  margarine, melted
50 g/2 oz dried apricots, chopped
50 g/2 oz dried pears, chopped
50 g/2 oz dried apples, chopped
275 g/10 oz hazelnuts
175 g/6 oz seedless raisins or
  sultanas
100 g/4 oz candied peel, chopped

Crumble the yeast into a small bowl and mash in 5 ml/1 tsp of the sugar and 125 ml/4 fl oz lukewarm water. Leave in a warm, draught-free place for 15-20 minutes, until frothy.

Sift half the flour into a mixing bowl with the spices and salt. Make a well in the centre and pour in the yeast mixture, 700 ml/23 fl oz lukewarm water, the sugar and margarine. Gradually draw in the flour and mix until all the flour is incorporated. Set aside for 15 minutes.

Sift the remaining flour into another bowl. Add the dried fruit, hazelnuts, raisins and candied peel and stir well. Mix into the dough, then turn out onto a floured board and knead until the dough is smooth and elastic.

Place the dough in a lightly-greased mixing bowl, cover and leave in a warm, draught-free place for 1-1½ hours, or until it has almost doubled in bulk.

Turn the dough out onto a floured board and knead for 2 minutes. Cut into three pieces and shape each into a ball. Place the rounds of dough on lightly-greased baking sheets and return to a warm place to rise for 30-40 minutes.

Heat the oven to 220C/425F/gas 7.

Bake the bread for 15 minutes, then reduce the heat to 190C/375F/gas 5 and continue baking for 30 minutes, or until the tops are crusty and golden brown. Test the bread by rapping the underside with your knuckles. When it is cooked, it should sound hollow. If not, return it to the oven for a few minutes. Leave the bread on a wire rack to cool.

*The quantities given in this recipe make three large loaves. To make less, you can of course halve the given amounts. Or you can freeze the completely cooled loaves and enjoy them when you do not have time for such therapeutic baking.

Makes 3 900-g/2-lb loaves
Calories per loaf 2420 (10650 kJ)
Protein per loaf 59 grams
Fat per loaf 65 grams

Eggless Fruit Cake

225 g/8 oz wholewheat flour
5 ml/1 tsp mixed spice
50 g/2 oz polyunsaturated
  margarine
100 g/4 oz soft brown sugar
350 g/12 oz mixed dried fruit
grated zest of ½ a lemon
30 ml/2 tbls dry cider
180 ml/6 fl oz skimmed milk
5 ml/1 tsp bicarbonate of soda

Heat the oven to 160C/325F/gas 3. Grease an 18-cm/7-in cake tin, line it with greaseproof paper and grease it again.

Sift together the flour and spice and tip in the bran remaining in the sieve. Add the margarine, sugar, dried fruit, lemon zest and cider and stir well.

Blend the bicarbonate of soda with a little of the milk, stir in the rest of the milk and pour it into the bowl.

Beat all the ingredients together until they are light and fluffy. Turn into the prepared tin and make a slight hollow in the centre using the back of a spoon.

Bake in the centre of the oven for 2½ hours, or until the cake is firm and a fine skewer pierced through the centre comes out clean. Cool on a wire rack before turning out of the tin.

Makes 10-12 slices
Calories 2395 (10150 kJ)
Protein 40 grams
Fat 45 grams

Walnut and Coffee Biscuits

175 g/6 oz ground walnuts
50 g/2 oz soft brown sugar
50 g/2 oz light Muscavado sugar
15 ml/1 tbls strong black coffee
3 egg whites, stiffly beaten

Heat the oven to 190C/375F/gas 5.

Mix together the ground walnuts, sugars, coffee and 30 ml/2 tbls of the beaten egg white. Gently fold in the remaining egg white.

Line a baking sheet with edible rice paper or non-stick vegetable paper. Drop heaped teaspoons of the mixture on to the baking sheet, leaving space for the biscuits to spread.

Bake for 15-20 minutes, or until the biscuits are golden and crisp.

Allow the biscuits to cool a little before lifting them from the sheet. If you used rice paper, cut out round the biscuits. Transfer them to a wire rack to cool completely. Store in an air-tight tin.

Makes 24 biscuits
Calories 1360 (5680 kJ)
Protein 30 grams
Fat 90 grams

Dairy-Free Orange Cake

100 g/4 oz polyunsaturated
　margarine
100 g/4 oz dark Muscavado sugar
225 g/8 oz wholemeal self-raising
　flour
5 ml/1 tsp mixed spice
100 g/4 oz sultanas
grated zest of 1 medium-sized
　orange
150 ml/5 fl oz fresh orange juice

Heat the oven to 150C/300F/gas 2 and grease an 18-cm/7-in cake tin.

Beat the margarine until it is light and fluffy and then beat in the sugar.

Sift the flour and spice into a bowl and tip in the bran remaining in the sieve. Stir in the sultanas and orange zest.

Put the orange juice into a small pan and bring it to the boil. Remove from the heat, allow to cool a little and then quickly stir into the flour. Stir the flour mixture into the sugar and margarine and mix thoroughly.

Transfer the mixture into the prepared tin, smooth the top and bake for 1¼ hours. Turn the cake on to a wire rack to cool. It will be very crumbly and needs handling with care.

*The flavour of this cake is so delicious that no-one will mind that it is not light and fluffy like a sponge cake. Actually, it can best be described as a cross between shortbread and cake in texture.

Makes 12 slices
Calories 2485 (10445 kJ)
Protein 33 grams
Fat 106 grams

GUIDELINES FOR A HEALTHY HEART

● **CUT DOWN ON ALL FATS AND OILS.** THIS INCLUDES BOTH VISIBLE AND INVISIBLE TYPES.

VISIBLE		INVISIBLE	
FATTY CUTS OF MEAT	SUET	CAKES	MAYONNAISE
BUTTER	TOP OF MILK	PUDDINGS	CHEESE
MARGARINE	SINGLE AND DOUBLE CREAM	BISCUITS	CRISPS
LARD	OILS	PROCESSED MEATS	NUTS
		SALAD CREAM	

Type of fat to use
The minimum of fat should always be used, but for preference use pure vegetable oils (high in polyunsaturated fatty acids). These include sunflower, corn (maize), soya bean, walnut, peanut, safflower and olive oils. Do not use blended vegetable oils. For spreading and baking use those margarines labelled 'high in polyunsaturated fatty acids'.

● **EAT MORE STARCHY FOODS** e.g. bread, rice, pasta, potatoes, pizza (with dough base), barley, muesli.

● **EAT MORE FIBRE** i.e. vegetables, pulses and fruit, wholegrain rice and wholemeal bread and pasta.

● **EAT MORE FISH AND SHELLFISH.** Both white and 'fatty' fish are included. (However note that smoked fish, boiled shrimps and cockles are high in salt.)

● **USE LESS SALT IN COOKING.** Beware of high salt foods e.g. processed meats, crisps, smoked fish, tinned and dried soups, processed cheese, Danish Blue, Camembert and Stilton cheeses, meat and yeast extracts.

WHICH FOODS?

EAT MORE OF THESE	EAT WITH CAUTION	AVOID

FRUIT   All types with the exception of avocado pears and olives
 	
VEGETABLES   All types including pulses (lentils and beans etc.), leafy and root vegetables. Potatoes are excellent!
 	
CEREAL AND CEREAL PRODUCTS   All types, preferably wholegrain e.g. bread   pasta
  rice   crispbread
  barley   muesli
  oatmeal breakfast cereals
  pizza   (with dough base)
 	
FISH AND SHELLFISH   All types including 'fatty fish'.
White fish are particularly good e.g. cod, haddock, plaice
 	
LOW FAT DAIRY PRODUCTS   As found in: skimmed milk
  egg whites
  low-fat yoghurt
  cottage cheese
	MEAT AND OFFAL 'Trimmed and skimmed' of all visible fat.
	
	EGGS 4-5 per week
	
	CHEESE: CHEDDAR TYPE 50g (2 oz) at any one meal
	EDAM TYPE 75g (2½ oz) at any one meal
	
	WHOLE MILK i.e. 'doorstep milk' up to 200 ml (⅓ pt) per day
	
	CANNED FISH Pour off the canning oil; it is not necessarily fish oil and may be high in saturated fatty acids
	
	CAKES AND PUDDINGS For treats only, and home-made low-fat recipes!
	
	NUTS Allow 25g/1 oz shelled weight in a main dish (except coconut). High in fat but low in saturated fatty acids. Avoid nuts as a snack
	
	Note: restrictions are per person
		ALL FATS, BOTH VISIBLE AND INVISIBLE
		
		VISIBLE FATS e.g. fatty meat
		  butter
		  margarine
		  lard
		  suet
		  dripping
		  cream, single and double
		  top of milk
		  oils
		
		INVISIBLE FAT, HIDDEN IN
		– MEAT PRODUCTS e.g. salami
		  liver sausage
		  luncheon meat
		  sausages
		  beefburgers
		– CAKES, PASTRIES & PUDDINGS BISCUITS & ICE CREAM (dairy and non-dairy)
		– SAUCES & SOUPS e.g. mayonnaise
		  salad cream
		  french dressing
		  cream soups
		– CONFECTIONERY e.g. chocolate crisps
		– COCONUTS
		– CREAM CHEESE

Menu Planner

Planning a menu is like putting together a very special jigsaw puzzle. At first all the separate pieces, the individual recipes, are spread out before you. And gradually you have to select two, three or four that go well together and make up the particular meal you are going to put on the table for your family or friends.

Something of a conundrum, you feel, with over 250 recipes in this book to choose from? Well, it is not, really, because every time you are planning a meal you have an occasion and a set of circumstances in mind. And they give you a lead in the right direction, pointing towards some recipes that would be suitable, and eliminating others that definitely would not be.

Whatever the time or occasion, and no matter how formal or informal it is, the most important thing to consider is the balance of the meal as a whole. Even when it is something as simple as a Ploughman's Lunch, it is made infinitely more enjoyable if you have chosen each separate component (each piece of the jigsaw) with an eye to the picture as a whole – the complete meal. Make each menu plan with an eye on the contrast in the colour of the various foods, their textures and of course their flavours.

In our example of a Ploughman's Lunch, with moist straight-from-the-oven Herb Soda Bread there might be one lightly spiced soft cheese, delicately tinged with pink, and one hard dairy cheese; with ice-green crisp pickled cucumbers there could be a soft, golden rhubarb and orange chutney, and in a large pottery bowl beside it all, a chilled salad of lettuce, spring onions, tomatoes and radishes. And so the picture builds up and you can see it all – fresh, wholesome and infinitely tempting, yet remarkably easy to prepare. This is the EAT WELL, STAY HEALTHY way of eating – mixing and matching simple foods prepared and served at their best.

Every time you are planning a menu, think carefully about what you will be doing on that day, whether you will have time to do the preparation in the evening or the morning before the meal, whether you will be away from home for a long time or want to be free for an hour or so in the afternoon. Consider whether friends will be staying with you, and you want to enjoy their company without dashing in and out of the kitchen, or whether people will be arriving after a long journey – and might be held up on the way, and arrive late. Take into account whether you or one of the group is on a special slimming or other diet. Or perhaps it is as simple as the fact that the weather has turned warm and you want to get out of doors and make the best of it, or it's turned cold and you want to close the shutters and huddle round a fire instead.

All these seemingly unconnected points have a strong bearing on the way you will plan your menu, and the way you use this book. Never fall into the trap of choosing a recipe first, and then having to reorganise your complete timetable to accommodate it.

Try to include some fresh fruit or fresh vegetables in every meal, and at least once a day choose one of the high-fibre foods. Slow Chicken Hotpot, or Beef and Butter Bean Casserole, for example, both leave you with a clear conscience and no last-minute worries! Nutritious, delicious – and easy, so you can be the perfect hostess, relaxed and free to chat with your guests.

When you want to create a fun atmosphere, it can be great to go for an 'ethnic' evening, choosing Chinese or Indonesian or, perhaps an Indian style curry. And even then, pick the long, slow-cooking dishes or the last-minute stir-fry ones according to your schedule on this occasion.

Think of the food balance; think of the colour balance; the textures, crisp to follow creamy. Think of the meal as a whole and you will EAT WELL, STAY HEALTHY.

Meal in 60 Minutes

One of the most precious assets a busy cook can have is a repertoire of dishes that can be prepared in minutes, but taste as if they took hours! Centre attention round a main dish of tender, lean pork simmered in a fruit-flavoured sauce, and you will have no worries. Vegetables served à la Grècque make a perfect opener, and baked bananas topped with toasted coconut round off the meal with a hint of Caribbean exotic.

Mushrooms à la Grècque
Pork Tenderloin in Orange Sauce
New Potatoes and Green Beans
Caribbean Bananas

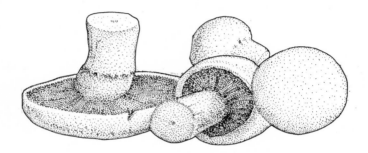

Mushrooms à la Grècque

90 ml/6 tbls dry red wine
30 ml/2 tbls tomato purée
30 ml/2 tbls sunflower oil
1 small onion or 3 spring onions, finely chopped
1 garlic clove, crushed
1 large pinch of mustard seed
salt and ground black pepper
30 ml/2 tbls chopped mint
450 g/1 lb small button mushrooms, thinly sliced

Put the wine, tomato purée, oil, onion, garlic and seasonings into a pan with 150 ml/5 fl oz of water, cover the pan, bring to the boil and simmer gently for 20-30 minutes, until the liquid is reduced by about one-third.

Add the mushrooms, bring back to simmering point and cook them in the uncovered pan over low heat for 15 minutes. Turn the mushrooms and sauce into a heated serving dish, sprinkle with the chopped mint to garnish and serve hot or warm.

If it suits your timetable better, you can cook the mushrooms in advance and leave them in the cooking liquor to cool. They are equally delicious if you serve them chilled.

Serves 4
Calories 330 (1360 klJ)
Protein 10 grams

Pork Tenderloin in Orange Sauce

Trim any excess fat from the pork and slice it into 3-cm/1¼ in slices. Put the flour into a bag, season it with salt and pepper and toss in the pork slices to coat them.

Heat the butter or margarine in a large frying-pan over a moderate-to-high heat. Add the pork and fry it quickly to seal the first side. Toss the slices over and seal the second side. The fat must be fairly hot or the meat will absorb it without sealing the surface. Lower the heat to moderate and cook for about 12 minutes, turning the meat once.

Grate the zest and strain the juice of the oranges. Reserve a little of the zest to garnish and add the remainder with the juice, the sherry and thickened yoghurt. Stir well, reduce the heat to low and simmer very gently for 5 minutes. Turn into a heated serving dish and garnish with the reserved orange zest, or with slices of fresh orange.

While the pork is cooking, steam new potatoes in their jackets and whole, tiny green beans. Arrange the vegetables around the dish.

700 g/1½ lb pork tenderloin (fillet of pork)
20 ml/4 tsp wholemeal flour
salt and ground black pepper
25 g/1 oz butter or polyunsaturated margarine
2 large oranges
30-45 ml/2-3 tbls sweet sherry
75 ml/5 tbls thickened yoghurt (see page 72)

Serves 4
Calories 1260 (5275 kJ)
Protein 132 grams

Caribbean Bananas

Cut 4 25-cm/10-in squares of foil and grease the centre of each with butter or margarine. Peel the bananas, put one on one end of each piece of foil and divide the honey and coconut between them. Fold over the foil and double-seal all around the three open edges, leaving plenty of air space between the banana and the top layer of foil. The parcels should look like fat little cushions.

You could cook the foil parcels in a large pan of boiling water under the vegetables as they steam. Or, if you intend to linger over the main course, steam the parcels when you remove the vegetables for serving. Allow 40-50 minutes.

Put the foil parcels on a serving dish and slash open the foil as you bring them to the table, or allow guests to open their own surprise packets. Serve the toasted coconut separately.

15 g/½ oz butter or margarine
4 large bananas
30 ml/2 tbls clear honey
40 g/1½ oz desiccated coconut
30 ml/2 tbls toasted coconut

Serves 4
Calories 1048 (4402 kJ)
Protein 9 grams

One-Pot Meal

It's fun to serve a one-pot meal, French farmhouse style, that can be cooking slowly for hours, mellowing all the time, and needs no last-minute attention. Make it the star of your menu, with a light and refreshing fruit dish to start, and a plate of cheese and fruit, or the frothiest of desserts, to finish. That's entertaining at its simplest and best.

Melon Cups
Slow Chicken Hotpot
Camembert and Fresh Fruits

Slow Chicken Hotpot

350 g/12 oz dried flageolets or haricot beans, soaked, rinsed and drained
175 g/6 oz onions, chopped
3 large garlic cloves, halved
1 bouquet garni
1 bay leaf
about 2 L/3½ pt unsalted chicken stock
2 kg/4½ lb chicken
½ lemon
salt and ground black pepper
175 g/6 oz carrots, scrubbed and sliced
400 g/14 oz canned tomatoes
30 ml/2 tbls tomato purée
100 g/4 oz fresh wholemeal breadcrumbs
15 ml/1 tbls chopped marjoram or 5 ml/1 tsp dried herb
15 ml/1 tbls chopped mint or 5 ml/1 tsp dried thyme (do not use dried mint)
225 g/8 oz potatoes, scrubbed and thinly sliced

Put the beans in a large saucepan and add half the onions, half the garlic cloves, the bouquet garni, bay leaf, and about 1 L/1¾ pt of the stock. Bring to the boil, cover the pan and simmer for 1 hour. Check the level of the stock during cooking and add more hot stock if necessary.

While the beans are cooking, skin the chicken and cut into serving pieces. Rub the flesh with the cut lemon.

Heat the oven to 150C/300F/gas 2.

Drain the beans with the flavouring vegetables into a colander. Discard the bouquet garni and bay leaf and reserve the stock. Season the beans well.

Spread one-third of the beans in a large oven-proof casserole and scatter half the carrot slices over them. Add the remaining garlic cloves and the onions. Arrange half the chicken pieces over the beans, then half the remaining beans, the carrots and the rest of the chicken pieces. Spoon in the rest of the beans.

Stir together the canned tomatoes, tomato purée and both the reserved and unused stock, and season. Mix well to break down the tomatoes. Pour this over the beans until it just covers them.

Mix the breadcrumbs with the herbs and sprinkle them over the beans to form a thick coating.

Cover the casserole and cook it for 1¼ hours. Push the soft crusty layer of breadcrumbs into the beans and arrange the potato slices over the top in overlapping rings. Return the casserole to the oven and cook, uncovered, for a further 1 hour, until the chicken falls off the bones, the sauce has mellowed and the potato topping is brown. If you like the topping browner, you can flash it under a hot grill for a minute or two.

Serve the hotpot straight from the oven with plenty of hot, crusty wholewheat bread.

Serves 6
Calories 2575 (10900 kJ)
Protein 278 grams

To make Melon Cups, cut a large cantaloupe melon in half, scoop out and discard the seeds and cut the melon flesh into ball shapes with a parisienne cutter. Put them in a covered container with 225 ml/8 fl oz fresh raspberry juice or unsweetened black grape juice. Serve well chilled, in glass goblets. (Calories: 520 (2205 kJ), Protein 21 grams).

In true French style, serve cheese following the main dish, then round off the meal with fresh fruits.

Ploughman's Lunch

Freshly baked wholewheat loaves, locally made cheeses, crisp pickled vegetables, chutneys from the storecupboard and perhaps a pot of beer to wash it down – these foods, in the best of country traditions, have become known as Ploughman's Lunch. Serve an informal meal of this kind on a busy Saturday, for a Sunday lunch in the garden, or when friends call in for an informal supper. When all the ingredients are 'home-made', the meal becomes a feast.

Herb Soda Bread
Mock Liptauer Cheese and Other Cheeses
Pickled Cucumber
Selection of Fresh Saladings
Nettle Beer

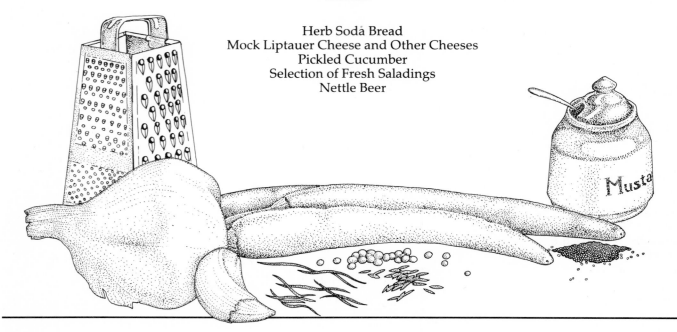

Herb Soda Bread

450 g/1 lb wholewheat flour
5 ml/1 tsp salt
ground black pepper
7.5 ml/1½ tsp bicarbonate of soda
25 g/1 oz margarine
2 medium-sized onions, grated
1 garlic clove, crushed
5 ml/1 tsp mixed dried herbs
5 ml/1 tsp chopped parsley
200 ml/7 fl oz milk
10 ml/2 tsp lemon juice
25 g/1 oz Cheddar cheese, grated

Sift together the flour, salt, pepper and soda and add the bran remaining in the sieve. Rub in the margarine until the mixture resembles fine breadcrumbs. Stir in the onion, garlic and herbs. Mix together the milk and lemon juice and stir into the dry ingredients. Mix to form a soft dough.

Turn the dough on to a lightly-floured surface and knead lightly until smooth. Shape into a 25-cm/9-in round and place on a floured baking tray. Score the top into 8 segments, brush with a little extra milk and sprinkle with the cheese. Bake at 200C/400F/gas 6 for 30-35 minutes, until the loaf is well risen and golden brown. Cool on a wire tray.

Makes 1 large loaf
Calories 1890 (7995 kJ)
Protein 75 grams

Mock Liptauer Cheese

Cream together the cheese and butter until soft and light. Add the other ingredients a little at a time, beating well between each addition. Blend well.

Press the cheese into a cylinder shape and smooth it with the blade of a knife. Make wavy ridges at intervals from top to bottom of the cheese shape. If you use the capers, press them in a decorative pattern, following the lines of the ridges.

Place the cheese on a serving plate and garnish with radishes and olives.

This strongly-flavoured cheese makes a good contrast to hard dairy cheeses or to less highly-seasoned versions of home-made yoghurt cheese.

Makes about 225 g/8 oz
Calories 850 (3500 kJ)
Protein 15 grams

100 g/4 oz cottage cheese
100 g/4 oz softened butter
15 ml/1 tsp anchovy essence
10 ml/2 tsp minced gherkin
2.5 ml/½ tsp crushed caraway seeds
5 ml/1 tsp French mustard
1.5 ml/¼ tsp salt
7.5 ml/1½ tsp paprika
capers, radishes, black olives

Pickled Cucumber

Wash the cucumbers but do not peel them. Cut them into 4-cm/1½-in pieces and cut each piece in half lengthways. Scoop out the seeds. Put the cucumbers into a colander or on a large plate and sprinkle 15 ml/1 tbls salt over the cut surfaces. Leave to stand for 15 minutes.

Cut the spring onion into 4-cm/1¼-in lengths and slice each one finely. Wash the cucumber under cold running water. Put the cucumber, spring onion, garlic, chilli and the remaining salt into an earthenware bowl and add 150 ml/5 fl oz water. Mix well and leave to mature for 2 days in a warm room or for up to 7 days in a cold place.

Once the cucumber has matured, spoon it into a covered container and keep it in the refrigerator.

Rhubarb and Orange Chutney (see page 140) would be a perfect contrast to this slightly spiced Korean recipe.

Serves 6-8
Calories 65 (275 kJ)
Protein 4 grams

3 large cucumbers
25 ml/1½ tbls salt
1 spring onion
1 garlic clove, finely chopped
2.5 ml/½ tsp finely-chopped red chilli

Nettle Beer

Wash the nettle tops, drain and put them in a very large pan with 4.5 L/1 gallon water and the root ginger. Bring to the boil and boil for 15 minutes.

Thinly pare the zest and squeeze the juice of the lemon. Strain the nettle liquid into a bowl, add the lemon zest and juice, the sugar and cream of tartar. Stir well, leave to cool, then add the yeast. Cover with a cloth and keep in a warm place for 3 days. Strain, pour into sterilized bottles and cork. Keep for 1-2 weeks before drinking.

Makes about 4.5 L/1 Gallon
Estimated calories 1670 (7035 kJ)

900 g/2 lb young nettle tops
15 g/½ oz root ginger
1 lemon
450 g/1 lb light brown sugar
25 g/1 oz cream of tartar
20 g/¾ oz fresh yeast or 5 ml/1 tsp dried brewers' yeast

No-Meat Meal

As a challenge to anyone who maintains that a meal can't be 'special' without meat – here's one that is! Even better, it entails no last-minute preparation. You can make the fish and vegetable casserole the day before. Keep it in the refrigerator and reheat it gently. The ice cream can be made up to a week in advance.

Leeks Vinaigrette
Fish and Courgette Casserole
Honey and Orange Ice Cream

Leeks Vinaigrette

12 small leeks
salt
1.5 ml/¼ tsp cayenne
30 ml/2 tbls red wine vinegar
grated rind and juice of ½ orange
60 ml/4 tbls olive oil
ground black pepper
watercress sprigs
1 lemon

Trim and wash the leeks as described in Leeks in Red Wine, (see page 65). Cut them into 5-cm/2-in lengths. Cook the leks in boiling, salted water until they are only just tender. Drain them well then pat them with absorbent kitchen paper to remove all excess moisture.

While the leeks are cooking mix together the cayenne, vinegar, orange rind and orange juice, then stir in the olive oil. Season the dressing to taste with salt and pepper and whisk it well.

Place the hot leeks in a shallow dish and pour on the dressing, turning them over and over to cover them thoroughly. Leave the leeks to cool, then cover the dish and chill for at least 2 hours, turning the leeks occasionally.

Garnish with chopped watercress and a few whole sprigs. Serve with lemon quarters.

Serves 4
Calories 675 (2780 kJ)
Protein 11 grams

Fish and Courgette Casserole

Heat the oven to 170C/325F/gas 3.

Skin the fish and cut it into 5-cm/2-in pieces.

Melt 25 g/1 oz of the margarine in a flameproof casserole, add the onion and courgettes and cook over a moderate heat for 2 minutes, stirring so that the vegetables become thoroughly coated in the fat. Stir in the flour and paprika and cook for a further 3 minutes, stirring.

Stir in the tomatoes and wine, fresh or dried herbs, bouquet garni and orange zest and season with salt and pepper.

Bring to the boil, stir well, add the fish pieces and cover the casserole. Cook for 30-35 minutes, until the fish is just tender. Taste and adjust the seasoning if necessary. Discard the bouquet garni and orange zest.

Heat the remaining margarine in a large saucepan and briskly fry the bread slices on both sides until they are crisp and golden brown. Drain them on absorbent paper to remove all excess fat.

Arrange the fried bread to stand up round the rim of the casserole so that they do not become soggy. Serve at once.

Wholewheat pasta makes a good accompaniment.

*Those who want to follow a low-fat or a general slimming diet should perhaps resist the temptation to indulge in the fried bread as a garnish!

700 g/1½ lb fillet of cod
75g/3 oz polyunsaturated margarine
1 large onion, sliced
350 g/12 oz courgettes, sliced
15 ml/1 tbls flour
5 ml/1 tsp paprika
2 large tomatoes, skinned and sliced
225 ml/8 fl oz dry white wine
5 ml/1 tsp chopped basil or thyme, or 2.5 ml/½ tsp dried herbs
1 bouquet garni including a strip of thinly-pared orange zest
salt and ground black pepper
12 thin slices French bread

Serves 4
Calories 1280 (5370 kJ)
Protein 118 grams

Honey and Orange Ice Cream

Turn the refrigerator or freezer to the coldest setting.

Beat the cheese thoroughly until it is smooth and creamy, then beat in the honey. Gradually beat in the orange juice, a little at a time, adding more only after the previous addition is absorbed. Beat well until the mixture is smooth.

Pour into a plastic container, cover and freeze for about 2 hours, or until the ice cream is hard.

Remove the container from the freezer 30 minutes before serving and leave in the main compartment of the refrigerator, to allow the flavour to mellow.

Spoon the ice cream into individual serving glasses. Cut one orange into thin slices and cut them into twists to decorate the glasses. Cut the other orange into quarters and put one on each serving, so that the guests can squeeze the juice on to the ice cream.

*A dash of orange-flavoured liqueur makes a delicious alternative to the extra orange juice.

450 g/1 lb yoghurt cheese
60 ml/4 tbls clear honey
75 ml/3 fl oz concentrated orange juice, frozen
2 oranges

Serves 4-6
Calories 825 (3425 kJ)
Protein 49 grams

Slimmers' Special

The secret of cooking meals for slimmers, we feel sure, is to forget that they *are* for slimmers. Nothing is more calculated to put the damper on a dinner party or the end to good intentions than the emphasis on what you 'must' eat and 'must' avoid. Here are three recipes, for a light and lovely savoury mousse, a low calorie but very tasty Italian dish, and a glowing golden dessert, chosen because they are simply delicious – and slimming, too!

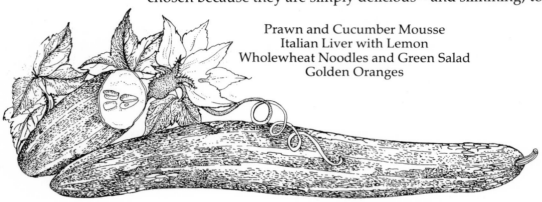

Prawn and Cucumber Mousse
Italian Liver with Lemon
Wholewheat Noodles and Green Salad
Golden Oranges

Prawn and Cucumber Mousse

50 g/2 oz cottage cheese,
sieved
150 ml/5 fl oz natural low-fat
yoghurt
1 large cucumber
100 g/4 oz peeled prawns
10 ml/2 tsp lemon juice
150 ml/5 fl oz light chicken stock,
skimmed of all fat
15 g/½ oz gelatine
salt and ground black pepper
2-3 drops of edible green food
colouring (optional)
1 lemon, quartered
1 green pepper

Mix together the cottage cheese and yoghurt. Peel and roughly chop the cucumber. Chop half the prawns. Add the cucumber, chopped prawns and lemon juice to the cheese mixture. Mix well and set aside.

Put 30 ml/2 tbls cold chicken stock into a small bowl or a cup, sprinkle on the gelatine and stand it in a pan of hot water. Stir occasionally until the gelatine has dissolved and the liquid is clear – about 5 minutes. Pour the gelatine mixture into the remaining chicken stock and stir to mix it thoroughly.

Pour the stock into the cheese mixture, stir well and add food colouring if liked. Season to taste.

Rinse a 400-ml/¾-pt ring mould with cold water, spoon in the mixture and level the top. Cover and leave in the refrigerator for 2 hours.

Cut the green pepper in half, cut away the white membrane and discard the seeds. Cut into very thin matchstick strips.

Dip the mould momentarily into hot water. Invert a plate over the top and turn out the mousse.

Arrange the reserved whole prawns and lemon quarters around the outside to garnish, and the pepper strips in the centre. Keep the mousse chilled until you are ready to serve.

Serves 4
Calories 325 (1360 kJ)
Protein 52 grams

Italian Liver with Lemon

Trim the liver, discarding any white parts, and cut it into 8 slices. Mix together the garlic, sage, breadcrumbs and mushrooms and set them aside.

Heat the butter or margarine in a large, heavy-based frying-pan over moderate heat until the foam has subsided. Add the liver and cook for 4 minutes. Turn the slices over, using a fish slice to avoid piercing the flesh, and cook for a further 4 minutes on the other side. Add the mushroom mixture and cook for about 3 minutes, stirring occasionally, until the breadcrumbs are crisp. Sprinkle on the lemon juice. Transfer the liver and mushrooms to a heated serving dish and scatter with the lemon zest.

Serve with wholewheat noodles cooked until they are just tender, and a green salad – watercress, chicory and Cos lettuce would be delicious.

450 g/1 lb lamb's or calf's liver
2 garlic cloves, crushed
6-8 fresh sage leaves, chopped
45 ml/3 tbls coarse wholewheat breadcrumbs
225 g/8 oz very small button mushrooms, thinly sliced
40 g/1½ oz butter or polyunsaturated margarine
15 ml/1 tbls lemon juice
5 ml/1 tsp grated lemon zest

Serves 4
Calories 1165 (4840 kJ)
Protein 93 grams

Golden Oranges

Thinly pare all the zest from 1 orange and reserve it to make the garnish. Skin all the oranges, removing all the bitter white pith. A swivel potato peeler does this efficiently.

Put each orange on a plate or a wooden chopping board with a groove to reserve the juice. Slice the oranges very thinly, using an electric carving knife if you have one. Remove the core from the centre of each slice. Re-form each orange again by threading the slices onto cocktail sticks. Place them in a single layer in a large, shallow dish and chill them.

Pour the reserved orange juice into a measuring jug and make it up to 350 ml/12 fl oz with water (or you could use extra fresh or unsweetened orange juice). Pour the liquor into a small pan, add the apricots and cinnamon stick and bring to the boil. Simmer for 30 minutes over low heat. Take the pan from the heat and remove the cinnamon stick.

Liquidize to a purée or rub through a sieve. Leave the sauce to cool, then chill it in the refrigerator.

Meanwhile, make the garnish. Cut the reserved orange zest into the thinnest possible slivers and cut them into matchstick lengths. Put them in a small pan of cold water, bring to the boil and simmer for 5 minutes. Remove the pan from the heat. Turn the strips into a sieve and refresh them under cold, running water. Drain thoroughly and dry them on crumpled kitchen paper.

Pour the chilled sauce over the oranges and garnish them with the julienne strips of orange zest. Serve the oranges chilled.

8 small, seedless oranges
75 g/3 oz dried apricots, soaked and drained
1 stick cinnamon

Serves 4
Calories 290 (1260 kJ)
Protein 7 grams

No-Cook Special

For all the lovely, lazy days when other things claim your attention, here is a well-balanced and nutritious meal that needs no cooking. The first course, a Middle-Eastern speciality, is Tabbouleh, a salad made from soaked cracked wheat grains tossed with fresh, fragrant herbs. Spend a few minutes to arrange the smoked pork and garnishes attractively for the main dish and round off the meal with a romantic flourish.

Tabbouleh
Smoked Fillet of Pork with Melon
Yoghurt Coeur à la Créme

Tabbouleh

225 g/8 oz burghul wheat
1 small onion, chopped
3 spring onions, finely chopped
75 ml/5 tbls chopped parsley
45 ml/3 tbls chopped mint
15 ml/1 tbls chopped coriander
   leaves
45 ml/3 tbls vegetable oil
juice of 2 lemons
450 g/1 lb tomatoes, skinned,
deseeded and chopped
salt and ground black pepper
12 lettuce leaves
4 firm tomatoes, quartered
about 12 black olives

Soak the wheat in cold water for 30 minutes to allow it to swell. Drain and put it into a clean tea towel. Wring the cloth to squeeze out as much moisture as possible.

Mix the wheat with the onion, spring onion, herbs, oil, lemon juice and chopped tomato and season well with salt and pepper.

Line a serving dish with the lettuce leaves. Pile the Tabbouleh in the centre, arrange the quartered tomatoes round the outside and scatter the olives over.

Serves 4
Calories 1240 (5210 kJ)
Protein 39 grams

Smoked Fillet of Pork with Melon

2 honeydew melons
350 g/12 oz smoked fillet of pork,
   very thinly sliced
30 ml/2 tbls lemon juice
10 ml/2 tsp finely-grated fresh root
   ginger

Cut the melons into quarters and scoop out and discard the seeds. Using a very sharp, long-bladed knife, cut round the melon pieces just inside the skin, cutting away the flesh in one section. Leaving the melon still in place, resting on the skin, cut it into 12-mm/½-in thick slices.

Insert a small strip of the smoked pork vertically between each slice and sprinkle with the lemon juice.

Loosely cover the melon slices with transparent film and chill them in the refrigerator for at least 30 minutes. Sprinkle with the ginger and serve at once, while it is well chilled.

Serves 4
Calories 910 (3840kJ)
Protein 84 grams

Yoghurt Coeur à la Crème

Beat the sieved cheese and gradually beat in the yoghurt. Stir in the sugar.

Stiffly whisk the egg whites until they stand in peaks, then carefully fold them into the cheese.

To drain the mixture, you will need four individual moulds (heart-shaped ones are traditional but by no means essential) or one large one. Yoghurt pots with holes punched in the base, or a well-washed flower pot are suitable. Line the container(s) with a double layer of scalded buttermuslin or cheesecloth and spoon in the cheese mixture. Press the mixture down and fold the cloth over the top. Place the moulds on a plate and leave in the refrigerator for 2 hours, or overnight.

To serve, turn the moulds out on to a serving plate and surround them with soft fruits such as strawberries, raspberries or blackberries. You can serve extra caster sugar and thin or thick cream for non-slimmers!

Serves 4
Calories 400 (1670 kJ)
Protein 49 grams

225 g/8 oz yoghurt cheese or
    cottage cheese, sieved
150 ml/5 fl oz natural yoghurt
15 ml/1 tbls caster sugar
3 large egg whites

Barbecue

In a climate where every warm, sunny day calls for a celebration, there's no nicer way to make the best of it than to invite friends for an impromptu party – or simply enjoy a family meal in the open. Kebabs are the perfect answer for the main course and you can choose from pork or lamb – or make both. If the sun goes down on your plans, you can cook the kebabs equally well on the grill for a meal in moments.

Pimms No 1 Cup with Fruit Cocktail
Pork and Dried Fruit Kebabs
Lamb and Bay Leaf Kebabs
Tossed Garden Salad

Pimms Cup with Fruit Cocktail

375 ml/13 fl oz Pimms No 1 base
1 L/2 pt low-calorie ginger ale or
*   lemonade, chilled*
ice cubes
4 small peaches, skinned and
*   thinly sliced*
16-20 strawberries, halved if large
slices of cucumber and lemon
sprigs of borage or mint

Put the ice cubes into a bowl and add the fruit. Pour on the Pimms base and top up with ginger ale or lemonade. Spoon an ice cube and a little of the fruit into each glass and pour on the drink. Decorate the glasses with sprigs of herbs and slices of cucumber and lemon.

For a complete 'appetizer' serve the drinks with toasted almonds and a selection of crisp Crudités with a chilled dip.

Makes 8 glasses
Calories 970 (4050 kJ)
Protein 3 grams

Pork and Dried Fruit Kebabs

700 g/1½ lb pork tenderloin (or
*   fillet)*
8 prunes, soaked, drained and
*   stoned*
12 whole dried apricots, soaked
*   and drained*
1 green pepper, cut into squares

For the marinade
45 ml/3 tbls vegetable oil
1 orange
15 ml/1 tbls red wine vinegar
salt and ground black pepper

Trim any fat from the pork and cut it into 2.5-cm/1-in cubes.

Mix together the oil, grated zest and squeezed juice of the orange, the vinegar and salt and pepper. Put it into a polythene bag, add the pork cubes and tie the top securely. Leave the pork to marinate for about 4 hours. Add the stoned prunes and whole apricots, tie the bag, shake it well and leave for a further 2-4 hours.

Light the barbecue at least 1 hour before you want to start cooking so that it is really hot.

Strain the pork and fruit and reserve the marinade. Thread the pork, prunes, apricots and green pepper on to 4 skewers. Grill them for 15-20 minutes, turning them often and basting them with reserved marinade.

Serves 4
Calories 2034 (8543 kJ)
Protein 149 grams

Lamb and Bay Leaf Kebabs

Cut all excess fat from the lamb. Cut meat into 3-cm/1¼-in cubes. Blanch the whole, peeled onions in boiling water for 3 minutes, then drain. Dry thoroughly on kitchen paper. Mix together all the ingredients for the marinade.

Starting and ending with a tomato wedge, thread all the ingredients on to 4 skewers and lay them on a flat dish. Pour over the marinade, turn the skewers to coat them thoroughly, then loosely cover them. Leave at room temperature for about 8 hours, turning the skewers once or twice if possible.

Lift the kebabs from the marinade and drain off any excess. Grill the kebabs on the hot barbecue for a total of about 8–10 minutes, or until the outside of the meat is crisp and charred, and the inside is tender and pink. Turn the skewers and baste them with any remaining marinade while they are cooking.

To make a complete barbecue meal you could cook large potatoes in their jackets, wrapped in foil. Or make a foil parcel of small scrubbed potatoes sprinkled with a little melted butter and chopped mint. (Baked potatoes – calories 225 (1092 kJ) protein 6 grams each).

700 g/1½ lb lean lamb, cut from the leg
8 small onions
4 large tomatoes, quartered
about 12 bay leaves

For the marinade
75 ml/5 tbls sunflower oil
1 lemon
15 ml/1 tbls red wine vinegar
5 ml/1 tsp dark Muscavado sugar
salt and ground black pepper
30 ml/2 tbls chopped parsley
parsley sprigs

Serves 4
Calories 1385 (5785 kJ)
Protein 130 grams

Tossed Garden Salad with Sunset Dressing

In a large bowl, toss together the lettuce, cucumber, chicory, tomatoes and herbs. If this is to be done well in advance of serving, cover the bowl and chill in the refrigerator. Toss again just before serving.

Mix or shake together the salad dressing ingredients, taste and add more seasoning if necessary. Serve the dressing separately.

If you prefer, you can toss the salad just before serving in a very little vegetable oil, or oil and lemon juice mixed. Use just enough to give the leaves a pleasant sheen.

1 large lettuce, washed and dried
1 small cucumber, thinly sliced
2 heads chicory, thickly sliced
6 medium-sized tomatoes, quartered
30 ml/2 tbls chopped mint
15 ml/1 tbls chopped parsley

For the Sunset Dressing
125 ml/4 fl oz tomato juice, chilled
125 ml/4 fl oz natural yoghurt, chilled
5 ml/1 tsp lemon juice
a pinch of paprika
salt and ground black pepper

Serves 4
Calories 190 (800 kJ)
Protein 15 grams

Springtime Celebration

When it's time to rejoice in the first of the spring lamb, plan a menu which more than ever places the spotlight on the main dish.
Rosy-pink Taramasalata served Greek-style with pitta bread is a happily informal start. For dessert, serve exotic but simple Paradise Islands, slices of fresh pineapple topped with cream and coconut.

Taramasalata
Spring Lamb
Paradise Islands (see page 76)

Taramasalata

Remove the skin from the roe. Soak the bread in water and squeeze out the excess. Put the cod's roe, bread and onion into a blender and blend to a smooth paste. Or mash and beat by hand – the texture will be a little coarser, but it is not difficult to do.

Very gradually pour on the oil and lemon juice alternately, a few drops at a time at first and then in a thin, steady stream, as when making mayonnaise. Blend or beat constantly until the paste is thick enough to hold its shape. Cover and chill in the refrigerator for at least 1 hour.

Serves 6
Calories 2050 (8495 kJ)
Protein 42 grams

125 g/5 oz smoked cod's roe
4 slices of dry bread, crusts removed
30 ml/2 tbls grated onion
175 ml/6 fl oz olive oil (or a mixture with a light vegetable oil)
juice of 1 lemon
lemon wedges, black olives and pitta bread or thin toast to serve

Spring Lamb

Trim any excess fat from the lamb and cut it into 2.5-cm/1-in cubes. Heat the butter and oil in a flameproof casserole and fry the meat in two batches, stirring frequently, until it is evenly browned. Remove the meat with a slotted spoon.

Strain off the fat from the casserole, return the meat and sprinkle it with the sugar. Stir over moderate heat until the sugar caramellizes.

Heat the oven to 150C/300F/gas 2.

Add the flour, salt and pepper and stir over low heat until the flour just turns brown. Gradually pour on the stock, stirring, add the tomato purée, garlic and bouquet garni and bring to simmering point. Cover the casserole and cook in the oven for 1 hour.

Skim off the fat on the surface of the sauce, add the onions, carrots and potatoes, stir well, cover and continue cooking for 40 minutes. Stir in the broad beans, cover and cook for a further 15 minutes, or until all the heat and vegetables are tender.

Skim the fat from the surface again, discard the bouquet garni, taste and adjust seasoning if necessary.

Serves 4
Calories 2960 (12460 kJ)
Protein 196 grams

700 g/1½ lb lean shoulder lamb
25 g/1 oz butter
15 ml/1 tbls vegetable oil
10 ml/ 2 tsp sugar
15 ml/1 tbls flour
salt and ground black pepper
450 ml/15 fl oz chicken stock
15 ml/1 tbls tomato purée
1 garlic clove, crushed
1 bouquet garni
16 small onions
12 baby carrots
12 small new potatoes, scraped
175 g/6 oz shelled broad beans

Chinese Supper

There's an air of informality about a Chinese meal, when all the dishes are arranged on hotplates on the table, the candles flicker and everyone is anxious to put their skill with the chopsticks (or a surreptitious fork) to the test. Take time and trouble with the preparation of the ingredients, have everything absolutely ready, then the last-minute cooking can be done in a trice. If your kitchen is large enough, serve the meal there and enjoy the conversation while you supervise the cooking. Served steamed long-grain brown rice with this meal.

Chinese Spare Ribs
Sliced Sweet and Sour Chicken
Quick-fried Beansprouts
Crab and Ginger Foo Yung (see page 136)

Chinese Spare Ribs

900 g/2 lb American cut pork spare ribs
5 ml/1 tsp salt
60 ml/4 tbls corn oil
2 garlic cloves, crushed
½ a small onion, finely chopped
2 thin slices root ginger, finely chopped
15 ml/1 tbls sugar
60 ml/4 tbls soy sauce
45 ml/3 tbls medium sherry
ground black pepper
150 ml/5 fl oz chicken stock

This course can be prepared well in advance of the meal.

Separate the spare ribs by cutting between each one with a sharp knife. Rub them well with salt to help crisp the skin.

Heat the oil in a heavy-based frying-pan or Chinese wok over a high heat. When the oil is hot, add the garlic, onion and ginger and stir-fry for 1 minute. Add the ribs, lower the heat to moderate and stir-fry for a further 5 minutes. Remove the ribs and keep them warm.

Add the sugar, soy sauce, sherry and pepper and stir-fry for 2 minutes. Return the ribs to the pan. Pour on the chicken stock and turn the ribs to coat them thoroughly in the sauce. Lower the heat so that the sauce is just simmering. Turn the ribs and sauce into a heavy-based saucepan. Place it over low heat, cover the pan and leave to cook gently for 20 minutes. Remove the lid, turn the ribs and cook for a further 10 minutes.

Heat the oven to 190C/375F/gas 5.

Arrange the ribs in a roasting pan and spoon over any remaining sauce. Leave them in the oven for 5-10 minutes until the surface of the ribs is dry.

If you have prepared the ribs in advance, reheat them for 15 minutes. Serve them at once.

Serves 4
Calories 2925 (12145 kJ)
Protein 203 grams

Sliced Sweet and Sour Chicken

Remove any small bones from the chicken breasts. Using a very sharp knife, cut the meat along the grain into 12-mm/½-in slices. Mix together the salt and cornflour and rub it into the chicken.

Heat the oil in a heavy-based frying-pan or Chinese wok over moderate heat. Place the sliced chicken in the pan and spread it out in a single layer. Stir-fry for 4 minutes to cook the chicken on all surfaces. Remove the chicken from the pan with a slotted spoon, drain on kitchen paper and keep it warm.

Mix together all the ingredients for the sauce. Add the bamboo shoots, green pepper, onion, root ginger and garlic to the pan and stir-fry over moderate heat for 1 minute. Return the chicken to the pan, pour on the sauce and stir-fry for 1 minute. Serve at once.

Serves 4
Calories 765 (3200 kJ)
Protein 56 grams

225 g/8 oz chicken breasts, skinned
2.5 ml/½ tsp salt
2.5 ml/½ tsp cornflour
45 ml/3 tbls corn oil
25 g/1 oz bamboo shoots, thinly sliced
1 green pepper de-seeded and thinly sliced
1 small onion, chopped
1 slice of root ginger, finely chopped
1 garlic clove, crushed

For the Sweet and Sour Sauce
15 ml/1 tbls soy sauce
15 ml/1 tbls red wine vinegar
15 ml/1 tbls soft brown sugar
15 ml/1 tbls tomato purée
60 ml/4 tbls chicken stock

Quick-fried Bean Sprouts

Heat the oil in a large heavy-based frying-pan or Chinese wok over a high heat. Add the onion and stir-fry for 1 minute. Add the bean sprouts and chopped Chinese cabbage or lettuce and stir-fry until they are all coated with oil – about 2 minutes. Sprinkle on the salt, stir-fry for a further 1½ minutes, then add the chicken stock. Stir-fry for 1 minute more. Serve at once.

Serve the chicken and bean sprout dishes with steamed brown long-grain rice (300 g/10 oz raw weight brown rice – calories 1045 (4450 kJ), protein 23 grams).

Serves 4
Calories 415 (1715 kJ)
Protein 8 grams

450 g/1 lb fresh bean sprouts, or canned ones, rinsed and drained
45 ml/3 tbls sesame seed oil
1 spring onion, finely chopped
45 ml/3 tbls Chinese cabbage or Cos lettuce
5 ml/1 tsp salt
30 ml/2 tbls chicken stock

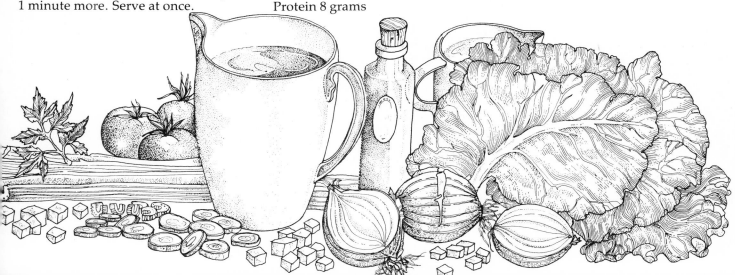

Index

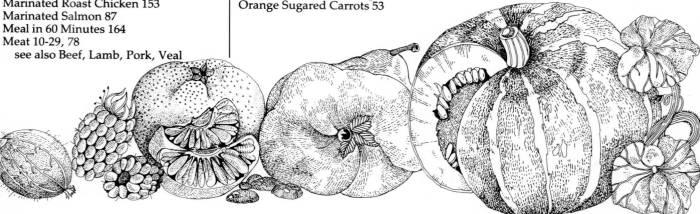